BLACK INTELLECTUALS,
BLACK COGNITION, AND
A BLACK AESTHETIC

BLACK INTELLECTUALS, BLACK COGNITION, AND A BLACK AESTHETIC

W. D. Wright

 PRAEGER

Westport, Connecticut
London

Library of Congress Cataloging-in-Publication Data

Wright, W. D. (William D.), 1936–
    Black intellectuals, Black cognition, and a Black aesthetic / W. D.
    Wright.
        p.   cm.
    Includes bibliographical references and index.
    ISBN 0–275–95542–7 (alk. paper)
        1. Afro-American intellectuals.   2. Afro-Americans—Intellectual
    life.   3. Afro-American aesthetics.   4. Afro-Americans—Race
    identity.   I. Title.
    E185.86.W96   1997
    305.896'073—dc21   96–37116

British Library Cataloguing in Publication Data is available.

Library of Congress Catalog Card Number: 96–37116
ISBN: 0–275–95542–7

First published in 1997

Praeger Publishers, 88 Post Road West, Westport, CT 06881
An imprint of Greenwood Publishing Group, Inc.

Printed in the United States of America

The paper used in this book complies with the
Permanent Paper Standard issued by the National
Information Standards Organization (Z39.48–1984).

10 9 8 7 6 5 4 3 2

For my mother,
Harriet Elizabeth Wright,
and my father,
Charles Noble Wright,
who both widened the boundary
of goodness in this world,
before going on ahead.

And to my sister,
Virginia May Wright,
who wrote her own pages
in the book of heroism
before passing to the
other side.

Contents

Preface

E. Franklin Frazier asserted in an article from the early 1960s that Black intellectuals had failed as intellectuals and had failed Black people.[1] Their failure was that they had not dealt adequately or at all with such intellectual matters as culture, personality, and human destiny or the impact of Western history and civilization and American history and civilization on Black people. Frazier also said that Black intellectuals had failed to adequately explain the Black community's relationship to the larger American society and the appropriate pathways this interaction should follow to benefit Blacks and America. Toward the end of the 1960s, Harold Cruse blasted Black intellectuals for being too dependent in their thinking, for not paying more attention to the cultural issues of Black life and of America, and for not helping Black people develop more cultural power and leadership in the country.[2]

Nearly three decades have passed, and it can be said that Black intellectuals have in the interim dealt with some of the matters that Frazier and Cruse thought were so crucial, although it would still be argued by them, as it is by this writer, that Black intellectuals have not provided the scope and depth of political and social analysis and commentary that they are capable of providing, either about Black life, or about the larger America. For instance, Black intellectuals still have not clarified, in a definitive manner, for Black people or for other

Americans such matters as assimilation, integration, segregation, and separation. Invariably, in their writings on these subjects, they confuse the first two terms with each other and use them interchangeably, as they do the other two terms. But then, it also has to be said that this kind of confusion and interchangeability can be found in the writings of white intellectuals. So it is a cultural thing in America, a lack of term and/or concept integrity, rather than a special deficiency of Black intellectuals.

But that does not get Black intellectuals off the hook. They consider themselves to be voices of Black people, some of their representatives, and have assigned themselves a role to help Blacks develop and to achieve full freedom in America—the obligations that Black history and social life have conferred upon them. But when Black intellectuals are confused and are too dependent on others for their own thought, their credibility is diminished and there are negative consequences for Black leaders, Black politicians, and other Black people. So, while Black intellectuals have come a long way in America, they still have more to do as individuals, as a group, for Blacks—and for America.

And the burden of Black intellectuals has increased. America itself is in a state of intellectual, moral, and spiritual crisis. The country has become incredibly profane, vulgar, and violent. The worst of American culture, social life, and personal life is paraded in a variety of media, as new ideals, as new standards, as a new realism, as *adult* behavior, and with all of it having great commercial value. Words like *perverted, debased,* or *degeneracy* or phrases like *intellectual decline, moral decline,* or *spiritual decline* are no longer in the public nor even in many individual vocabularies. There are the so-called conservatives in America who see America hitting the intellectual, moral, cultural, and social skids; these people have of course voiced their objections publicly. But their voices have almost no credence, because it is no secret to anyone, except to themselves, that their historical and current social behavior have helped significantly to put America in its present crisis.

It is not just America's crisis. It is also the crisis of Western civilization itself, where the latter, despite its last half century of economic prosperity and abundance, still shows the intellectual, moral, and spiritual malignancies that produced Hitler and the Nazis, the communists, an enormous inhumanity, and which are vividly revealed as ongoing by the horrors in the former Yugoslavia, the resurrection of malevolent politics in various countries of Europe, and by the threat that the continuing malaise presents to the aspirations for a greater and unified European Community.

The problems of Europe are the problems of America and vice versa. They are, combined, the problems of Western history and civilization. Black intellectuals still show an incredible indifference to Western history and civilization, of which they and Black people are a part, and which has significantly shaped both. They also do not deal satisfactorily, intellectually, with *American* history and *American* culture. All of these things inevitably impact Black people, but they also inescapably affect the ability of Black intellectuals to fulfill their self-images, of spokespeople, representatives, and helpers of Black people.

The whole blame cannot be laid on Black intellectuals. The long and continuous racist history of America has been very anti–Black intellectual, even investing white Americans with a belief that Blacks and intellectuals, or Blacks and intelligence, are contradictions in terms. White intellectuals, in the main, have never taken Black intellectuals seriously, and this arrogant and blighted behavior continues. It also has to be said that Black intellectuals have taken a beating from other Black intellectuals when they have tried to write on subjects that did not pertain directly to Blacks or Black life in America, even though they might have thought that indirectly they did, and in a serious manner. Such individuals have been accused of trying to be "White" or trying to gain White approval, or trying to attain White largesse, or of betraying Black people and Black interests. So there has been historical and social pressure on Black intellectuals in America to stay at home and also to limit their intellectual range.

But Black intellectuals can no longer let these matters act as inhibitors for them. The general crisis of Western civilization, and its specific manifestation in America, calls for Black intellectuals to come forward and provide some intellectual and moral leadership. This has become an imperative because so many white intellectuals are caught up in what is called *postmodern* thinking, in which they show acute hostility to any thought that seeks to provide a broad or narrative explanation or which seeks to promote a consensus or social morality, such as philosophies of history or general political or social theories. These intellectuals are part of the malaise of Western civilization, but they are incapable of perceiving this, believing that they are precisely the intellectuals, with precisely the modes of thought that Western civilization and America desperately need at the present moment.

These intellectuals will be the first to rip Black intellectuals who seek to come forward with some intellectual offerings to America or to Western civilization that are directional or that have consensual or moral orientations. The situation is not disconnected from racism. Most postmodern thinkers are white, especially white men, who have only in the rarest instances been willing to accept intellectual fare from Black people, even Black intellectuals—and they do not wish to become innovative now.

So another element has been added to the burden. But Black intellectuals have to shoulder it; they really have no choice in the matter if they see themselves as spokespeople for and representatives of Black people and see themselves as having a messianic role to help Blacks in America. But to help them in the most propitious manner, they have, of necessity, to relate intellectually and critically to Western civilization and America itself, because the problems and needs of both affect Black people and their future in America. It is the thesis of this book that Western history and civilization and America itself are calling upon Black intellectuals to play a new and critical intellectual and moral role in regard to both, for the purpose of trying to aid both and also Black people in America.

Black intellectuals will have to demonstrate their capabilities in many subject areas. One area that beckons them to make a display of their capabilities is in the area of cultural thought. Black intellectuals have taken only small steps in this direction. Black cultural thought lags far behind the aesthetic cultural capabilities of Black people, which are second to none in America and which may be preeminent in the country by the way so many different Americans go to this aesthetic trough for inspiration and nourishment. Black intellectuals and artists in the 1920s began their efforts to develop a Black Aesthetic to help guide the development and performance of Black art— broadly conceived—and the Aesthetic's relationship to the development of Black people in America and their quest for full freedom in the country. A stronger effort was made in the 1970s, and it is one that continues, although without making giant strides forward. Aesthetic culture is the strength of Black people. If Black aesthetic thinking could ever match this strength, it would be proof enough that Black intellectuals were capable of taking on the horrendous historical assignments that have been handed to them.

I wish for Black intellectuals to take up this challenge of constructing a Black Aesthetic philosophy or theory, or several of each, to show their intellectual capabilities and their ability to be intellectual leaders. Hindrances are strewn in the pathway, in the form of intellectual and cultural problems that Black intellectuals have to resolve through historical knowledge and also through analysis and discussion, such as the reality of racism and the difference between racism and race, the identity of Black people, the cognitive methods of Blacks, the relationship between Black thought and postmodern thought, the relationship between Black art and African art, and the relationship of a Black Aesthetic to a Black American Aesthetic. All this is necessary before they can move vigorously and successfully to the larger aesthetic intellectual efforts. I have dealt with these issues and others in this book, mainly to identify them in a clear fashion and to suggest the direction that might be pursued to achieve resolution, as a personal effort to try to help Black intellectuals get on with their aesthetic and intellectual objectives and demonstrations, preparatory to engaging the new and large demands of history.

I have also done one other thing in writing this book and in my personal effort to stimulate Black intellectuals into action. I have tried in this work to provide some coherence to the spelling of the words *black* and *white* and also to invest the words with a better understanding and meaning, which I believe is necessary and which I feel will be helpful to Black intellectuals as they take up their new intellectual and leadership tasks. When the word *black* is spelled in the lower case in this book, it will be a reference to color or race. When the word black is spelled in the higher case, as *Black*, it will be a reference to ethnic group, ethnic status, ethnicity, or community, that is, Black ethnic community. The Black ethnic group and the Black ethnic community are descendants of the Africans brought to this country as slaves between the seventeenth and nineteenth centuries, and their slave descendants. An individual designated as *Black* in this work will be a reference to an individual who is a member of the Black ethnic group or the Black ethnic community. The word *Blacks* will be a reference to a few, many, or all Black people who are members of the Black ethnic group or the Black ethnic community. The phrase *black* ethnic group or *black community* will be references to the color and racial attributes of the ethnic group or the ethnic community, but not references to culture or social life.

The word white receives similar treatment in this book. When that word is spelled in the lower case it will be a reference to color or race. When it is spelled in the higher case, as *White*, this will be a reference to ethnic group, ethnic status, ethnicity, or community, that is, White ethnic community. White people form a large White ethnic group and ethnic community in America forged over the course of their history in the country. An individual designated *White* will be a reference to an individual who is a member of the White ethnic group or White ethnic community. The word *Whites* will be a reference to a few, many, or all White people who are members of the White ethnic group or White ethnic community. The phrase *white ethnic group* or *white community* will be references to the color or racial attributes of the ethnic group or the community, but not references to culture or social life. White people in the Western world are part of Western civilization and, therefore, are part of a civilizational group and have a civilizational status. In this context, and in this book, the word *White* will be a reference to an individual who is a member of this civilizational group. The word *Whites* will be a reference to a few, many, or all White people who are members of this civilizational group.

As can be seen from the above discussion, the spelling of names and identities is not just grammatical activity. Such spellings can have historical, cultural, social, and political significance, which requires that the spelling of words or names and identities be done with great care.

Acknowledgments

I wish to thank professor Richard Garner of the Department of Classical Languages of Yale University and his graduate student, John Dyan, as well as Margaretha and Johaan Bischoff, for their assistance in translating passages from ancient Greek and Latin.

1.

The Reality of Black Intellectuals

The Black Liberation Movement of the 1950s and 1960s had many successes. One of these was the ending of the public, blatant, and violent racism of Whites in the United States as a normal and acceptable way for them to relate to Black people in the country. A second success was the restoration of the national citizenship and national political and civil rights of Black people that had been gained in the 1860s and 1870s, but which had been taken away between the 1880s and early 1900s by Supreme Court decisions, national government enforcement of the decisions, state statutes, and by national and local racist practices. A third success was the firm establishment of the Black middle class as the leadership class of Black people, and as the class that would, and that had to, carry out the vigilance to see that Whites did not restore the openly blatant and violent racism that had been strongly eclipsed, as well as to remain vigilant about and to attack the subtle White racism that had, in the late 1960s, emerged as the new dominant form of White racism in America, and that has continued ever since. A fourth success of the liberation movement was to publicly catapult Black intellectuals as a sizable, knowledgeable, capable, and permanent critical group in Black America and in the larger American society.

The last success may not seem all that outstanding and, indeed, might be regarded as some kind of normal attainment or normal reality. After all, there are white intellectuals in America; why shouldn't there be Black ones? But the apparent normalcy or expectancy of the whole matter actually hides reality; namely, the reality of the resistance to having Black intellectuals in the United States.

In the seventeenth century, white people and black people came together in North America. Unfortunately, they did not come together on a strong basis of individuality or equality. By the 1640s, Whites were passing laws enslaving black people. By the late seventeenth century and the first half of the eighteenth century, Blacks were nailed down by racist beliefs, slave laws, and political, individual, or group violence to a condition and reality of perpetual slavery that carried over from the colonial into the early national period of American history. Slave laws were passed determining that black slaves were not to be taught how to read and write. And those Blacks who were not slaves were discouraged from pursuing education, with the discouragement taking many forms.

Consciously making Blacks slaves and consciously removing them from formal education makes it clear that white slaveholders and other Whites were determined to suppress the mental and intellectual capabilities of black people. And at this time, the latter seventeenth and the first half of the eighteenth centuries, and even more so thereafter, there was a belief—a racist belief—that black people were naturally, or innately, incapable of significant cerebral functioning or attainment. During the colonial period of American history, there were Whites who thought Blacks were anatomically and cerebrally akin to apes. There were Whites less mephitic in their racism, such as Thomas Jefferson, who accepted and argued the view that Blacks did not have the innate capacity for intellectual activity but showed a great ability to employ the senses. Jefferson was not willing to say that Blacks were apes, or akin to them, but he left no doubt that he did not think that they were fully human either.

Thus, Whites joined racism and slavery together to carry out a double assault against Black humanity, and particularly, Blacks' human capacity to think and reason, or to be rational. This facilitated maintaining slavery, but it also became a rationale to justify exclusion, segregation, and the denial of human as well as political and civil rights to Blacks in America. Indeed, in the eighteenth and nineteenth centuries, white men, especially, the ones who were most insistent that Blacks were incapable of significant intellectual activity, developed theories to prove their contentions. One of these theories was phrenology.[1] Phrenologists argued that the shape of a head determined brain size and cerebral capacity. Human races had different head shapes. The white race had the best-shaped head; therefore, white people had the largest brain size and the greatest capacity for intelligence. The black race had the worst-shaped head of all racial groups, and, thus, had the smallest brain size and virtually no capacity for intelligence. Another racist theory at the time was the "Two-Creation" theory. This one stated that God engaged in two acts of Creation. He created the white race and white people and endowed them with great innate intellectual ability. In a second Creation, he created the black race and black people and endowed them with very little intellectual ability. In the latter nineteenth century, Charles Darwin's theories of evolution (variation), natural selection, and the survival of the fittest (which was actually taken from Herbert Spencer) were invested with racism and were used to prove that the white race evolved into the highest type of humans, with a commensurate high capacity for intelligence and that the black race was arrested in its anatomical and cerebral development, leaving it at the level of apes in both physical and cerebral attributes. In the latter nineteenth century, there was the theory of craniology. This was actually a different version of the phrenological theory that had passed out of existence by the 1850s. Physical scientists, as well as medical doctors, resurrected the deceased theory, giving a new name to it: craniology. This theory argued that a large skull denoted elaborate brain organization and a great capacity for intelligence, while a small skull denoted little brain organization and very little capacity for intelligence. As the racist argument went, using science as a handmaiden to validate it, the white race had a larger skull than the black race and, therefore, had a much larger capacity for intelligence. A special theory regarding the intelligence of the black race, and aimed specifically at Blacks in the United States, was advanced by the southern-born Harvard University biologist, Nathaniel Shaler, from whom W. E. B. Du Bois took a class and who, Du Bois said, treated him very well. Indeed, as Du Bois said in his *Autobiography*, "Shaler invited a Southerner, who objected to sitting beside me, out of his class."[2] Shaler obviously found Du Bois to be a Black "exception." But Shaler's general view of Blacks, as he expressed it in his "regression theory," first made public in 1884, was that they were arrested in both their physical and intellectual development. They survived in America only because slavery had kept them in close association with Whites, whom they had enough brain capacity to imitate in various ways. By imitating Whites, Blacks became "Whitelike" and were able to survive with White help, which was provided throughout slavery. But now that slavery was over and Blacks were on their own, Shaler argued, they were quickly reverting back to their original African savagery. And this would only get worse unless Whites intervened in this situation and offered some kind of help, because Blacks did not have much innate ability for intellectual and creative efforts. They were, and could be, good imitators, but this was not a "racial trait" that could carry Blacks very far on their own. He writes "Here, as in the Old World, the Negroes have not only failed to exhibit a capacity for indigenous development, but when uplifted from without have shown an obvious tendency to fall back into their primitive estate as soon as the internal support was withdrawn."[3]

As can be seen in these comments, white men, especially, have been *obsessed*, with believing and trying to prove that Black people in America are naturally or innately intellectually inferior to them. In the early twentieth century, craniology finally succumbed to its own ineptness and unscientific character. It could no longer withstand the main criticism that some animals had larger skulls than humans, and that, therefore, logically, these animals should be more intelligent than humans, including white men. Moreover, craniologists had a difficult time trying to explain why white women had smaller skulls than white men, and even more troubling for them was trying to explain how small-skulled people gave birth to large-skulled people. At a point where there was some despair about not being able to prove, in a scientific way, that black people were innately intellectually inferior to white people, along came intelligence tests, which became the new so-called scientific device that continued the white male obsession of trying to prove the intellectual superiority of Whites—especially of white men—and the intellectual inferiority of all black people.

I have mentioned several reasons why white men have been preoccupied with their great obsession. But there is another. White men also did not want a Black middle class in America. The only Blacks who were welcomed were slaves, or Blacks who would not resist a subordinate, lowly status and condition in America. Black middle-class people were considered to be a problem. This was what was initially meant by the *Negro Problem* or the *Negro Question*—the problem of the Black middle class and the question of what to do with it.

These matters aggravated Whites because of their own racist beliefs and thinking. There was no difficulty in American ideals with a Black middle class, but White racist beliefs and feelings made it an impossible concept, as did the belief and insistence that Blacks ideally be slaves in America. In the latter eighteenth and early nineteenth centuries, two events occurred that initiated the fear of a Black middle class. During this period, slavery in the North was put on a program of gradual abolition. By 1830, slavery was officially abolished by state statutes in the North. This meant that prior to 1830, and then, of course, at that date, there were thousands of nonslave Blacks in the North. These nonslave Blacks began (actually going back to the latter eighteenth century and continuing with efforts initiated then) building a Black community in the region. This community construction was being led by individuals who could be classified as middle class, and who sought, with their constituents, to build a Black community of middle-class people in the northern part of the United States. The alarm that a number of northern and southern white men saw in these developments was reflected in their creation of the American Colonization Society in 1817. It was established by prominent northern and southern Whites for the purpose of trying to persuade, with a willingness to aid, nonslave Blacks to leave America and repatriate to Africa. Indeed, the society established the colony of Liberia in 1822. Prior to the mid-nineteenth-century war, about 12,000 to 15,000 Blacks returned to Africa. But most who did were emancipated southern slaves, who were emancipated on the basis of their returning to Africa. Northern nonslave Blacks put up a strenuous fight against the American Colonization Society and its efforts, which many regarded as a deportation scheme. In the 1850s, and because of the new Fugitive Slave Law, thousands of northern nonslave Blacks fled from the United States to Canada, fearing being kidnapped and declared fugitives and being taken to the South as slaves.

But most northern Blacks, who numbered about a half a million in 1860, were determined to stay in the United States. They regarded themselves as Americans and asserted that they were entitled to the rights and opportunities of American citizens. Many were building a middle-class life in America, and this was the hope as well as the goal held out to all northern Blacks, and to which Black middle-class people, including intellectuals among them, religious and secular, endeavored to lead them. Between the 1820s and the midcentury war these Black intellectuals and other Black middle-class people created a Black Public and a Black Public Voice in America. That Voice not only protested racism, slavery and American Colonization Society efforts; it also protested against Blacks, in the ranks of this emerging Black middle class, who advocated emigration from America, to Africa or to elsewhere. America was home. This was where Blacks now had their roots, and this was where all future mainline battles of Black people would be fought.

It wasn't just the Black slaves, as historians sometimes remind us, who engaged in resistance in America. The emerging Black middle class was born out of resistance to racism and slavery and efforts of deportation. Black intellectuals evolved out of this resistance. But Black middle-class people, including Black intellectuals, also emerged from cooperating or working with Whites and even White racist power and institutional racism. This was reflected in the accommodation to White religious institutions, which saw Black clergy and Black congregations accept affiliation within racist white churches. There were northern Blacks who agreed not to try to integrate schools attended by white children, in return for Whites accepting Blacks having their own schools; these Whites even aiding Blacks in establishing the schools, selling them land on which to build or buildings in which to establish schools. The Black middle class fought for its existence in the United States against white and Black elements that it perceived seeking to do it harm, which sought to drive it away, or which sought to suppress it to a nonnoticeable status in America. Black intellectuals played a critical role in these fights. They publicly condemned racism, slavery, and repatriation and were strong public advocates of an American identity for Blacks and Black freedom in America.

This was the kind of development that many American white men did not want to see. They did not wish to see a stratum of Black people existing between Whites and the mass of Blacks. They especially did not want to see a stratum that constituted a middle class, with intellectuals. They saw what they specifically feared: a public critical voice. Their racist beliefs, which spoke of Black innate inferiority, an even nonhuman or subhuman status, said these kinds of developments were not to take place. These developments among Blacks confused and angered many Whites and made them feel intellectually, psychologically, and morally vulnerable. What eased this kind of vulnerability and psychic stress, and pain, was the segregation of Blacks, either legally or in a de facto manner; both of these things occurred between the late nineteenth and early twentieth centuries. These racist power displays were augmented by public verbal and physically violent racism, which continuously, for decades, denigrated and assaulted the humanity, intelligence, and physical being of Black people and which denigrated the black race in general.

But Blacks had their own understanding about who they were. They knew they were human beings, no matter what white people said. Listening to white people talk, and reading what they wrote, they could see that intellectual ability and intelligence were not confined to the white race or white people. Intellectuals among Blacks saw how white intellectuals made a mockery of science, scholarship, and political and social thought. During the decades reaching into the early twentieth century, when racism and segregation were their most vicious in American history, the Black middle class and Black intellectuals continued to grow. The Black Public and the Black Public Voice continued and even expanded. This was aided by Blacks, usually led by Black middle-class people, turning inward and focusing on internal cultural and social, or community development. Booker T. Washington and his newly created Black middle class leaders, and the new Black middle class he sought to build in the South, were preeminent in turning Blacks in on themselves and their condition to improve their lives in America. The other aid to Blacks was the continued development of the newly established Black colleges and universities, primarily in the South. By the close of the nineteenth century, these institutions were more like high schools than colleges and universities. But under Black middle-class leadership and Black intellectuals, along with White help, they continued to grow and strive toward full college and university status. Many southern Whites, functioning as vicious racists at this point in time, did their very best to suppress or thwart any kind of Black educational development, which only southern Black determination and northern white philanthropists—and the leadership genius of Booker T. Washington— saved from the fires of ruin, and that kept U.S. Black education alive and developing. Southern Whites put millions of southern Blacks into another form of slavery, in the form of racist labor practices, peonage, generational indebtedness sharecropping, violence, and political suppression that lasted until the 1930s and 1940s, when the depression and mechanized agriculture in the South ended this new slavery. Strongly racist, as most were, between the latter nineteenth and early twentieth centuries, southern Whites were not only opposed to a

Black middle class and Black intellectuals, particularly in the South, but also generally in America. Moreover, they could not understand how something like this could happen anyway—not given how inferior Black people were. This had always been something incomprehensible to white racists in America. But southern Whites were so beastial in their racism in the latter nineteenth and early twentieth centuries that an understanding of these matters was wholly beyond their capabilities. They were not even able to understand how their own racism and segregation helped to create the Black middle class and Black intellectuals they feared and sought to suppress in the South. They feared a critical voice. They feared a Black leadership that would take Blacks away from their control or that would make Blacks under their domination and control restless, disobedient, or dangerous.

In *The Souls of Black Folk* Du Bois wrote about the southern White fear of a Black critical voice, seeing it as continuous, fearful reaction since the first phase of slavery.[4] In his article "The Training of Negroes for Social Power," also written in 1903, he discussed the fear southern Whites had of losing control over the mass of Blacks, and especially to Black intellectuals and a Black middle-class leadership. Southern Whites feared Black intellectuals and a Black middle-class leadership helping Blacks in the South develop a group power that would be used against Whites and racism in the region:

> Such social power means, assuredly, the growth of initiative among Negroes, the spread of independent thought, the expanding consciousness of manhood; and these things today are looked upon by many with apprehension and distrust, and there is systematic and determined effort to avoid this inevitable corollary of the fixing of social responsibility. Men openly declare their design to train these millions as a subject caste, as men to be thought for, but not to think; to be led, but not to lead themselves.[5]

For white racists in the South or the North, Black Power was not permissible. One reason for this, as they saw it, was that Blacks were nonhumans or subhumans and were not entitled to power, as they were not entitled to political and civil rights—both of which only human beings were entitled to. There was another racist belief that black was evil, which meant that Black Power would be evil power.

White Power was all right (when white racists admitted to exercising power against Blacks), because it was presumed to be good and beneficial. But the deepest White racist fear was that Black Power would be used by Blacks to seek to end White domination, control, and exploitation of Blacks and as a means to try to help Blacks achieve full assimilation, integration, and freedom in America. Historically, Whites have sought—in a myriad of ways—to steer Black intellectuals and the Black middle class away from Black Power. Whites also did not want Blacks to think of rights and opportunities nor of aesthetic cultural development, that is, art, literature, drama, or music. They preferred that Blacks focus on these matters, or pursue these matters, rather than attempting to build effective group power in America.

Because of White racist thought and social behavior, Black intellectuals and the Black middle class are something close to anomalies in America, social realities that were not even supposed to appear in the country, sanctioned by the belief that Blacks were innately incapable of producing either. But when white racists saw Blacks doing what they believed impossible, it produced confusion, vulnerability, and determined efforts by Whites to suppress or to impede these developments.

Of the two realities, in time, Black intellectuals were considered by white racists to be the most troublesome and dangerous. Thinking Blacks were troublesome and dangerous. They contradicted the very basic, operational racist belief that the black race generally, and Black Americans, in particular, were incapable of significant intellectual activity and that this was a fixed or permanent condition. The low-grade intellectual capability and the low level of morality believed to be part of the natural inferiority of black and Black people meant that neither of the latter groups could produce sophisticated social or aesthetic culture. This thinking was all part of what I called in my article "The Faces of Racism"[6] *ebonicistic* racist beliefs, that is, racist beliefs against black people (race) or Black people (ethnicity) which non-white people could hold. *White supremacy* is a racist doctrine pertaining to white people, and white people only, that refers to their alleged innate superiority. In the United States white supremacy and ebonicism have been the two chief forms of racism, as the White-Black social relation has been the primary social relationship in the country. Historically, and following the pattern of the implementation of racist beliefs in the society, white supremacy and ebonicism have been joined at the hip, paired together, and have functioned together in America as white supremacy/ebonicism. This means, to be perfectly clear, that when white Americans have acted and continue to act in a racist manner toward Blacks, they act from two racist doctrines simultaneously and interactively, never from just one set of racist beliefs. The other doctrine might not be stated explicitly, but it will always be there implicitly as a source of motivation, attitudes, thought, or social behavior. White people have always been more explicit in their ebonicistic racism when relating to Blacks than their white supremacist racism. The latter may never be mentioned but is there all the time. Thus, White racism toward black people or Blacks in America has always been, conceptually and in practice, white supremacy/ebonicism. It is this paired racism that has been chiefly embedded in American history, culture, and social life.

But there have been other paired racisms in American history, culture, and social life because other forms of racism have been concocted and practiced. There has been and continues to be white supremacy/*redicism,* the latter meaning racism against red people or Native Americans. There has been and continues to be white supremacy/*xanthicism* (with the latter meaning racism against yellow or yellowish-brown Asians). *Aryanism/anti-Jewism* (or Nordism/anti-Jewism) is another form of paired racism practiced in America, and even more so in Europe. *Anti-Jewism,* in my view, is a more accurate term than the usual *anti-Semitism* because Arabs are Semites as well, and they certainly are not anti-Semitic. There is one last form of paired racism to mention: *maleism/sexism. Sexism* refers to racist beliefs that men have toward women. But when men function as racists toward women, they do so from a second set of racist beliefs simultaneously, which relates specifically to them that refer to their alleged natural superiority, and which I call *maleism.*

A truism, and a sad one at that, is that it is not recognized, not even by many scholars, that there are many forms of racism, that racism can take many specific forms. I had been one of those scholars functioning from a limited understanding of racism. But reading Du Bois's discussion of racism more closely, and by studying racism on a comparative basis, in two ways—comparing racism as it occurred in America and Europe and by comparing racist phenomena from numerous instances—I came to see that racism could and did assume many faces. My study showed that there were more faces than names for such faces, so I provided some names for some of the forms.

My study of Du Bois's writings on racism, as well as my other study, also indicated clearly to me that racism and race were not the same things. Indeed, it was made clear to me that racism was not necessarily predicated on race and did not necessarily have anything to do with race. Maleism/sexism, for instance, were two separate forms of racism, but they are predicated on gender rather than race. Ebonicism was based on race and ethnicity. Aryans, who were of the white race, treated Jews in a racist manner, even though the Jews could be of the white race as well, as most were and are in Europe and in America. This means that race is not the main consideration in the racism toward Jews. Something else is. And what is that something else?

That something else applies to all forms of racism and speaks to what the racist doctrine and racism are about. Racism is about being *anti–human being* or *anti-humanity*. Racists seek to relate to people as if they were nonhuman or subhuman—on the assumption that they themselves are gods or godlike (which also means that they are non-human as well). The race that racists have always been concerned about is "race," meaning the "race" of godly or godlike entities, and the "race" of nonhumans or subhumans. Racists see themselves as their racist beliefs—their maleist, Aryan, or white supremacist beliefs—tell them as being of the race of gods or godlike entities. Racists see others, as their racist beliefs tell them—their ebonicistic, xanthicistic, redicistic, anti-Jewish, or sexist beliefs—as belonging to different, individual "races" of nonhumans or subhumans. Was this not what the American scientist Louis Agassiz was saying in the 1850s about the black race (and Blacks in America), when he wrote that the brain of black people bore a strong resemblance "in several particulars to the brain of an ourangoutang."[7] Years earlier, the German philosopher Georg Hegel, showing his strong racist orientation, wrote: "The Negro represents natural man in all his wild and untamed nature. If you want to treat and understand him rightly, you must abstract all elements of respect and morality and sensitivity—there is nothing remotely humanized in the Negro character."[8] There was no humanity in black people, at best only subhumanity. At a later time in the nineteenth century, the French thinker Georges Cuvier wrote:

> The Negro race . . . is marked by black complexion, crisped or woolly hair, compressed cranium and a flat nose. The projection of the lower parts of the face, and the thick lips,

evidently approximate it to the monkey tribe: the hordes
of which it consists have always remained in the most complete state of barbarism.[9]

These eminent white intellectuals were saying that black people,
also Black people in America, were animals, or near animals; that they
were nonhuman or subhuman; and that they belonged to the "race"
of nonhumans or subhumans; while white people, as their remarks
implied, belonged to the "race" of gods and godlike entities. As the
comments of these three racist intellectuals also showed, each one
believed that the attributes that their racist beliefs concocted about
black people constituted the actual attributes of black people (or
Black people). They invested these concocted attributes in black (and
Black) people and then claimed that these were their real traits, their
true representations, deeply embedded in their nature, and that determined their thought and social behavior. It did not matter to either
one of these thinkers who black (or Black) people really were or what
their actual racial or ethnic traits were. These white racist intellectuals
simply related to these groups of people on the basis of their racist
fantasies about them, which *invisibilized* black people or Black people
and their actual natural or cultural attributes.

But this is what racism signifies. It is not synonymous with race, although racist beliefs can be imposed on a race, as ebonicistic racist beliefs have historically been and continue to be imposed on black
people—which conveys the impression that race is the main
consideration, when it is not. What is paramount, and the primary motivation, is "race": black people or Black people as a so-called "race" of
nonhumans or subhumans. Many Black intellectuals have remarked
how Whites have treated Blacks as if they were nonhumans or subhumans. But this understanding has always been predicated on the assumption that race, that is, color or physiognomy, was the primary and
even the only motivating factor for Whites. It was not. The basic motivating factor was always "race," as concocted by ebonicistic racist beliefs. Sexism was not really a reference to female gender. Sexist racist
beliefs were imposed on female gender, to convert women into a
"race" of nonhumans or subhumans, which would be proclaimed by
the sexist beliefs to be their real attributes or true representations, and
which determined their thought and social behavior. This kind of racist
thinking, falsification, and invisibilization would be applied to all victims of racism. The object of racists is to reduce all their victims to

the conception (which to the racists constitutes the reality) of being nonhumans or subhumans, so that they can be treated that way. Racists do not wish to relate to people as if they were *Others*, which is what they would be doing if they related to them on the basis of their actual race, gender, or ethnic status. Racists seek to relate to people, namely, those they make their victims, on the basis of their being *Non-Others*, as belonging to something other than the human race, as belonging to a nonhuman or subhuman "race," or "races." This also means that racists view themselves as Non-Others as well, when they relate to themselves on the basis of racist beliefs about themselves, such as white supremacy or maleism, or when they relate to their victims as racists. Thinking of themselves as godly or godlike makes them Non-Others, too, as belonging to something other than the human race or something other than humanity itself.

Black intellectuals in America have been no better than white intellectuals in the country, or intellectuals elsewhere in the world, in clarifying the phenomenon of racism. Even Du Bois, who understood that racism and race were not the same things, that racism was not even necessarily predicated on race, and that it could take numerous specific forms, obscured this brilliant insight by the way he usually wrote on this subject, by focusing on race. Throughout the history of Blacks in America, Black intellectuals have equated racism with race, although throughout that history, until about the 1960s, using words and phrases such as *prejudice, discrimination, race prejudice, caste, color caste,* or *racial caste* to do so. When Black intellectuals began employing the concept of racism, they employed the new concept in the old manner, as something relating exclusively to race, and the old notions of racial denial, racial exclusion, racial discrimination, racial segregation, or racial subordination. They failed to perceive and apply the more primary understandings of racist denial, racist exclusion, racist discrimination, racist segregation, and racist subordination—meaning that Blacks were denied, excluded, discriminated against, segregated, and subordinated in American history and American society, on the White racist belief and assumption that they were not human beings, or not full human beings, and that this was a permanent condition. The confusion is actually understandable. For centuries in America Whites made race such a stark reality and jammed it down the throats of Black people, as well as down their own throats and those of others in America. Black intellectuals, as well as other Blacks, had to deal with this persistent inundation of race. It was something they had to confront from birth to death and in a myriad of ways, all of which were insulting and assaulting. It was necessary to fight against race, as well as it was necessary to try to speak positively and to relate positively to race, namely, the black race. This was a historical, social, and intellectual preoccupation, and it was hard to see clearly, or always clearly, the larger and even different realities of racism and "race" that were involved. Unfortunately, present-day Black intellectuals are still mainly in a time-warped posture understanding racism.

But, on the other hand, over the history of Blacks in America, the fight against race as racism, and the support of race, as a biological reality by Black intellectuals and other Blacks, was helpful to Blacks. Indeed, at the close of the nineteenth century, a group of Black intellectuals decided to put themselves and all Black intellectuals on the task of dealing intellectually with racism and race. These same intellectuals felt that it was necessary for Black intellectuals to show a strong affinity with the Black middle class that was continuing to evolve in America, and of which they were a part, so that they could help strengthen this class, and specifically to help strengthen it as the leadership class of Blacks in the country. In 1897, in the midst of virulent verbal and physically violent racism, these intellectuals established the American Negro Academy, the subject of a recent monograph by Alfred Moss.[10] The prime mover behind the Academy was Bishop Alexander Crummell. He drew up the constitution for the academy, which would have a limit of forty members, and who would be college or university "graduates or Professors . . . (or) Authors, Artists, and distinguished writers."[11] Crummell was elected president of the academy and served for eighteenth months in that capacity until his death.

The intellectuals that Crummell drew into the American Negro Academy agreed to promote "Letters, Science, and Art" among Blacks. This was the general objective of the academy, but there were other objectives as well. As Alfred Moss has written, "the chief concerns of the men who founded the ANA were to strengthen the intellectual life of their racial community, improve the quality of black leadership, and insure that henceforth arguments advanced by 'cultured despisers' of their race were refuted or at least challenged."[12]

Crummell had remarked to historian John W. Crogman before the establishment of the American Negro Academy that "The [race] battle in America [was] to be carried on in the world of the minds."

The bishop of the African Episcopal Church looked upon the forty members of the academy, as well as Black intellectuals in general, as elites among blacks—a "Talented Tenth" among them, and saw that it was the moral and political duty of this Talented Tenth to fight racism on an intellectual basis, to promote thought and culture among Blacks, to strengthen the Black middle class and its leadership capabilities, and to help Blacks achieve full freedom in America. In a paper at the inaugural meeting of the academy, "The Conservation of the Races,"[13] Du Bois echoed Crummell's views and added that if the intellectuals of the academy and black intellectuals in general were to accomplish their various goals, they would have to do so by working closely with Black cultural and social institutions. They would have to help mobilize these institutions and Black people to produce, for instance, "a Negro school of literature and art." These cultural and social efforts meant that Blacks would have to hold onto their racial identity in America and never give it up. Intellectuals of the academy and other Black intellectuals would help Blacks function in America as Blacks as well as Americans. But the Black identity and the Black culture had to be held onto firmly because, as Du Bois saw it, Blacks in America, as he saw black people generally, had an intellectual and cultural "Message" to give America and the world.

Taking Crummell and Du Bois's remarks alone, one can see that the intellectuals of the American Negro Academy were seeking to foster a kind of organic relationship between Black intellectuals and Black people. The concept *organic* is taken from the Italian intellectual Antonio Gramsci, who posited it years later in his writings. Cornel West employs this term, taking it from Gramsci, and suggests that Black intellectuals make use of it in their present efforts in America. West does not seem to know that such a conception of a relationship between intellectuals and masses was nearly a century old among Blacks, even if the specific concept *organic* had never been used; nor does he note that its practical conceptualization among blacks had preceded Gramsci's theoretical formulations by decades.

The American Negro Academy lasted until 1928. It passed right into the period in Black history known as the Harlem Renaissance, contributing to it. Here was another time when black intellectuals, a group that now included many black literary elements and artists, functioned as a collectivity and in an organic relationship with Black people to augment Black aesthetic culture. Other black aesthetic elements, such as singers, musicians, dancers, and comedians, also par-

ticipated in this collective, organic situation, to help Blacks develop
and advance their aesthetic culture in America or, to put it another
way, the aesthetic dimension of their ethnic culture in the country.
This question of Black ethnicity will have to be discussed further, as
it will be in this book.

But it is to be noted that the Black intellectuals of the Harlem
Renaissance went against two of the primary goals for Black intellectuals as laid out by the American Negro Academy. One of these goals
was that Black intellectuals had to try to strengthen the Black middle
class and Black middle-class leadership in America. The truth was
many black intellectuals during the Harlem Renaissance, and especially among the literary elements, ridiculed the Black middle class
and Black middle-class leadership. The ridicule was so devastating that
neither has regained the stature that each had had in the earlier part
of the twentieth century. Indeed, it is presently fashionable for black
intellectuals, of various kinds, to ridicule the Black middle class and
Black middle-class leadership. And the irony and contradiction of it
all is that it is mainly intellectuals from the Black middle class doing
the ridiculing and undermining of their own class and its leadership
role and abilities.

The second violation of the American Negro Academy's code for
Black intellectuals was that many Black intellectuals abetted White
racism, namely, white supremacy/ebonicism, rather than attacking it.
They did this by focusing heavily on what contemporary Black social
psychologist Allison Davis said were the "primitive" and "low-life"
dimensions of Black life in America. A number of Black intellectuals
and other Blacks made this criticism of Black literati and Black artists
and other aesthetic elements. Du Bois was one of them. Jesse Faucett
was another. Black historians and other Black intellectuals who have
analyzed the Harlem Renaissance have called the critics of the Black
"primitive" and "low-life" portrayers, such as Langston Hughes and
Rudolph Fisher, conservatives or even reactionaries; as individuals
against the liberation of Black artists and Black literature and art, and
other manifestations of Black aesthetic culture. This has been a raging
debate among Black historians and other Black intellectuals since the
1920s. But Davis had raised a vital point.

He had done so in an article in 1928, published in *The Crisis*, the
house organ of the National Association for the Advancement of Colored People (NAACP), and entitled "Our Negro Intellectuals." The
writing represented one of the first serious critiques of Black intellec-

tuals in America, concentrating on the aesthetic intellectuals. Davis denied that he wished to thwart Black artists and Black art, but his criticism of Black literati and artists was that they dwelled on the "primitive" and "low-life" dimension of Black existence, to the virtual exclusion of any other people or aspects of Black life in America.

> Our "intellectuals" then, both those in literature and those in race criticism, have capitalized the sensational aspects of Negro life, at the expense of general truth and sound judgment. Primitivism has carried the imagination of our poets and storytellers into the unhealthy and abnormal. . . . With regard to the primitivists, the first thing to be settled is whether our lives are to be interpreted with relation to the Negro race or the human race. Are there any traits peculiar to Negro character, and if so, are those traits especially crude emotions? It will appear, I think, that the qualities of fortitude, irony, and a relative absence of self-pity are the most important influences in the lives of Negroes, and that these qualities are the secret strength of that part of us which is one with a universal nature. Our poets and writers of fiction have failed to interpret this broader human nature in Negroes, and found it relatively easy to disguise their lack of a higher imagination by concentrating upon immediate and crude emotions.[14]

Davis was, as his comments show, raising the question for black intellectuals generally and Black literati, artists, and literary critics in particular whether Black literature, poetry, and art were ingrown and only Black or were also to have a universal dimension and appeal. If the latter was to be the interest, then psychological and cultural traits peculiar only to Black people would make the broader orientation for literary and artistic efforts impossible.

Without conceptualization, Davis (as well as other contemporary Black critics of Black literati, Black artists, and Black aesthetic critics) raised another important point in his critique. This was about *essentialism*, as it related to Black people, as a people, and to their aesthetic culture. In a recent work, *The Rhythms of Black Folk*, Jon Michael Spencer defined what he called "black essentialism" in the following manner: "the notion that there is a black essence that biologically or ontologically distinguishes us from other human beings."[15] Spencer was talking about a *racial essentialism*, and he asserted that this viewpoint had derived from the thoughts of the racist French thinker of the nineteenth century Joseph de Gobineau and been modified by black thinkers in the nineteenth century and even in the twentieth century and from whom he was claiming his intellectual heritage. The forebears he referred to were "Edward Wilmot Blyden, Alexander Crummell, W. E. B. Du Bois, Kwame Nkrumah, Leopold Senghor, Langston Hughes, and others."

What the black thinkers of the late nineteenth century had done—Blyden, Crummell, and Du Bois (and others of the American Negro Academy)—had been to react to the *racist essentialism* of Gobineau and other white Western thinkers of the late nineteenth century that emphasized the low intellect and innate emotionalism, hedonism, degeneracy, and savagery of black people, as well as other alleged innate traits that were actually opposite to the others, but which were alleged to be in black people, such as being childlike, innocent, devoted, affectionate, good-natured, docile, and patient.[16] Racist essentialism had it that these alleged innate traits of the black race or black people were absolutely fixed and unchanging. What Blyden, Crummell, Du Bois, and other black intellectuals did was to take some of the second kind of racist essentialist traits, the "positive" ones, and make them part of racial essentialism, without necessarily seeing them as innate or permanent, and even accepting that history, culture, and social experience had something to do with this investment, such as making black people more open and caring.

In his critique of Black intellectuals of the 1920s, and without conceptualization, Davis accused many of them of subscribing to racist essentialism to describe or portray Black life at the time; doing so, he argued, played into the hands of White racism. Davis gave indication that he and other black intellectuals, and this would certainly include Du Bois, were subscribers to racial essentialism, as reflected in his view of positive Black traits, as already presented and also because of other racial traits he said that Blacks possessed, such as "fortitude, an oriental spirituality and unworldliness, and a faculty of laughing at any tendency towards self-pity."[17] For Davis and for other Black thinkers of the 1920s that he could identify with, the positive racial traits that Blacks had were what gave them and their historical experience a universality, which could be reflected in literature, drama, and art.

Jon Michael Spencer is a strong believer in racial essentialism and sees as its central feature the *basic rhythm* to be found in Black culture and social life (as well as among all black people in Africa or those derived from Africans). Spencer regards it as appropriate and necessary to do racial thinking or racialist thinking. There are Black intellectuals today who reject the idea and reality of race and who would strongly object to something called racial thinking or racialist thinking. The latter is a particularly problematic phrase that Spencer does not seem to be aware of or does not wish to acknowledge. There are black African and white European intellectuals, especially, who use phrases such as *racialism* or *racialist thinking* that are synonymous with the words *racism* and *racist* and, thus, are actually discussing these phenomena in their commentary, not race or racial realities.

Molefi Asante is another Black intellectual who believes in and advocates Black essentialism. But he does it differently. He refers to it, as he did in *Malcolm X as Cultural Hero*,[18] as *African essentialism*. Asante believes that Black people in America, as well as all black people in the Western Hemisphere, are Africans, just like the black people on the large island continent. An African identity is part of Asante's conception of African essentialism, as are an African historical tradition, African culture, African institutions, and African modes of thinking. Asante deemphasizes race or biology and focuses more on history and culture. He is one of the foremost exponents in America of what he and others call Afrocentricity and the Afrocentric Perspective, which I prefer to call Africancentricity and the Africancentric Perspective. Asante feels that the "recentering" of Africa and Africans in their own history will result in a profoundly new way of looking at both and will be a boost to the intellectual and aesthetic cultural development of Blacks in America and among black people elsewhere in the Western Hemisphere. In the 1920s, Black intellectuals turned to Africa for inspiration in art, music, and dance. But it was the view of Davis and others that all this did was to orient Black literary and artistic people to primitivism and what I myself have denoted as racist essentialism. There were other contemporary critics of the Harlem Renaissance who felt that the inclusion of Black folk-cultural material in Renaissance efforts also promoted racist essentialism and abetted White racism in America. What was missing during the Harlem Renaissance was a general and adequate aesthetic philosophy or theory to guide Black intellectuals, Black artists, and other Black aesthetic elements in developing black aesthetic culture and in dealing with such specific matters as the essentialisms associated with Black thought and life, the role of folk culture in aesthetic literary and artistic efforts, the relationship of Black aesthetic culture to black African aesthetic culture, and the way that aesthetic culture should or had to aid Blacks in their march to full freedom in America. This kind of general Black Aesthetic was developed in the late 1960s and 1970s, but it had a short life. A Black Aesthetic is needed for Black aesthetic cultural production in America. In another chapter I focus on the subject of a Black Aesthetic.

A primary reason why a Black Aesthetic fell essentially (but not totally) by the wayside after the 1970s was because of the negative impact of postmodern thought on it. (I will deal with what is called modernity and postmodernity, or postmodernism, in a separate chapter.) I regard both modernity and postmodernism to be colossal fantasies and deceptions. Not enough Black intellectuals, of any kind, have recognized this and, therefore, have not recognized how they have been bamboozled. There is a belief, for instance, that deconstruction is a method of critique invented by postmodernists. I will argue later that Black people have been using that method since the seventeenth century, during what postmodern thinkers refer to as one of the centuries of European or Western modernity, with some postmodern thinkers regarding the seventeenth century as the inaugural century of that modernity, when René Descartes made metaphysical philosophy and the individual human subject epistemology supreme in Western thought. Blacks in America had also had long experience dealing with the question of the relationship between representations and reality that became the concern of postmodernists in the 1960s and thereafter. And while white postmodern thinkers attack and denounce philosophical foundationalism, they have neither understood nor dealt with racist foundationalism that continues on in the Western world and, therefore, the racism embedded in postmodernity itself, when one accepts that designation to analyze it.

As will be seen in the chapter on a Black Aesthetic, postmodern thought affects the ability of Black literary and artistic elements to determine the *position* they write or perform from to construct and promote Black aesthetic culture. Postmodern thought is against race and any notion of racial essentialism. It denounces any form of humanism. Postmodernists claim that they are against any kind of general narratives or general theories, which would pit them against a general Black Aesthetic, which would affect the way Black literati and artists and other Black aesthetic creators positioned themselves to do Black aesthetic culture.

But these kinds of Black intellectuals had difficulty positioning themselves to pursue this objective long before postmodern thought crippled and thwarted this effort. The basic difficulty has always been the problem that Black people have had with their own identity. It has to be said, however, that this has been a problem mainly for some Black middle-class people, and particularly some Black intellectuals of that class. I take up the question of black identity in America in the next chapter, where I will endeavor to show how and why Black people are black people (racially) and Black people (ethnically). Black people are not, nor have they ever been, Africans, Afro-Americans, Afri-Americans, AfraAmericans, or African Americans. There are Black intellectuals, including Black literati and Black artists and musicians, and other aesthetic figures who use many of these names to describe Black people. But one can see the great difficulty this presents in positioning. One can see the great difficulty this presents to canon formation or to constructing a general aesthetic cultural intellectual framework.

At the heart of all of these problems is the problem of historical knowledge, namely, the knowledge of Black history in America. This knowledge has to be provided to all Black intellectuals and all Black people. It is crucial to developing Black aesthetic culture and having the ability to analyze and evaluate it critically. Thus, a knowledge of Black history is crucial to developing a Black literary or Black art criticism. I myself am a Black historian (actually, historical sociologist), and I am critical of much of the Black history written in this country, and particularly by many Black historians. A number of these historians are heavily romanticizing Black history, which drew a sharp rebuke from Clarence Walker in his book, *Deromanticizing Black History*.[19] There are Black historians who call themselves Black Nationalist historians. But what their discussions invariably point to is Black ethnicity, or the Black community, and nothing remotely relating to nation-state construction, or nation-state living, which is what nationalism is about. Black historians have not helped other Black intellectuals and other Black people to know that all Black people in America who are descendants of the slaves who had been brought to these shores directly from what is known as Africa comprise a large ethnic group, and which is a new ethnic group of the black race that stretches from the Western Hemisphere to the African continent. Black ethnicity is a legitimate foundation on which to position oneself to produce Black literature, Black art, Black music, Black dance and other Black aesthetic cultural forms: But most Black aesthetic elements do not position themselves on the basis of Black ethnicity. Nor do they (usually) position themselves on the basis of an American identity, or a Black American identity, which are also proper positioning points from which to do Black aesthetic culture in America. Black ethnicity is a legitimate position from which to do Black history as well. There is something rather unique about Black history in the United States, which cannot be captured by referring to Blacks as Africans, or to their history as African history or African-American history. Indeed, conceiving of and writing about Black history under either of these conceptions distorts and suppresses that uniqueness and distorts and suppresses Black history. I think there has to be a close collaboration between Black historians and all other Black intellectuals, to help the latter better understand black history, black culture, and Black social life—as historical realities—so that they can better utilize the knowledge of them in their intellectual and aesthetic cultural efforts. I see this essay as a contribution to this collaboration, which has to be interminable.

A particular historical contribution I wish to make, which will actually be historical-psychological, is to discuss the subject and reality of *Black Cognition*. Philosophers and psychologists have long dealt with the subject of cognition. Some clinical psychologists have long practiced cognitive psychology and cognitive therapy. Cognition is a special way to talk about an intellectual orientation and intellectual activities that involve beliefs, ideals, values, thinking, memory, perception, and observation. Cultural anthropologists now make extensive use of cognitive theory, employing cognition as a method to understand other cultures. The point I will make in a separate chapter of discussion is that Black people, as a people—as an ethnic group in America—have evolved and use a unique cognitive method that is very different from the way white people in this country engage in cognition. Actually white people employ several methods or systems of cognition. There are Black people who know and utilize these methods, too, namely, some Black middle-class people, and particularly Black intellectuals and Black leaders. But these Black people and other Black people—the mass of Black people—mainly employ the single but complicated form of Black Cognition, which I call *diunital cognition*, taking the name from the book *Beyond Black or White*[20] published in 1971 by Vernon Dixon and Badi Foster and other black scholars. The book has long since been out of print, but it contains a discussion of Black Cognition, without the authors themselves knowing how deeply this form of cognition was embedded in Black history and Black ethnicity nor how commonplace it was among Blacks. Black Cognition is part of the uniqueness of Black history and Black life in America. It is the key to working out the problems involved in researching and writing Black history, in constructing a general Black Aesthetic, and in helping Black literary, artistic, and other aesthetic elements contribute to the construction and augmentation of Black aesthetic culture in America and how this culture can help Blacks achieve full freedom in the country. But the discussion of Black Cognition has to be preceded by a discussion of Black identity, which immediately follows.

2.

From an African to a Black Identity

In the first half of the nineteenth century, some Black intellectuals in the United States gave birth, without conceptualization, to the Africancentric Perspective. This was when lay Black historians appeared in America, and they wrote histories that showed that Black people had origins beyond slavery and beyond America and which could be located on the African continent. Such historians also talked to some extent about the impact of Africa on the Greek and Roman civilizations and, thus, on the history and civilizational development of Europe. Other Black intellectuals at the time and in later decades of the century took up this theme: "Henry Highland Garnet . . . Frederick Douglass, and Martin Delaney among others appealed to the writings of Homer, Herodotus, and other classical writers to argue that Egypt and Ethiopia had been great and progressive civilizations—and that they had been Negro."[1]

The above comments were made by Eric Sundquist in *To Wake the Nations*, who continued:

> A number of the significant black historical and sociological works on Africa and African America in the late nineteenth and early twentieth centuries—among them George Washington Williams's *History of the Negro Race in America* (1883), William T. Alexander's *History of the Colored*

Race in America (1887), C. T. Walker's *Appeal to Caesar*
(1900), Pauline Hopkins's *Primer of Facts Pertaining to the
Early Greatness of the African Race* (1905), Booker T.
Washington's *Story of the Negro* (1909), William Ferris's
African Abroad (1911), and Du Bois's . . . *The Negro*
(1915)—eloquently refuted the regnant white argument,
summarized by John T. Morgan, that Africans have not
contributed a thought, or a labor, except by compulsion,
to aid the process of civilization.[2]

These historical works reflect their inadequacies of scholarship and
many of their mistaken claims about black Africans and black Africans
in antiquity. They were written at the height of White racism in the
Western world, which centered in a virulent white supremacy/ebon-
icism, white supremacy/xanthicism, and very heavy Nordicism/anti-
Jewism. They were written at the time when Whites/Westerners or
Whites/Europeans were finishing up the process that they had
initiated back in the late fifteenth century of establishing their hegemony on the planet, employing racism, colonialism, imperialism, military power, and many aspects of Western civilization, including
science, technology scholarship, and political thought to do so. Black
intellectuals in America were countering this effort, saying things
about Black people in America and black people in Africa and about
Africa that were not said or which were distorted. Much of what Du
Bois said about ancient Egypt and ancient Ethiopia in *The Negro*
would be upheld by present scholarship, as would his discussion
about the role of black people in the ancient Near East and in Asia.
J. A. Rogers, from the 1920s on, and in a number of books[3] and
through many revealing photographs, tells the story as it has never
before been told, about the presence of black Africans and people of
black African descent in the world and their participation in world
civilization—notwithstanding St. Clair Drake's recent two-volume
discussion of the subject.[4] There have been other later and more
scholarly writings with greater presentations of facts, accuracies, and
truths that have all contributed to the construction and presentation
of the Africancentric Perspective, with a number of them preceding
the formal construction of this concept and which speak to the black
Africans' and Africa's impact on Western history and civilization.
George James published his important and influential *Stolen Legacy*.[5]
Chancellor Williams published *The Destruction of Black Civilization*

in 1971,[6] and it was reissued in 1987. Frank Snowden published two important studies, *Blacks in Antiquity* and *Before Color Prejudice.*[7] Cheikh Anta Diop published two important works, *The African Origins of Civilization* and *Civilization or Barbarism.*[8] John Jackson, who had written a number of works within the Africancentric framework since the 1930s, published *Introduction to African Civilizations* in 1970.[9] Likewise Yosef ben-Jochannan published *African Origins of the Major "Western Religions"* and *Africa: Mother of Western Civilization*[10] in 1970 and 1971 (originally), respectively. In 1976, Ivan Van Sertima published *They Came Before Columbus.*[11] He is also the editor of the *Journal of African Civilizations*, which has concentrated on ancient Egypt, depicting it primarily as a black civilization and one that had made enormous contributions to Western civilization. There are other black and Black historians and other scholars who have written on ancient Egyptian or other ancient African civilizations. There have also been a host of white scholars who have done the same, going back to the late nineteenth century, and usually writing on these civilizations as if they were composed of white people, that is, "dark Caucasians" or white civilizations. What present-day black and Black scholarship is out to do is to strengthen its reclamation that the ancient Egyptian and Ethiopian civilizations were black civilizations. There are white scholars who are willing to support this contention with respect to ancient Egyptian civilization, although not always so clearly or forcefully, such as Basil Davidson and Martin Bernal (see, for example, Bernal's *Black Athena*). Legrand Clegg II has recently expressed great outrage at the way that white Western scholars have sought to take the blackness out of the ancient Egyptians and the ancient Egyptian civilization:

> Ancient Egypt was stolen from Africa by nineteenth-century Egyptologists whose doctrine was nourished by the African slave trade, the sugar empire, and the cotton kingdom. Many scientists during this period were loathe to associate black folks with the human race, much less with civilization. Hence it was early determined that not only black people be excluded from Egypt, but that Egypt itself, through ingenious anthropological manipulation, be excluded from Africa. . . . Never before or since has such a mockery been made of human history in the name of racial superiority and under the auspices of anthropological pur-

suit. Science bowed before race prejudice and truth re-
coiled in panic.[12]

A point to be made here is this: that while the Africancentric Perspective was initiated by Black intellectuals in the United States and
augmented by them and by other black intellectuals, the writings on
ancient African civilizations by white intellectuals can be utilized by
them. Thus, and in fact, there is a vast scholarly corpus of works that
Black and black intellectuals can use to develop the Africancentric
Perspective more fully.

And then there is the physical science evidence to draw into this
Perspective to broaden it and to augment it and to validate it. Since
the nineteenth century, paleontologists and anthropologists have
been digging up fossil remains of early humans, called *hominids,*
meaning prehistoric creatures that fall roughly in the "human family." In 1959, Louis Leakey found fossil remains in Kenya that carbon
dating proclaimed to be 1.8 million years old. In 1972, the year Leakey died, he found a skull that he regarded as being a human skull
that he concluded, from dating, was about three million years old.
Subsequent evaluations by paleontologists reduced the age of the
skull to just less than two million years old, but with discernible human characteristics. Then, in 1974, Donald Johnson and his exca-
vation team discovered the remains of a young female fossil in
Ethiopia, which they called Lucy and dated at 3.5 million years of
age.[13] This fossil had definite human characteristics, and it suggested
that human beings, Homo sapiens, had a longer ancestral history than
had previously been believed. Then in 1994, a skull was found in
Kenya that was carbon dated at three million years old, the oldest
human fossil skull ever found.[14] This discovery also brought a raging
controversy among paleontologists to a close—at least for the time
being. Some paleontologists had adhered to a theory that human
origins had occurred in two places simultaneously: Asia and Africa.
But the three-million-year-old humanlike skull, which greatly exceeds
the age of any skull found in Asia, has discredited that theory, in what
could be a permanent resolution. Some paleontologists had resisted
accepting the African origins of human beings and had kept looking
for them in Asia. Adding to the African origins of human beings, a
recent discovery was made of sophisticated tools in Zaire by anthropologist Allison Brooks and her husband John F. Yellen, that have
been dated at 90,000 years old. This predates the use of sophisticated

tools in Europe and Asia, where it was long argued that such tools were first used, by 75,000 years.[15]

There had also been another earlier body of evidence to suggest that human beings had originally emerged in Africa. About three decades ago, some geneticists discovered the mitochondrion gene. This was genetic material on the outside of the DNA cell that was transmitted only by women. Geneticists began searching the world to see if they could find the oldest pool of mitochondrion genes. They found the oldest pool in Kenya. This discovery was actually the discovery (without fossil remains) of Homo sapiens indicating that anywhere from 250,000 to 300,000 years ago, human beings emerged in Africa, given birth by what the geneticists call Eve (having not as yet found an Adam). The conclusion is that these human beings, the first to appear in history and on the earth, were black people: "If Eve lived within the past 200,000 years, she may have been a modern human, perhaps one of the first to appear. In that case she might have looked like a more muscular version of today's Africans. . . . She was certainly a hunter-gatherer, probably much like today's Bushmen in southern Africa."[16]

Paleontologists have put forward two separate theories that relate to hominid and human-being emigration from Africa. One theory is that the Australopithecine, Homo erectus, which had originated in Africa, emigrated from that continent about a million years ago (some paleontologists now say two million) and populated the world with itself and its descendants. The second theory is that Homo sapiens left Africa anywhere between 180,000 and 100,000 years ago[17] and populated the world with human beings. These early human beings were black; thus they underwent color and biological mutations in other parts of the world, giving birth to yellow people, white people, red people, and others.

While theory is always subject to change, when new evidence and interpretation require it, theory holds, is *durational*, until something replaces it. There are those geneticists still looking in Asia for the oldest mitochondrion gene pool. The mitochondrion genes found in Kenya and the three-million-year-old humanlike skull found there have not dissuaded these searchers. But the present theories about human origins and emigration are the ones that must be given the greater weight and validity. What these theories generally say is that human beings originated in Africa and were originally black people. The current theory also states that these original black human beings inaugurated human history, human culture, human social life, and human language. In regard to the latter, the German zoologist Josef Reichholf recently indicated that linguists had backed up the mito-chondrion theory of human origins "by comparing the 5,000 human languages to find the common root—in Africa."[18]

Thus, the Africancentric Perspective is not as some would have us believe some romantic, unrealistic, irresponsible intellectual frame-work for historical, cultural, and social analysis. Moreover, it can be seen that it is not a new perspective and that it is more than a hundred and fifty years old. It was formally conceptualized in the 1980s and still remains underdeveloped, but there is a lot of historical, fossil, and other physical evidence to draw into it and to be worked on to augment it, and there is now theory and philosophy being injected into it by Molefi Asante and other Africancentrists.

There are two prominent Black intellectuals who object to the Af-ricancentric Perspective. One of them is Henry Louis Gates, Jr., and the other is Cornel West. Gates thinks that Africancentrism is "secessionist," reflects "cognitive relativism," also "epistemic segre-gation," and is also "incoherent." Perceiving the Africancentric Per-spective and Africancentrism in this manner, Gates objects to its becoming a main feature of American higher education:

> Of course, my vision of the academy centers on dialogue and mutual interrogation, not proud secessionism. And so I worry that the sort of cognitive relativism promoted by many Afrocentrists eventuates precisely in this sort of epi-stemic segregation, where disagreement betokens only a culpable failure to comprehend. This explains my own skepticism about such approaches; I believe cognitive rel-ativism to be incoherent.[19]

My reaction to these comments is that they are nonsensical. They remind me of the white scholars of antiquity who will not let Egypt reside in Africa. Africancentrism is not secessionist, as it is essentially excluded from American higher education. Africancentrists would love to dialogue with white scholars on what they are about, and the kind of knowledge and interpretations they are trying to bring forth. But white scholars, in the main, will not engage in dialogue with them. This means that Africancentrists are not against Whites sharing their epistemic practices or learning from them or even helping to construct Africancentrism, as Whites are presently doing that and have been doing so even when it was not intended. And for a postmodern thinker like Gates to be against relativism, which is a byword for postmodernists, makes no sense.

Another prominent Black intellectual, Houston Baker, Jr., has an entirely different view about the Africancentric Perspective and Africancentrism. He recently remarked:

> Now with Afrocentricity, I have always assumed that what scholars were talking about was a different orientation in the American academy toward African history, literature, culture, etc. To the extent that the study of such areas of world knowledge has been sharply limited in the American academy, Afrocentric scholars consider themselves redressing an imbalance. It has never seemed to me that they have called for any person of goodwill to stay away from the domain of study they have marked out for themselves.[20]

Cornel West's dislike of the Africancentric Perspective and Africancentrism is rather peculiar. It has a tragic dimension. West simply does not seem to like black intellectuals, at least not many of them. He does not think that many of them are worth their designation. He once remarked in *Prophetic Fragments*[21] that W. E. B. Du Bois was not a major socialist thinker, and yet I have my own unpublished dissertation of Du Bois's socialist analysis and a draft of a manuscript of his prescriptive socialist theories to disprove that notion; they indicate that he was one of the most significant socialist thinkers that America has ever produced. In a recent article entitled "The Dilemma of the Black Intellectual," West said: "And to be honest, black America has yet to produce a great literate intellectual with the exception of Toni Morrison. There indeed have been superb ones—Du Bois, Frazier, [Ralph] Ellison, [James] Baldwin, [Zora Neale] Hurston—and many good ones. But none can compare to the heights achieved by the black preachers and musicians."[22] West believes there is much "mediocre black intellectual production," which includes "the latest fashion of writing, which is often motivated by the desire to parade for the white bourgeois intellectual establishment." As regards parading, I would have to regard this as an instance of the pot calling the kettle black—because this is precisely what West does. Molefi Asante is right, it seems to me, when he says of West that he "has an awesome disregard for reading African-American intellectuals."[23] This is reflected by the fact that when West recommended intellectual help for Black intellectuals to try to help shape them up in America, to make them more useful to the Black community and to America, and to help advance both, he recommended three bodies of White thought for them to take up with. He recommended no Black thinker or collective Black thought. He shied totally away from an African-centric Perspective and Africancentric knowledge and probably would have shied away from what I call a Blackcentric Perspective and Black-centric knowledge, which I will talk about later in this chapter.

West did not want Black intellectuals to be deferential to the White thought or white intellectuals he wanted them to follow, and he even pointed out to them what he regarded as being of value in the recommendations that he made and they should work with. One of his recommendations was bourgeois humanistic thought and action, from which Black intellectuals should take "the emphasis on human will and heroic effort . . . this model privileges collective intellectual work that contributes to the communal resistance and struggle."[24] Who has exerted human will and been more heroic in American history than Black people? So why would Black intellectuals wish to turn to white intellectual or white social models on this? And Black intellectuals have often functioned as a collectivity in America to aid Blacks in their struggle in the country. So what would be new about this? What would make more sense would be to suggest to Black intellectuals that they read and digest the vast body of Black thought on the Black struggle in America and seek to change or augment that, as a way to aid Blacks and America. This could be a foundation from which to reach out for White thought that might be deemed useful.

Cornel West recommended to Black intellectuals the thought of the French postmodern thinker Michel Foucault. Foucault is something of a rage among many white Western thinkers, and some Black ones as well, such as West. Foucault considered intellectuals to be very important in society, but he did not believe that they should be seeking truth, because truth was not to be found because language, ideology, theory, and other things blocked the ability to get at truth. What intellectuals had to do was expose how what was projected or promoted as truth was done—what he called "truth regimes"—and how they were perpetuated. This meant that knowledge had to be perceived as power. Foucault felt that power took more forms in society than just political, military, judicial, or sovereign power. It was pervasive in society and was reflected in language and discourse. Foucault was an advocate of resistance to power.[25]

West felt that Foucault was really who Black intellectuals should follow. In his mind, Foucault was a thinker on the Left, which West seems to think is the only valid form of thought. Left and Right thinking is White thinking to begin with, flowing from White cognition. West wishes black intellectuals to be white intellectuals in thought and cognitive habits. But one certainly questions the notion of intellectuals not seeking truth. The power to make anything pass for truth would seem to make it imperative to seek out truth. Would Foucault and West be in favor of ending criminal investigations or court trials? But then, if there is no truth to be had, then what is the point of doing research? What is the point of philosophical or critical reflection? Like so many postmodern thinkers, and in so many instances, Foucault wished to throw the baby out with the bath.

And, or course, it has to be said, that "truth regimes" are hardly something new for Black intellectuals or Black people. Both have been dealing with the racist truth regime of America for centuries and all the ways that Whites have upheld it.[26] And Blacks, more than any other people in America, know how pervasive power can be in the country and how it can be found in every nook and cranny of it. White supremacist/ebonicist power has been pervasive in American society since the late seventeenth and first half of the eighteenth centuries, and Blacks have had to deal with it. Did not Black intellectuals see white racist power embedded in the Declaration of Independence and the Constitution? In representative government and capitalism? Did not Black intellectuals and other Blacks know that when white people said progress, they did not mean the same progress for Blacks as for Whites and that there was ensconced in that understanding that Whites would use power and even violence to deny or limit progress for Blacks? What can be said about Foucault is that he learned in the 1960s, and thereafter until his death in 1984, some things about power that had been commonplace among black intellectuals and other Blacks for centuries. And Blacks have had a history of resisting pervasive and multifaceted white racist power. But they have also had a history of having, in a necessary way, to cooperate with White racist power and using it—as Booker T. Washington did so effectively. Foucault would have been against Black Power. But West is against it, too—and wants Black intellectuals to be against it. Foucault's thought might be of some help to Black intellectuals, but they would

be helped more by studying how Black thinkers, Black leaders, and
Black people have dealt with vast, pervasive power, and then maybe
looking at someone like Foucault.

The third body of thought that West wanted Black intellectuals to
make use of, in a modified manner, was Marxist thought. This recommendation is the least satisfactory that West made. Marxists in
America and Europe, and particularly white ones, have shown little
ability to understand racism. Their emphasis is on social class and
social class domination. Black people have been dominated in America primarily by white men. This is gender, not class domination. And
since white men dominated black people in a racist manner, from
their gender position, that makes the domination gender-racist.
Marxists and Marxist analysis would not be able to relate to these
situations easily. Nor could they to the situation that Black people in
America constitute an ethnic group in the country, because Marxist
thought, driven by class analysis, does not deal with ethnicity very
well. Marxists and Marxism do not like capitalism, but Black people
are overwhelmingly capitalistic. There is the concept of class struggle
among Marxists, but Blacks hardly need conflict between their social
classes. How would that strengthen Black people? Black ethnicity?
How would Blacks be aided in their struggle against White domination divided among themselves? How would they build power in
America, divided among themselves? West calls himself a radical democrat, a euphemism. He is really a socialist, namely, a social democrat
or, as he might also say, a democratic socialist. Black people in the
United States are overwhelmingly not socialists. Most socialists who
remain in America are white. How would Blacks, as West seems to
wish, be helped by following white socialists?

And one more final thing about West: He seems to think that any
Black intellectual's turn to Africa will be done in a romantic or irresponsible manner. He said in his article on Black intellectuals: "The
future of the black intellectual lies neither in a deferential disposition
toward the Western parent nor in a nostalgic search for the African
one."[27] One thing that Black intellectuals, and other Black people
have shown is that when they have taken ideas or culture from
Whites, intellectuals and other Blacks have shown a tendency to mod-
ify what was taken. This is their history, and this is what people usually
do when they borrow culture. Neither element of Blacks had to be
instructed in that. And it goes without saying that Africa is a parent
of Black people. They originally, through their ancestors, came from

there. Their original culture, which was the culture they brought to North America, came from there. Their biological heritage, that is, their racial heritage, originated from there. So there is, inescapably, African parentage of Blacks in America. The task before Black intellectuals and other Black people is to clarify the extent and quality of this parentage. Put another way, these two groups, with Black intellectuals leading the way, have to clarify the relationship of Black people, Black history, and Black cultural and social life to Africa. That has to be a serious scholarly and intellectual effort. And Black historians have to play a crucial role in that. Black African scholars also have to help Blacks in America with these understandings. This is where the Africancentric Perspective and Africancentrism become aids in understanding. They function to help Blacks understand their continental origins and the kind of historical and civilizational backgrounds they came from through their ancestors who came to America as slaves. Whites in America and Europe have done a lot to disparage Africa and its peoples and its cultural and civilizational attainments, even often denying that black Africans had produced civilizations. There has been, since the nineteenth century, an effort to discredit ancient Egypt. And when that has not been done, there has been an effort to deny that it was primarily a civilization of black people. Even when the ancient Egyptian civilization has been called an African civilization, there has been the concomitant assertion that the ancient Egyptians were white, "dark Caucasians" or "brown Mediterraneans." These are all manifestations of a white Western obsession, rooted fundamentally in the White racist obsessive effort to prove that black people are innately inferior to white people and do not have the innate intellectual ability to create a glorious civilization. This racist obsession continues in 1997. So who is being romantic, nostalgic, and irresponsible?

As always with racists, it is the victim who is to be criticized, ridiculed, or blamed. And it is not always the racists who do that. They can find or encourage others to do it for them. Recently, the black British intellectual Paul Gilroy was critical of Black intellectuals in America and black intellectuals elsewhere trying to claim ancient Egyptian civilization as primarily a black civilization (or, worse yet, as an all-black civilization).

The difficulties involved in projecting the typologies of modern racism back into a past where they are wholly ir-

relevant can be illustrated through the problems that arise
in attempts to name the Egyptians black according to contemporary definitions rather than seeing them as one African people among many others.[28]

This comment reflects shortsightedness, among other things. There
are white American and white European scholars who are saying in
their writings, directly or indirectly, that the ancient Egyptians were
white people. One indirect way is to remove ancient Egypt from Africa. Another indirect way is to talk of the ancient Egyptians as being
simply Africans. This would make them what kind of people racially:
white, black, brown? Or would they be colorless? What people in the
world are colorless? The Germans are Europeans. Are they also white?
Will anyone deny that? Not likely. If it were now only said of the
Germans that they were Europeans, and there was no reference to
their race, would people still know that they were white? Yes, because
they know they're white. The instruction on that has been so thorough and continuous that people just know this fact. And that instruction continues on in many indirect, subtle ways. The world has
been told for a long time that the ancient Egyptians were white.
Calling them Africans, and making no reference to their color, will
continue to make them, in the eyes of white people, and other people,
as well, white people. Ivan Van Sertima tells the story of how a white
person said to him that pictures he had seen of ancient Egyptians
showed that the men were red in color and the women were orange.
Van Sertima said that he had remarked to the person that no group
of people in the world, or at any time in human history, have had
men one color and women another. And then he explained that red
was the color and symbol of masculinity and that orange (or yellow)
was the color and symbol of femininity in ancient Egypt.

But was not the person's position absurd? Is it not absurd to remove Egypt from Africa? Is it not absurd to try to make the ancient
Egyptians colorless? Why, on a continent that people know is made
up mainly of black people, do people insist on having one area on
this continent as it existed in ancient times, when there were even
fewer white people on it, that contains only white people? And would
this be done if that area had not housed a great civilization?

And what about the ancient testimony? The ancient Egyptians
called their country Kemit, not Egypt, an ancient Greek word. In
Egyptian hieroglyphics, the world *kem* means black, and when female

and male figures or symbols are put together with this hieroglyphic, as Cheikh Diop says, the reference is to black people. The ancient Greeks called the ancient Egyptians and other black people in northeast Africa Ethiopians, meaning "burnt-faced" people. White people are not burnt-faced people. As historian Frank Snowden said in *Blacks in Antiquity*, both the ancient Greeks and ancient Romans used the word *Ethiopian* to refer to people who were black, blackish-brown, and brown in color.[29] And then there are Herodotus's comments about the color of ancient Egyptians. And what is one to do with Aristotle's comment that the ancient Egyptians were "excessively black"[30] in color? And to say, as Dinesh D'souza recently said in *The End of Racism*, that ancient Egypt could not have been primarily a black civilization, when it was, as he said—basing his contention on the testimony of hostile "Egyptologists"—a "multiracial civilization,"[31] is like saying that America's population is not predominantly white, because America is a multiracial society. Or that the former Soviet union was not made up mainly of white people, because it was multiracial.

Thus, it is not a matter of transposing contemporary racist theories to ancient times, as Gilroy said. If that were the case, then it would not be race that one would be concerned with, but rather concerned with "race." Gilroy seems not to know the difference between racism and race. And he (like others) seems to be operating on the assumption that everybody in a race has the exact same biological features. This would make a race pure. But there have never been pure races, because individual races have color and other biological variations within them. As biologist Richard Osborne has written: "There has never been such a thing as a 'pure' race. Race formation and breakdown is a dynamic process subject to constant change."[32] There are white people who are white, palish white, reddish or pinkish white, cream color, and brownish white. There are white people with blond hair, red hair, brown hair, and black hair. There are white people with blue eyes, brown eyes, green eyes, hazel eyes. There are white people with thin noses and some with long noses and broad noses. There are white people with thin lips and broad lips. These kinds of variations within the white race can be observed by observing northern and southern, and eastern Europeans and white people in America. But presumably what is true about white people is not applicable to black people. White people, especially, insist that all black people have to be biologically alike. Any variation among black people would be interpreted by these Whites to mean that some people did not belong to the black race. This is racist thinking at work, and this is the basic reason that there is all this furor, denial, ambiguity, and contrived confusion about the color and race of most ancient Egyptians.

But Black intellectuals and other Black people in America, or black intellectuals elsewhere, do not have to participate in this behavior, which is political behavior disguised as scholarship. What it shows is how racist scholarship is used to promote racist political and social behavior, how it is still being used to promote these things. It should be clear to black intellectuals anywhere that it would be illogical and absurd for them to accede to white intellectuals and other white people as the ones who should have the authoritative judgment about race, concept and reality, which they have greatly fouled up and have bent to the most atrocious uses.

But on the other hand, I have my own critical stance toward the Africancentric Perspective and Africancentrism. I object to the phrases Afrocentricity and Afrocentrism. If African people are Africans, then they must be called Africans and not Afros. There are no Afros, Afris, Afras, or Africos in this world. This is an instance of Black or black intellectuals playing around with the identities of black or Black people, and, therefore, joining with the white racists they despise, in playing with, distorting, deprecating, and confusing the identity of black or Black people.

Molefi Asante uses phrases like Afrocentricity, Afrocentrism, or the phrase *Africology* for his conception of a body of knowledge about African people and their histories, cultures, and social lives. But another objection that I have to Asante's conception of Afrocentricity, as generally conceived and used, is that he recognizes no limitations to his conceptualization. He is not the only Africancentrist who does this. But he is one of the leading lights in this field, if not the foremost developer in this field, at least in America. So what he says will have considerable carriage. I like much of what he has brought forth so far, as reflected in *Afrocentricity, The Afrocentric Idea*,[33] and other writings. But I object to the absolutist orientation of Asante's thinking and writing—in short, to the 100 percent African parentage that he thinks black people in America have. He also believes this to be so with other black people in the Western Hemisphere. To Asante all black people in this region of the world are Africans. The cultures of all these black people are African cultures. In Asante's Africancentric perception and philosophical or theoretical project, there are not significant distinctions between Africans and people of African descent. Indeed, he does not even recognize the latter classification: "the misoriented African assumes that he or she is not African and therefore takes exception to those who remind him or her that he or she bears all the major characteristics of resemblance to those who are African."[34] This is ignoring, or downplaying—and even suppressing—a lot of historical, cultural, and social reality.

Older generations of Black historians and other kinds of Black and black intellectuals in America referred to all black people in the Western Hemisphere as black people, or as Negro or colored people, and as being of *African descent*. They had recognized that the descendants of the original slaves had undergone historical, cultural, social, and even linguistic transformations. Asante rejects this interpretation and even these realities, even though his own language and discussions might blur his sharp rejection, as when he says that: "The Afrocentrists have been very clear that there exists an African-American cultural history that is distinct from other cultures. We believe that this distinction is based on our multiple African backgrounds, augmented by our enslavement experience, and refined by our resistance movements."[35] What is missing from these comments is any reference to the White, American, or European cultural contributions that went into the early construction of a Black culture in America and which continue to go into the construction and reality of a Black culture in America. Asante and others like him accept only an African parentage for Blacks in America, and ignore, mainly, the Euro-American parentage and also the Black parentage I will discuss.

According to the black African philosopher Kwame Appiah, who teaches at Harvard University and who is a soul mate of Henry Louis Gates, Jr., and Cornel West, the name and identity of African should be confined to the black people on the African continent, and should not be extended to any other black people anywhere.[36] Asante would find this totally objectionable. Jon Spencer strongly rejects the argument, saying that Africa remains the racial homeland of all black people in what he calls the African Diaspora—that is, black people in the Western Hemisphere—and the homeland of the rhythmic tradition of all black people from Africa to the Western Hemisphere. I reject the concept of African Diaspora. I prefer the concept of *Western African Extensia* in regard to this specific external reach of Africa. Diaspora is associated with the African slave trade to the Western

Hemisphere, which dispersed Africans to the region. It conveys the understanding that black Africans had never been in that region of the world until the slave trade put them there. As Ivan Van Sertima has shown in *They Came Before Columbus*, there had been black Africans in the Western Hemisphere thousands of years before the African slave trade dispersed them there. I also have the concept of the *Northern African Extensia*, meaning the black Africans who moved into Europe, going back thousands of years ago, even before the Greeks moved into the Peloponnesus and the concept of the *Eastern African Extensia* to refer to the Africans who emigrated to the Middle East and Asia from early times on. These concepts I see as being part of an Africancentric Perspective, with the knowledge they convey being part of Africancentric knowledge or Africancentrism. I assert the view, as part of an Africancentric Perspective, that when black Africans moved to other parts of the world, they not only moved into different geographical areas but also into different time and spatial zones, and into different historical, cultural, and social contexts. In each geographical and time and spatial zone, they took their original African culture with them, and it also became modified. Asante allows for no transformation or relativism in his concept of Afrocentricity. He would not accept the notion that any black person from Africa would lose his African identity. Spencer is less concerned with an African identity than he is with a black racial identity, from Africa to the Western African Extensia. Appiah accepts the notion that black Africans underwent transformations of identity and culture in the Western African Extensia, leaving the African identity confined to the African continent. He recognizes the African identity to be a continental identity, not a national or ethnic identity. In *In My Father's House*, he argued that black African culture reflected great diversity, that has always stood in the way of a universal black African culture. Because of this, he indicated, an African identity is not fully developed but is in the process of being developed. And this developed identity would be for black Africans and not for black people in the Western African Extensia.

I can accept this argument from Appiah, but I would suggest that this matter of the identity of black African people, and even black people in the Western African Extensia, is more complicated than he seems to realize. It is more complicated than Asante, Spencer, and other Africancentrists seem to realize. Reflect on the following comments by the Kenyan political scientist Ali Mazrui in 1963. In an article of that year, he said: "in colonial schools young Bakongo, Taita and Ewe suddenly learned that the rest of the world had a collective name for the inhabitants of the landmass of which their area formed a part."[37] That collective name was African. But what is important to observe here is that, according to Mazrui, the little black children learned they were Africans from white Europeans, not from their own peoples. Is that because their peoples did not consider themselves Africans? That they did not even know the name *African*, or *Africa*? People outside Africa knew that the black people on the continent were Africans, but the implication of Mazrui's remarks was that the black people on the continent did not know that they were Africans and did not regard themselves as Africans.

In the early 1990s an African intellectual, about to attend an international conference, lamented to another African intellectual:

> Whatever it is, my mind keeps getting pre-occupied with one topic: "The problem of the African being." Or put less philosophically, the problem of being African.
>
> We both know the problems and have discussed them often. So that is not really the topic this time. The real discovery is that the problem of the African is that he *cannot* and does *not* wish to be an African. Examples abound to support the above theory. So I skip that issue also. The real issue therefore is, why can he not and why does he not wish to be an African?[38]

In *In My Father's House*, Appiah, as I have said, indicted that an African identity had to be further developed. But he insisted that an African identity already existed on the continent and had meaning and was accepted by the black people there:

> I do not want to be misunderstood. We are Africans already. And we can give numerous examples from multiple domains of what our being African means. We have, for example, in the OAU and the African Development Bank, and in such regional organizations as SADDC and ECO-WAS, as well as in the African caucuses of the agencies of the UN and the World Bank, African institutions. At the Olympics and the Commonwealth games, athletes from African countries are seen as Africans by the world—and, per-

haps, more importantly, by each other. Being African already has a "certain context and a certain meaning."[39]

But a certain context and meaning for whom? Institutions or organizations can have African names. But the people who participate in them do not have to regard themselves as Africans, as witness the Blacks in America who put the name African in institutions and organizations, but who did not regard themselves as being Africans, but rather as Negroes or Colored people. And what intellectuals and leaders accept as an identity is not what the mass of people might accept. The lament from the African intellectual was that the mass of black people on the island continent did not regard themselves as Africans, even though, as Appiah remarked, there were transnational, continental institutions. Appiah admitted that a continental identity was the weakest kind of identity, with a national identity next in line. The stronger identities were the tribal or ethnic, clan, family, or religious identities in Africa. But, in the case of black Africans, save for those who lived and were educated in Europe or America or other places or who were educated in colonial or missionary schools in Africa, most never really heard the names *African* and *Africa*, until sometime in the twentieth century, principally after the Second World War, when they heard slogans such as Africa for the Africans, African Nationalism, or African Unity. While people outside Africa had been referring to the continent as Africa, and the people in it as Africans, for thousands of years, most of the black people on it, for millennia, were ignorant of these names and identities and did not claim them as their own.

This peculiar situation can be explained. The name *Africa* comes from outside the continent and the indigenous millennial people who lived there. The word is an ancient Greek word, *phrike*, meaning "shuddering." A pun was made on the word, but it remains unclear who made it, the ancient Greeks or the ancient Phoenicians of Carthage, who lived in north Africa (present-day Tunisia) and traded with the Greeks and were their rivals for control of part of the northern portion of the African continent. But at some point either the ancient Greeks or the ancient Phoenicians made a pun on the word, and the pun converted it into *afrike* (fully written out with the proper article, *he afrike*), meaning "without cold, without shuddering."[40] For some reason or other and at some point in time the Carthaginians called their country *afrike*. It was also called that in ancient Phoenician as well, but the word in this instance was *Aourigha*, which was pronounced Afarika.[41] When the Romans conquered Carthage in the third century B.C., the Carthaginians told the Romans, a dictionary of ancient Latin has said, that their country was called *he afrike*[42] perhaps, Aourigha or Afarika as well. But the Romans seemed to have picked the word *he afrike*, which became Africa. The Romans made Carthage a colony and called it Africa. They also called other colonies on the continent Africa. They referred to the northern part of the continent as Africa and sometimes applied that name to the whole continent. The Romans referred to anyone from the continent, as *Afer*, a Latin word meaning African. It was the Romans who popularized the words *Africa* and *African* in history. But they were popularized among people outside the African continent, with most black people on that continent, over millennia, never hearing them and hearing them with any frequency only after the Second World War. As can be imagined, European colonial imperialists in Africa would not often use the words *African* and *Africans* on the continent. These would be universal names and identities. The Europeans dominated and controlled Africa and the black people on the continent, aided by the device of emphasizing tribal or ethnic names, by dividing the tribes or ethnic groups, and also by pitting them against each other. An African identity could have helped to unite the various black ethnic groups against the Europeans.

What the above discussion also makes clear is that the black people who came from the island continent to the Western African Extensia as slaves did not know the names *African* or *Africans* and did not have them as their identities. Thus, the Black historian Joseph Holloway was in error when he wrote in *Africanisms in American Culture*, "Thus this debate has come full circle, from *African* through *brown, colored, Afro-American, Negro,* and *black* back to *African*, the term originally used by Blacks in America to define themselves."[43]

And Sterling Stuckey was in error when he said in his book that the slaves in America functioned as Africans on a "profound level."[44] That would not have been possible without an *African* identity and an *African* consciousness. Nor could it happen given the amount of culture that slaves lost—had stripped away from them by the slave trade and slavery and by the introduction and acculturation of Euro-American cultural traits. The slaves in North America were the black slaves most stripped of what historians have called "African cultural traits," or "Africanisms," but there are Black historians and other

Black intellectuals who insist on a 100 percent African parentage for Blacks in America and an African or African-American identity for themselves and Black people. The following reflects a glimpse of the cultural loss of the slaves that came to North America and inaugurated a new history and new life here. Religious beliefs, religious cults, religious rituals and ceremonies, and ancestral beliefs and ceremonies were lost. Ancestors and spirits were lost. Philosophies and artistic and magical practices were lost. Political and judicial institutions and legal thinking were lost, as were the rituals and ceremonies associated with political and judicial institutions. National and ethnic loyalties and rituals and ceremonies were also lost. Languages were destroyed. The drums were lost (save for their small use in Louisiana) and the large number of events, rituals, and ceremonies associated with them, including the ceremonies involved in naming drums. Ceremonies and music associated with ethnic or village diplomacy or national diplomacy were lost. The various rites of passage (for boys and girls), the rituals and ceremonies surrounding birth and death and those surrounding the birth and death of animals were lost. The warrior cultures, military institutions, secret societies, as well as economic institutions, and the cultural and social practices that regulated them, including the religious practices that did, were destroyed. Courtship, other kinds of premarriage cultural and social practices, and marriage practices passed away. Patrilineal and matrilineal lines of descent and inheritance and the many rituals and ceremonies involved in them went down. Medicine man functions and medical and culinary practices were lost. The roving griots and the tribal memory historians were lost. Circumcision, scarring and painting the body, and the rituals and ceremonies that pertained to these activities, as well as the practices of identifying with totems and worshipping animals, demised. The hunting culture, including weapon making, initiation practices, training activities, and the hunting itself was lost. Many other cultural traits were lost. The traits that survived usually did so in a fragmented or diminished manner and meaning or were significantly transformed in form or meaning.

The slaves themselves were transformed. But to talk about this matter, it is necessary to talk about the matter of an African identity in a different way that will make it possible in a special and necessary way to relate this identity to Black people. For millennia people of the world have been calling a continent Africa and the people on that continent, Africans. This continues. Now the black people on that continent are, hesitatingly, but nevertheless, accepting those names and identities as if they were their own, as if they were indigenous and natural to them. This means they are accepting an African identity in *retrospect*, as an identity that had had long recognition, but which they had not known or recognized, but which they now seem headed to accepting as their own. Some of the slaves who came to North America heard the names *Africa* and *African*, and some of them accepted them as names and identities that were theirs, or as names and identities that they were supposed to accept and use. Thus, these black slaves in North America accepted an African identity in retrospect. That seems to me how Black people in America have to do this thing as well. I recommend they accept an African identity as some black slaves, and as some non-slave Blacks had done long ago, and as black people on the African continent are now in the process of doing, as a retrospective identity. This will allow them to talk of Africa and Africans and even to call black slaves Africans, which they themselves did not call themselves, and to say that these slaves came from Africa. In the seventeenth, eighteenth, and in the first half of the nineteenth centuries Africans came to North America as slaves. This is the Africancentric Perspective on the situation. But then what I call the *Blackcentric Perspective*, has to take over. This Perspective recognizes that the history of the Africans (the identity of these people accepted in retrospect) took a new turn in North America (and elsewhere, too, in the Western African Extensia). These Africans began making history in an entirely different geographical area and in an entirely different historical-cultural-social context. The new context was far removed, politically, culturally, and linguistically from what the Africans had known. This was the new general context (including new geographical and physical features) in which they would have to live, work, and continue to evolve. But they would not be able to continue evolving as Africans. Black slaves seldom heard the words *Africa* or *Africans*. What they overwhelmingly heard, and continuously, were words and names like *Negroes, slaves, niggers, savages, heathens*, and sometimes *Guineas*. They might also on occasion hear their tribal or ethnic names. The slaveholders of North America were not anxious to give the slaves a common identity of African. That could be a rallying point or a motivation for resistance. The slaveholders used common names and identities that could not inspire unity and resistance among the slaves, such as Negroes, slaves, and niggers.

The Blackcentric Perspective indicates that the Africans became Black people, who beget Black people, who beget Black people, who beget Black people. What all this begetting means is that Black people in America have two ancestral groups—the original Africans who came here and the Black people that they produced, making a new history, living in a new culture, and living in and making a new culture for themselves. Thus, *there is a Black parent of Black people, as well as an African parent.* There is also a *European-American* parent. Blacks have three ancestral parents, because they have three sources of their historical, cultural, and social development. These facts, knowledge about these facts, and interpretations about them constitute early contributions to what I call *Blackcentrism*, that knowledge and thought (analysis, interpretation) of the history, culture, social life, and psychology of Black people in America and out of which a Blackcentric Perspective is created. The latter gives Black people a special perception on their own history and existence in America, as they occurred separately from Whites and others in America and as they interacted with Whites and others in America. The Perspective gives Blacks a view of how they have contributed to the history, culture, and social life of Blacks. By functioning from the Blackcentric Perspective, and Blackcentric knowledge, or Blackcentrism, and drawing on the Africancentric Perspective and Africancentric knowledge, or Africancentrism, Blacks gain a view of how Africa and Africans, or black people of African descent from the Western African Extensia, have contributed to these developments.

The Blackcentric Perspective and Blackcentrism accept the notion that Black people in the United States are of African descent. They are descendants from black Africans racially and culturally, more racially than culturally. Most of their African culture was destroyed. Whites engaged in sexual activities with Blacks and thus produced a biological variation in them. But the Africans were not of a pure black race on the island continent, and there was racial variation among them when they came to North America as slaves. These slaves held onto the African cultural traits they could, as best they could. In other instances, indeed, in most instances, they clung to their original traits, as much as was left of them, by attaching them to, or mixing them with, the Euro-American cultural traits in the new environment. Thus would be the combining of African religious music with Protestant religious music, with the stronger emphasis being on the African heritage; or associating the trickster cultural trait with animals, physical objects, or social situations now found in the new environment. This lamination and synthesizing of cultural traits initially reduced and then ultimately eliminated the *African* orientation of traits, making it possible for that orientation to become *Black*. As Black people were produced from Africans, it was they who took up the tasks of holding onto and utilizing original traits, and drawing on Euro-American traits in their environment and then combining the two, creatively, into a new Black culture. This in turn produced a new Black ethnic group in America, a new ethnic group of the black race that stretched from Africa to the Western African Extensia. The Black ethnic group has been evolving in America since the late seventeenth and first half of the eighteenth centuries.

But during these years and during all the years thereafter that the Black ethnic group has evolved in America all the way up to the present day, there have not been many Blacks or Whites who have looked upon Blacks—the descendants of the African slaves—as an ethnic group. Racism and race have always played deterring roles here. Functioning as racists, Whites wanted Blacks to identify with being nonhuman or subhuman, and when not with that, with color and race. And for a very long time, it was all of these things along with the identity of slave. Whites, functioning as racists, slaveholders, or supporters of slavery, did not want Blacks to associate their identity with history or culture. But behind slave and racist segregationist walls, Blacks continued to evolve as a people, and specifically as an ethnic group, the same as other ethnic groups evolved in America, such as the Anglo-Saxons, German, Irish, or Jewish ethnic groups. It was the responsibility of Black intellectuals to help Black people in America know that they had moved from a simple racial group to an ethnic group that also included their racial status (ethnicity has a racial component, as witness the Greeks, Poles, and Italians of the white race, and the Sachems, Sioux, and Hopi of the red race in America). The Black intellectuals have failed to enlighten Blacks about their ethnic status, the failure being that of the Black intellectuals who have had the word and knowledge of ethnicity at their disposal to make the clarification. But Black intellectuals are still inundated with thoughts of race. Black literary people and Black artists and Black performing artists still overwhelmingly position themselves on race, to do their cultural thing. These Blacks come under criticism from various kinds of Black intellectuals who claim there is no such thing as race, which reflects their confusion about racism and race. A po-

sitioning on Black ethnicity would eliminate this squabble and confusion, but not totally, because there are Black intellectuals who say
that Black people in America are Africans, Afro-Americans, or African-
Americans and have been saying so since the 1980s.

Black historians have aided this cry, because these names and identities are found in their writings. There are the Black historians who
have written and who continue to write on Black slavery in America,
who contribute to the claims and efforts to promote an African identity, of some sort, among Blacks. These historians show less of an
interest to understand slavery, than to identify what they call the "African rententions" or the "Africanisms" of slavery. They can never
identify many, because there are not that many to identify anymore.
They seem to resist calling these traits "Black" cultural traits, as part
of the Black ethnicity that the slaves created during the centuries of
slavery. This is what the Blackcentric Perspective would require. But
these historians are looking at the Black slave experience from an
Africancentric Perspective. And their point is to try to prove that
Black people are Africans. They tend to look at the Black slave experience in America more like historical anthropologists than historians, not wanting to see change or transformation, which historians
focus on, but rather to focus on the unchanging, timeless realities.
But an equally important observation to make about these historians
is that they essentially ignore the dictatorial, oppressive, and tragic
character of Black American slavery and thus suppress the Blackcentric
knowledge that Black slaves created a new culture and with the aid
of that erected themselves as a new people in America and in the
world in these arduous and debilitating conditions. This was a heroic,
creative achievement, and this achievement can be fully fathomed
only by dealing with the dictatorial, oppressive, and tragic character
of Black slavery in America.

But Black intellectuals—scholars, literati, playwrights, artists, or
musicians, who view Blacks in America from an Africancentric Perspective should pay attention to how Black people themselves regard
themselves in America, which is from a Blackcentric Perspective,
which was originally created by Black slaves. In a poll conducted by
ABC News and the *Washington Post* in September and October of
1989, 66 percent of Blacks polled said that they preferred being called
Black, while 22 percent were against this identity.[45] In the fall of
1990, the Joint Center for Political and Economic Studies conducted

a similar poll and discovered that a majority of Blacks preferred to be called Blacks and Black Americans. The results of the poll were as follows:

> Specifically, 72 percent of young Blacks (18–29 years old) preferred Black instead of African American, as did 81 percent of Blacks ages 30–40 and 83 percent of Blacks 50 and older. Additionally, the vast majority of Black men, and women—72 and 85 percent respectively—preferred to be called Black.[46]

In 1994 a research group functioning from the University of North Carolina at Chapel Hill conducted an identity poll among southern Blacks. According to that study, 75 percent of the respondents said that they were Black and members of the black race.[47] Gwendolyn Brooks recently remarked that she preferred to be called Black.[48] Nikki Giovanni recently wrote: "I am a black American. Period. The rest is of no particular interest to me. Afro-American, African-American, whatever."[49] In accepting Black and Black American identities, Giovanni was not clarifying whether she was viewing "black" as race or as ethnicity. As I argue, a lower case spelling of black makes reference to color or race. The upper case spelling of black—Black— makes reference to ethnicity or the Black ethnic community, or the Black community, without the words *ethnic* or *ethnicity*, but which would be presumed with an upper case spelling. The word Black, singularly expressed, refers to a Black individual of the Black ethnic community, while the word Blacks refers to individuals or a group of Blacks of the Black ethnic community, or all Blacks of that community. Historically, there has been an orthographic problem dealing with the word *black* as a word relating to Black identity. Viewing *black* and *Black* as words referring to two different identities of Blacks solves this problem.

It seems to me that Black intellectuals have to enter this resolution. It also seems to me that they have to get with the people they claim to represent and whom they wish to help lead in America. Leaders and led must have the same name and identity, or the same names and identities, as the case may be. Many Black intellectuals are lagging behind, or are out of step with the mass of Black people, and that includes the mass of Black middle-class people.

I can see three reasons why this continues. There is a fundamental hostility toward Whites at work here and a determination not to accept any name they provide Blacks. That hostility in my view induces some Black intellectuals to engage in some romantic and nostalgic thinking: namely, about Blacks having lost their homeland; or that they are without a homeland; or that they have lost their identity and that there has to be an effort to reclaim it at all costs. It is like the southern Whites who keep after their "lost cause"—the country that southern Whites almost established once in continental North America, which is symbolized in the Confederate flag and various monuments.

The third reason that some Black intellectuals are out of step with the identity that most Blacks claim for themselves is that they have the wrong conception of Black history. They believe it is African history and that Black people are Africans in another physical place. This thinking is not unrelated to the first two kinds; and, indeed, the first instances spur it and encourage it. What I see in the writings of Black historians who are motivated in these ways, which are manifestations of their Africancentric orientation in looking at Black people in America, is that they are endeavoring to ignore or to jump over the Black experience in America. When the focus of historical scholarship on Black slavery is the African retentions, the focus is not on Black people, or the Black experience, but rather Africa, Africans, and a believed African experience in America. This kind of thinking and historiography suppresses Black history and the Black experience in America. This is what Sterling Stuckey did in his book *Slave Culture*, in which he made a desperate effort to make it appear that African history and an African way of life continued on in America.

This kind of writing not only suppresses Black history; it also suppresses the uniqueness of that history and the uniqueness of Black people. Writings like Stuckey's ignore or downplay a focus on the African Holocaust, which John Henrik Clarke recently described, which included not only the African slave trade but the establishment of slavery in the Western African Extensia.[50] The slavery in North America inaugurated the Black Holocaust, which, seen from the Africancentric and Blackcentric Perspectives interactively, would be the *African-Black Holocaust*,[51] with one growing out of the other. The African-Black Holocaust makes it impossible to put Black slavery in any kind of idyllic light and makes it necessary to see it as a situation of oppression and as a great human tragedy. But strangely or oddly enough, some Black historians have portrayed Black slavery in an idyllic fashion, by concentrating on African retentions and not really dealing with slavery or only as a secondary matter. This is that historical anthropological approach to writing Black history that I spoke about. Indeed, it is Black people in America who suffered the most from the African Holocaust, because it was the African slaves who came to North America who lost most of their African attributes. It was the Blacks in North America who had to do the greatest amount of adapting and creating to survive and evolve as a people.

Paul Gilroy has recently written that Black intellectuals should take a greater interest in the Jewish Holocaust, because there are things they can learn from it that would aid them in understanding the Black slave and the general Black experience in America, or what I would call the Black Holocaust. I not only believe that Gilroy is right; I also believe that there are things that Black intellectuals can also learn from their own Holocaust, the Indian Holocaust, and the African Holocaust, which occurred simultaneously and which lasted for several centuries. What is a unique feature of Black people in America is that they were born out of a holocaustic experience, whereas other people have had holocausts carried to them. Blacks have exhibited another unique feature of evolving as a new people within a holocaustic context—chattel slavery—under which people denied them rights and opportunities and who, as often as they could, treated Blacks as non-humans or subhumans, as property, as things, as objects of plunder, as objects of humiliation, as objects of wild, perverse imagination, and as objects of violence.

There was something else, as there remains something else, that is unique about Black people and their experience in America, and that is, or that should be, of particular interests to Black intellectuals. This is the unique method of cognition that Blacks evolved in America, as part of their ethnic development, and which they still engage in as their main method of cognition. To understand this situation fully, it is necessary to combine the Blackcentric and Africancentric frameworks and Blackcentric and Africancentric knowledge. These things will be done in the next chapter to provide a discussion of Black Cognition.

3.

Black Cognition

One way to get to know how people of a country or community or group think is to examine their ideals, beliefs, and values. However, this would not tell you if the people lived up to these idealities and implemented them or how often they did or how much significance or meaning the ideals, beliefs, and values had for the different groups of people. There could be a big gap between what people professed and the way they actually behaved. The Swedish social scientist Gunnar Myrdal noted this kind of situation when he studied white and Black people in the United States in the 1940s. He observed how Whites professed high-flown idealities, such as human dignity, liberty, equality, individual and equal opportunities, and justice—American idealities—but related to Black people in ways that were in violation of and that were just the opposite of the public professions. Myrdal described this situation, which he put into the title of his book, a proclaimed classic, *An American Dilemma*.[1] Myrdal knew and indicated that racism, namely, what I call white supremacy/ebonicism and the social practices that flowed from these beliefs, values, and ideals played the primary role to create the ideational-social gap that he observed in America. What this meant was, and which Myrdal did not clearly see, that Whites held their racist idealities just as high as they held America's lofty nonracist ideals, beliefs, and values—and even higher and certainly when Whites interacted with Blacks. Indeed, what actually happened in America, was that Whites, functioning as racists toward Blacks, invested their racism into their nonracist idealities so that they would all function as racist idealities when they related to Blacks. For instance, liberty was a high-flown American ideal. Whites invested racism in it when they related to Blacks, and this led Whites to interpret *liberty* to mean the individual right to own Blacks, the individual right to discriminate against them, or the individual right to deny them rights and opportunities. And equality, invested with white supremacy/ebonicism, gave Whites the idea that they had the equal right to do these thing to Black people. Thus, what Myrdal did not see in his study of Whites and Blacks in America is that Whites only ostensibly left a gap open between what they professed and the way they behaved. They bent the lofty idealities downward, with inundations of racism, which closed the gap, and enabled Whites to relate to Blacks as if there were no difference in the ideals they professed and the way they acted. Liberty, interacting with Blacks, meant denial, exclusion, and subordination. The ideal of progress, invested with white supremacy/ebonicism meant progress for white people and no progress, or not the same kind or amount of progress, for Blacks. Thus, to know how Whites have thought and continue to think about Blacks in America, it is necessary to know their racist beliefs, ideals, and values, and how they used them. This is actually still a wide open area for research and discussion. Both Black and white intellectuals focus on race in this country, not racism. To focus on racism is to focus on the racists, which in America would mean focusing on the thought and behavior of white people. When the focus is on race, the discussion is invariably on Black people, as the victims, and all the problems of victimization. This can be done without talking about white people at all, or not very much, and giving the impression that white people are not involved in the victimization of Blacks in America. In the eyes of white racists, they are not involved. They are guiltless, innocent, and nonresponsible. Blacks are in their depressed condition because of their innate inferiority. Today, Whites are not inclined to be this explicit in their racist thinking. They are more subtle in their racism today. A manifestation of this subtle racism is to take the idea of Black natural inferiority and shift it to the environment in which Blacks live. The environment is then proclaimed to be, not naturally, but intrinsically, inferior, that is, having deep pathologies that act continuously in Black life, making it pathological and low level. Since Whites are geographically and physically removed from the Black social environment, they have nothing to do with it and are not in any way responsible for it; therefore, they are guiltless, innocent, and nonresponsible. But Whites want a double insurance for their alleged lack of complicity and for not having to feel guilt or responsibility for the situation of Blacks. They still hold onto their ebonicistic racist beliefs, even as subtly as they might, which talk of the innate inferiority of Blacks that produces their low-level thought and social behavior.

Another way of learning how people think is to live among them and observe their thinking and their cultural and social behavior. This is what diplomats and missionaries have done and still do. There are some academics who do this as well and have been doing it for some time. Earlier, in the nineteenth century and also in the twentieth century, there were social anthropologists who went among what they invariably called "primitive" people, to study them and their thinking and cultural and social patterns on the assumption that these people were on the road to extinction. Many of these people have shown remarkable staying power, so social anthropologists still function and still anticipate extinction. There are also cultural anthropologists, indeed more of them today than social anthropologists. They are more flexible than the latter. Cultural anthropologists will study what are now called "traditional" people or "traditional cultures," or "traditional societies," meaning people and structures that have not been affected or affected much by what the cultural anthropologists call modernity. They also study transitions that traditional peoples and traditional societies might be making toward what they call modernity or a modern society. Cultural anthropologists will also study groups of people in a "modern" society, those that they think are marginal or separatist. Blacks and the Amish and other groups of people in America have been studied by cultural anthropologists.

Cultural anthropologist George Foster has provided the field with what many cultural anthropologists believe is a good investigatory tool. This is Foster's concept of "cognitive orientations." It is employed to observe what traditional or other people are doing, their "basic assumptions about social relations (what values motivate individuals, how one deals with others in social relations, and matters of interpersonal style), and . . . the . . . basic assumptions and expectations about the way the world functions phenomenologically (for instance, beliefs about causality, and how particular causes are revealed"[2]). Eminent cultural anthropologist Clifford Geertz feels it is perfectly possible to get to know a people of a different culture well, their thinking and social behavior, by learning how to interpret their symbolic life. This does not require immersing oneself in another culture, that is, strongly empathizing with a people and trying fully to share their culture. The investigation can be more detached and cognitive. With the proper education and training in academic disciplines and methods of investigation and analysis, the symbolic action and the "symbol systems" of peoples of other cultures can be deciphered and understood.

Geertz's thinking, especially, has had an impact on the thinking of some Black literati, which has induced them to turn to the field of cultural anthropology and cultural anthropological theory. One of these is Michael Awkward, who recently wrote in *Negotiating Difference*:

> If the major issue in such debates is, as I believe, whether racial and gendered experience can be adequately interpreted across "class" lines or boundaries, we find ourselves discussing matters traditionally associated not with literary interpretation but with the field of anthropology. Because of the nature of the enterprise, this field has historically had to concern itself with the question of whether it is possible for an investigator to achieve accurate analyses of alien (usually third world) cultures.[3]

Awkward was reacting to the question, or to the point that some black literati had made that white literary elements were incapable of interpreting black literary texts correctly. Black literary critic Joyce Joyce was of this view. She also did not want "black critics" to be seduced by a "poststructuralist-informed emphasis on the language of the text," which would prevent them from engaging in a "serious analysis of black literature's" ability to liberate them and other Blacks.[4] Joyce holds strongly to the view that Black literary and other aesthetic elements need a Black Aesthetic to help guide their efforts, and that the Aesthetic construction and Black aesthetic culture have to be done by Black people. Houston Baker, Jr., had once held the view that white literary critics were not able to correctly interpret black literary texts, but he had come to change his mind. He had seen some good work done by white critics, but he had also come under the influence of Clifford Geertz and his critical work *The In-*

terpretation of Cultures. Geertz was of the view that anthropology could "enlarge . . . the universe of human discourse."[5] This was Baker's view of literature, too. "A work of literature, for example, is a manifestation of the human capacity for symbolic behavior, and an entire field of anthropology is currently devoted to the study of men and women as agents who represent and transmit knowledge in symbolic form. Their literary work is also a form standing in a peculiar relationship to all other forms of verbal behavior in society."[6] For Baker, as for Geertz, as for Foster, one had to be equipped with the cognitive tools to study human expressive behavior, and to be able effectively and accurately to interpret symbolic expressions or symbolic social behavior. Baker adduced a phrase the "anthropology of art" and then explained the significance of it for him:

> The phrase expresses for me the notion that art must be studied with an attention to the methods and findings of disciplines which enable one to address such concerns as the status of the artistic object, the relationship of art to other cultural systems, and the nature and function of artistic creation and perception in a given society . . . the "anthropology of art" signals an investigative strategy that I am striving to apply to black literature and culture.[7]

This might also be called Baker's cognitive strategy or, taking from Foster's construction, his "cognitive orientations," to engage in aesthetic cultural investigations. And it is Baker's view that an "anthropology of art," which he would also doubtlessly say of Foster's "cognitive orientations," can be developed by drawing together appropriate knowledge and analytical tools to fit the investigative situation. This would make it possible for someone outside a cultural context to enter it with the ability to do serious, accurate, and important interpretive work. There are Black literary and other Black aesthetic cultural elements who still have reservations about white literati and other white aesthetic cultural agents having significant interpretive success with Black aesthetic culture, no matter how well cognitively tooled they are, because there is the belief that their racism will get in their way. And then there are those Black literary and other intellectuals who feel that Whites should not even seek to do it. They have other vineyards in which to do their work.

But in the discussion of cognition, even by cultural anthropologists, there is something seriously missing. This is also true of discussions by psychologists, where cognition has its greatest number of utilizers and theorizers. As said earlier, there is a special field in psychology of cognitive psychology, and there are clinical cognitive therapies. Philosophers are also heavily involved with the concept and activity of cognition. For all of these different academic or intellectual groups, cognition is an intellectual activity, which involves things like memory, perception, intellectual ability (reasoning and analytical abilities), beliefs, values, and language. This approach to cognition invariably excludes or strongly plays down what are called *affective* qualities, such as emotion, intuition, attitudes, feelings, or motivations. Of course, even psychologists know that affective psychological traits affect intellectual ability, even learning or remembering anything. But there is still the slashing and either-or conception of cognition. As Anthony Sanford has remarked, "it would be true to say that cognitive psychology and the associate discipline of cognitive science have at their core the study of the actions of the intellect. . . . This is not to say that cognitive psychologists are not concerned with the emotions or with motivation . . . but rather to say that these issues have been less well treated in cognitive psychology than cognition itself."[8]

Another thing that is seriously missing from the study and use of cognition is the role that *organizational* or *relational logics* and the *thinking patterns* that these logics help to create play in cognitive activities. Cognitive psychologists and other psychologists speak of cognitive schema, or different modes of cognition. I prefer the concepts *cognitive system* or *cognitive systems*. A given cognitive system, in my view, contains ideational elements, such as ideas, beliefs, and values, psychological features, such as emotions, attitudes, and feelings, and intellectual features, such as ratiocination or reasoning logic, organizational logic, and a thinking pattern. A concept like *cognitive orientations* does not apprehend the complexity of cognition just described. Nor does the concept of an anthropology of art. Both would likely ignore the psychological dimensions of cognition. And neither would likely be aware of organizational logics and related thinking patterns, and their functioning in cognitive activities. It is not enough just to have ideational attributes in a cognitive system. And it is not enough to have academic methodologies or investigative tools when probing an indigenous or a different culture or even in examining literary texts from an indigenous or foreign culture. These instruments will be greatly affected in their use by the organizational logics and related thinking patterns of cognitive systems. Different systems have different organizational logics and thinking patterns. For instance, in America, an individual white person functions from several different cognitive systems; that is, a given white person can possess more than one cognitive system and use more than one in cognition. This is also true of an observing, investigating, or analyzing scholar or other kind of intellectual. The cognitive systems that Whites employ in America are embedded in American history, culture, and social life. They are invested in individual white Americans in the early socialization process and in the early stages of formal education. There is then continued reinforcement of the cognitive systems. Whites employ four cognitive systems, some employing all of them, others just some of them. The four are *vertical cognition, domination-subordination cognition, dualistic cognition,* and *dialectical cognition.* These forms of cognition had been used in Europe for centuries and then were transferred to North America (and elsewhere in the Western Hemisphere as well), when Europeans established themselves and their cultures there. African and then Black slaves were introduced to some of these cognitive systems, but their life in America made it difficult for them to imbibe them fully and use them often. Indeed, their oppressive and extremely contradictory existence forced them to develop a very different kind of cognitive system than the ones used by Whites to cope with the kind of life they found themselves in and had to live. Their original African method of cognition will be the basis for this new cognitive construction. The nonslave Blacks, South and North, and over the early centuries of America, were the ones who had the most interaction with Whites or were the ones who were more concerned to be, and who made the effort to be, more like Whites culturally and socially. This brought them into greater contact with White cognitive systems, which they assimilated more extensively than slaves and used more often than they. But nonslave Blacks, early Black middle-class people, also had to live a very contradictory life in America, and that forced them to devise a different cognitive system to cope better with their existence, which also had its origins of construction in African cognition that had been passed on to them by Africans and early Black predecessors.

In the discussion that follows about White cognition, I will be less concerned with the ideational or psychological component of each system than with the organizational logic and related thinking pattern of each. Idealities might differ from cognitive system to cognitive system and make them different and distinctive that way. But the only way to tell if cognitive systems are different in a functional sense, that is, to determine if they represent different cognitive strategies or approaches to investigation or analysis, is to focus on and disclose their organizational or relational logics and the thinking patterns these logics produce.

The first form of White cognition I want to discuss is the form I call simple vertical cognition. This cognitive system, owing to its ideational components, that is, its ideas, beliefs, values, ethics, and the psychological traits that support it, looks upon natural (physical), cultural, and social realities in a rigid dichotomous manner. The reasoning or analytical logic of this system is directed by ideational and psychological traits to see only incompatibilities, contradictions, or dichotomies in a reality or realities, with the understanding that one of these incompatible, contradictory, or dichotomous elements must go. This takes the functioning of this cognitive system up to the matter of organizing, meaning organizing the reality or realities discerned. Simple vertical cognition calls for organizing reality or realities in a one-dimensional fashion. One of the oppositional elements has to be eliminated from reality, from the physical, political, cultural, or social reality to effect this single or monistic reality. The vertical organizational or relational logic of vertical cognition gives rise to *either-or thinking.* The latter insists (actually aided by all elements of the cognitive system) that two things cannot occupy the same space at the same time. One thing has to go. Vertical cognition can be described as either-or cognition.

Another form of White cognition is dualistic cognition. Like vertical cognition, this form also perceives physical, cultural, or social realities in an incompatible, contradictory, and dichotomous manner. But this system, owing to its ideational orientation, seeks to keep contradictory realities in existence, because it sees various kinds of value in that. Thus, when reasoning logic, aided by ideational and psychological attributes, discerns realities such as good and evil, war and peace, crime and law abiding, Black and White, capitalists and socialists, the organizational logic of this cognitive system is called upon to organize these realities in a way that they remain totally separate from each other, having no practical contact with each other, and only enough intellectual contact to discern the differences, and the need to keep the different realities separate. The dualistic organizational logic of dualistic cognition produces rigid *parallel thinking* which helps to implement this form of cognition and to keep reality organized in an essentially noninteractive manner.

The third system of White cognition is domination-subordination cognition. The latter, like the other two systems of cognition, looks upon reality in a contradictory and dichotomous manner, but not in a fully incompatible manner. Reasoning logic, aided by other components of the cognitive system, discerns realities in their contradictions and differences, but this cognitive system seeks to organize the contradictory and different aspects of realities in a domination-subordination relationship. One aspect of reality is given more value or importance or utility than another. But the lesser reality has some value, some importance, and some utility. Thus, the less-perceived reality, which is not totally incompatible, is brought under the other in a domination-subordination or hierarchical relationship, such as men over women, Whites over Blacks, good over evil, capital over labor, with the subordinate reality being of some aid or value to the dominant or superordinate reality. The relational logic and the other components of the domination-subordination cognitive system produce *hierarchical*, or *more-than*, or *prioritized thinking*. Either term is appropriate.

The fourth form of White cognition is dialectical cognition. This is a form used primarily by intellectuals, who would also use some or all of the other forms of cognition as well. The dialectical cognitive method also perceives reality as dichotomous and contradictory, with the contradictions acutely antagonistic toward each other. This cognitive method upon perceiving, by its functioning, the contradictory and antagonistic character of reality, pits the antagonistic elements in a fierce struggle with each other, so that one of the elements has to overcome and subdue the other and put the subdued aspect of reality in a subordinate position, whereby its reality is diminished by the absorbing activities of the dominant reality, which increases in size. This more or less makes the two different realities a single reality, from a process of synthesis (absorption), that will then find itself in an antagonistic relationship with another reality. This will lead to an overcoming process and another synthesis, which will lead to a new, synthetic reality that will interact with an opposite and antagonistic reality that will lead to an overcoming and synthesis—ad infinitum. Dialectical cognition, like vertical cognition, seeks monism. But the approaches are different. Vertical cognition seeks monism, or a one-dimensional reality by excluding or eliminating an aspect of reality from a situation. Dialectical cognition seeks an essentially one-dimensional or monistic reality by bringing two aspects of reality into a domination-subordination relationship in which the dominant aspect enlarges itself at the expense of the subordinate aspect. Dialectical organizational logic, along with the other components of dialectical cognition, produce *overcoming* or *transcendental thinking.*

As can be seen, all of the White forms of cognition take an essentially negative view of reality, and a very aggressive view, in which given realities are put under attack to discern them, to evaluate them, or to organize them—or to use them. All of these cognitive systems function on the basis of being a power system, even if this is not discernible to those who employ them. But these cognitive systems seek domination, control, and even exploitation. This presupposes a power value and a power motive. It also presupposes thoughts or intentions of winning and defeating somebody or something.

White racists in America have historically used vertical, domination-subordination, and dualistic cognition in this country when relating to Blacks. Years ago, the psychiatrist Joel Kovel wrote a book called *White Racism: A Psychohistory.*[9] In it, he discussed the white racist response to Blacks in a historical fashion, indicating that in different periods white racists responded to Blacks in different ways. For much of American history, he said, white racists took a domination or, as he said, *dominative* approach. Later in American history, he said, it was an avoidance or *aversive* approach. These two approaches indicated two different cognitive orientations, domination-subordination and vertical cognition. It suggested that white racists had only one cognitive system with which to relate to Blacks at a given time. In truth, however, as Blackcentric knowledge fully attests, Whites, functioning as racists in America against Blacks, have always sought to dominate and control them—and exploit them—and avoid them. Dominating them took the form of making them slaves or segregating them, which made it possible for most Whites to avoid Blacks. Segregation and avoidance were also done by using dualistic cognition.

When white cultural anthropologists from America or Europe study people of different cultures, they will be doing so on the basis of the cognitive systems outlined here. White literati from Europe and America would use these same discussed cognitive systems if they were to examine literary texts of another culture. It can be seen that if four cultural anthropologists investigated a given different culture, with each functioning from one of the different cognitive systems outlined here, each would come up with a different interpretation of that culture. This would also be true of four investigators of a literary text of a given different culture, if each investigator examined the text with a different cognitive system.

Any one of the White cognitive systems discussed here is not capable of dealing with totality or wholeness. These forms of cognition aggressively slice up reality and seek to exclude aspects, to dominate aspects, or to overcome and diminish aspects of reality. There is also a great distortive understanding and use of dialectical cognition. There are intellectuals who understand the dialectic as just a matter of opposites interacting with each other. Analytical reasoning, as well as the organizational logic and thinking pattern of dialectical cognition embedded in Western culture, requires going beyond just interaction. The cognitive system requires an act of overcoming and, thus, an act of dominating to achieve an essential monism.

There are Blacks in America, and that includes Black intellectuals, who know and who use White forms of cognition. They are embedded in the culture, social institutions, and in social interactions and social relationships in America, and there are Blacks who have assimilated the forms and who use them, especially when interacting with white people, to be on the same cognitive wave links with them. Thus, Black intellectuals and other Blacks can be heard to say "either-or" or "prioritize" or "set priorities." There are Black intellectuals and others who use White cognitive methods to investigate or to analyze Black history, or Black culture and social life. Or who do so to offer Blacks political advice or political leadership, such as saying to Blacks that they should function and struggle in a Left manner in America, and avoid or fight against a Right posture. Or who seek to get Black middle-class people or other Blacks to think that the individual is more important than the group or community or that a Black individual is more important than the Black ethnic group. There are Black historians who employ either-or cognition, who seek to write on Black history in America or Black culture in America as if neither has been affected by white people, or America, or Europe. Employing White forms of cognition is not to be able to understand or to analyze Black history, Black culture, or Black social life in a comprehensive or whole manner. It cannot even be done by putting various forms of White cognition together, for these cognitive systems are not structured to deal with wholeness. Each one is against wholeness, and each one will leave out something, or much, that is necessary to analyze and understand wholeness. With respect to the latter, Black intellectuals and other Blacks can do better by employing Black Cognition, which is a form of cognition that focuses on individual parts and the whole reality.

I am going to discuss Black Cognition, but first I have to take a step back into history, even into antiquity, to trace its origins. It is necessary to go back to ancient Egypt, and to what is called "traditional" African societies, which were the societies from which Africans would be snatched to be turned into slaves in the Western Hemisphere. Someone might ask why not just start with the traditional societies of West and Central Africa? That could be done. But the Africancentric Perspective suggests that there are cultural similarities between ancient Egypt and the African cultures on the other side of the continent,[10] and one of the great similarities is the cognitive system of both places, which the Egyptian civilization might have passed on to other African cultures and civilizations.

In ancient Egypt there was a very complicated form of cognition, complicated because it seemed to be comprised of several cognitive systems in one, namely, the domination-subordination, dualistic, and dialectical forms of cognition, all interacting with each other, to produce the single, complicated form. The ancient Egyptians had the philosophical view that reality was one, but at the same time, it showed different manifestations, or different specific realities. Thus, reality was at the same time plural. But for the ancient Egyptians, the oneness of reality and the plurality of reality were not separable from each other. One could not be understood apart from the other, could not have meaning apart from the other. The oneness and plurality of reality represented harmony and unity that were held together by what the ancient Egyptians termed the universal life force, which was symbolized by the *ankh*, a cross (which also symbolized the notion of eternal life), that would become the Christian cross at a later time, with a modification of the design. This universal life force was always dynamic and always changing things. In his book, *Foundations of African Thought*, Chukwunyere Kamalu indicated how the *Book of the Dead* spoke of the universal life force in ancient Egyptian history, culture, and social life:

> He createth but was never created; He is the maker of his own form, and fashioner of his own body—God himself is

existence. He endureth without increase or diminution. He multiplieth himself millions of times, and He is manifold in forms and in members—God hath made the universe, and He hath created all that therein is; He is the creator of what is in the world, and of what was, of what is and of what shall be.[11]

The universal life force (which was God, existence, and reality in Egyptian thought) inundated reality in its oneness and in its plurality. This means then that it also inundated reality in its harmony and unity, that is, the harmony and unity of its oneness and plurality. The oneness and plurality also represented a duality. Indeed, for the ancient Egyptians, reality or existence was comprised of dualities, such as the body and soul, good and evil, life and death, strong and weak, science and religion, this life and the afterlife. These dualities were constant, but they were not static, or simply parallel or oppositional to each other. The opposite elements, or dualities, owing to the movement of the universal life force, interacted with each other in a dialectical manner that saw the oppositional elements, at moments, transcend their opposition and duality and through a synthesis or union become one, a oneness that was a small manifestation of the absolute oneness or absolute reality. The dialectical transcendence of all dualities pointed to the absolute reality or absolute existence and how it stood in a hierarchical relationship with synthesized oneness or even all synthesized onenesses combined. For the ancient Egyptians, the dialectical organizational logic was the critical one in their cognitive system, as it was the logic of movement and dynamism that utilized and overcame dualism, and that helped to establish domination-subordination or hierarchical organizational logic that made it possible for reality or existence to have a oneness and plurality, or a harmony and unity of its oneness and plurality. The dialectic, driven by the universal life force, was the organizational logic means, along with other aspects of Egyptian cognition, ideational, psychological, and intellectual, such as perception and reasoning logic, to continue expanding reality or existence in its oneness and plurality. It also has to be said that the ancient Egyptian form of the dialectic was not used—and certainly not primarily—as it was and continues primarily to be used by Western intellectuals, to establish domination, subordination, and control, and an essential monistic reality. The ancient Egyptians primarily used this form of cognition to produce changes and to strike *balances* in thought or between objects, to make it possible to achieve the dynamic reality of oneness and plurality, or oneness and diversity, and in harmony and unity, and on a continuous, unending basis. This rends the past and current understanding of Western intellectuals, that ancient Egyptian history and life were static and essentially unchanging.

I find myself wanting to give the Egyptian method of cognition, with multiple organizational logics, a formal name. I choose *monointeractive* cognition. This denotes, on the one hand, monointeractive organizational logic, composed of three separate but interactive organizational logics functioning as a single or general organizational logic. On the other hand, it refers to the way this cognition functions to enable reality to interact with itself to endeavor to understand itself in its entirety or wholeness. This kind of cognition gives rise to what I choose to call *wholeness thinking*, or *holistic thinking*. Apprehending something in its entirety is not usually possible. But this can be a conception and an ideal, and a cognitive method can be devised to try to achieve this objective as much as possible, which was what ancient Egyptian monointeractive cognition was about. It is even possible to believe that some Egyptians might have used one or two of the organizational logics of monointeractive cognition at times, rather than all three. But the ancient Egyptian quest for harmony, unity, and wholeness was cultural, and the cognitive methodology to achieve these results was cultural; that is, like the ideals, it was generalized among the ancient Egyptians, and clearly was the preferred method of cognition.

Monointeractive cognition was also found embedded in the traditional societies of West and Central Africa. It was there when Africans were taken from these cultures and societies and transplanted in the Western Hemisphere as slaves. It continues on in West and Central African traditional life. European social and cultural anthropologists have studied this cognition. Their purpose was to try to "fathom" African thought. The assumption was—the racist assumption was—that black Africans were primitive or savages and that they had some primitive or savage way of thinking, that flowed from a primitive or "savage mind." The French anthropologist Lucien Lévy-Bruhl made his study of cognition and thinking among traditional black Africans. He approached the subject not only with feelings of superiority and Western ideational attributes, but also with Western organizational logics and thinking patterns. As said earlier, White/

Western cognitive systems slice up reality, to eliminate it, to freeze it, or to dominate it, but not to see it in its entirety or wholeness. White/Western cognitive systems are intensely, that is, narrowly and aggressively analytic and mechanistic or intensely rationalistic or instrumentalistic. The idea of White/Western cognitive systems is to eliminate, freeze, suppress, or to destroy contradictions or differences in reality or in history, culture, or social life. Those white American or European scholars who studied ancient Egyptian medicine saw that the ancient Egyptians did not separate medicine from religion. They also saw that the ancient Egyptians did not separate astronomy from religion. They also discovered that the ancient Egyptians did not separate the secular from the sacred. Monointeractive cognition produced a harmony, unity, and oneness of opposites. White Western scholars saw this as nonrational, mystical, or unscientific thinking. The white Western scholars like Lévy-Bruhl who studied traditional West and Central African thought and cultures saw the same monointeractive cognition, the same fusion or unity of opposites into synthesized realities, and the same preoccupation with wholeness. They also observed the vitalist principle at work among traditional West and Central black Africans, which had also functioned among ancient Egyptians. That principle was that reason or rationality alone was not sufficient to attain knowledge, truth, and understanding. It was necessary to employ, along with reason, imagination, intuition, emotion, and feelings. The reason for the emphasis on the latter was that it was necessary to decipher symbols. In the latter were embedded knowledge, truth, understanding, and meaning. And it took affective qualities, and rationality, and these elements in monointeractive motion and union, effectively, to decipher symbols. As Janheinz Jahn wrote in *Muntu*, Lévy-Bruhl described traditional West and Central black African thought, and traditional black African cognition and thought generally, as "pre-logical."[12] Other white Western observers did the same, providing additional descriptions, such as "nonlogical," "mystical," or "savage." What also bothered Lévy-Bruhl and other white observers of traditional black African culture and life was that there was not a separation between thought and culture and thought and social life. Thought was intertwined with both, meaning that thought could not become abstract and divorced from culture and social life, as if it were an entity or reality apart from both, or standing above both, which was the way thought functioned in America and Europe, because of the high value placed on abstract thinking, and the functioning of White cognitive systems that separated thought from culture and social life. White Western scholars and others also noted that traditional black Africans were a very *oral* people, who put a great deal of emphasis on verbal expression and the word, or message. They also were *sense* and *visual* oriented and were preoccupied with *rhythm* and *sounds*.[13] For the white Western observers, this all added up, in most of their discussions, to the inferiority, primitiveness, uncivilized, or savage character of black Africans. In the 1960s, Western anthropologists especially began looking differently at traditional black African cognition and culture when they began to alter their own view about aspects of Western culture. They began to see that there were similarities between art and science, between myth and science, or magic and science. Now, what had been learned about traditional black African cognition and culture (as well as cognition and culture of other people in the world, that differed from White/Western cognition and culture) could be viewed differently. The French anthropologist Claude Lévi-Strauss now claimed that the "primitive" or "savage" mind was not prelogical and that it displayed logic.[14] Lévi-Strauss did not really understand the mind he now regarded as not being savage, and which he now felt displayed logic. What he did, for instance, was to cull the dualistic organizational logic and parallel thinking from traditional West and Central African monointeractive cognition, which enabled him to perceive the dualities of this traditional thought and these traditional cultures, such as the dualities of magic and science, myth and science, or the religious and the secular. But the West and Central black Africans continued on with their traditional method of cognition, which went beyond duality to establish harmony and unity in reality, and in pursuit of wholeness. Recently, an African intellectual from Nigeria, Tejumola Olaniyan, described the traditionalist West and Central black African method of cognition (monointeraction), which continues in these broad areas in full force:

> The African worldview, on the other hand, is characteristically thorough and catholic: a "relative comprehensiveness of vision" in which parts are apprehended in all their fullness, that is, in their dynamic relationships with themselves, in their constitutive identities as parts and whole. For this worldview, history is not a threat that disperses understanding into unyielding "separatist myths (or

'truths').'' On the contrary, new experiences, in either harmonious or contradictory relationship to the stock, are absorbed, dealt with, and allocated their proper berths within a vision that resolutely refuses to conceive life and death, evil and good, heaven and earth, past and present, inside and outside, and so on, as irreconcilable absolutes.[15]

The Africans who came to North America, as well as to other parts of the Western Hemisphere, who mainly came from West and Central Africa, brought their monointeractive cognitive method with them. That method would have a greater holding power in the West Indies and Central and South America than it would have had in North America. As said earlier in this essay, the Africans who came to North America as slaves were stripped of most of their culture by the slave trade, slavery, and the taking in of Euro-American cultural traits. There simply was not much of a cultural base to sustain the original monointeractive cognitive system. But the kind of life that Black people had to live in America, slaves and nonslaves, and which went on for centuries and continues on for millions of Blacks to this day, forced them, consciously and unconsciously, to devise a different cognitive system from the one that had been the original inheritance. And the life that Blacks, slave and nonslave, had to live motivated and even forced them to seek wholeness and to develop a cognitive system to enable them to do that.

Blacks lived a more complicated life in America than Whites, and that was because it was, as Blackcentric knowledge reveals, extremely contradictory. They lived in a society that sang the phrases of freedom, but in which they were slaves. America was portrayed as the land of opportunities, but they were denied opportunities. Blacks heard continuously that America was an open society, but it was closed to them. America had political and civil laws for white people and slave and racist laws for Black people. Black slaves were told that they were lazy and poor workers, but they made great wealth for their white masters. Whites talked about how they took care of Blacks and how Blacks were dependent upon them, but Whites and America were dependent upon the labor of Blacks, especially the labor of Black slaves. America put a great emphasis on education but made education illegal for Blacks or restricted their ability to be educated. Blacks were denied rights, education, and opportunities but were told to be moral, responsible, and not to engage in crime. Blacks were denied

political and civil rights but were told that they had to prove that
they could be responsible citizens. Blacks were told that Whites were
always superior and that they were always inferior. Blacks were told
that they were too inferior to produce aesthetic culture, but they
produced aesthetic culture such as music, dance, and humor. Whites
told Blacks that they were imitators, but Blacks, over their existence
in America, witnessed Whites imitating their aesthetic culture. There
was not supposed to be a Black middle class in America, but there
was one. When Blacks attained middle-class status, they were still
discriminated against. There were not supposed to be Black intellectuals in America, but there were. Whites told Blacks that they were
nonhumans, but white men had sexual relations with Black women.
White women were publicly proclaimed beautiful, and Black women
were publicly proclaimed ugly. White women were projected in front
of Black men as beautiful and desirable, but Black men were told to
leave white women alone on the pain of great punishment, including
death. Blacks were told to make cultural and social progress, and they
would be accepted by Whites. But Blacks discovered that their progress brought on White resentment and hostility. Black women, as
slaves and as nonslaves, nourished and raised white children who, at
a later time, would abuse or even kill the children of the women who
cared for them. Blacks fought in American wars that were proclaimed
as wars for freedom, but Black soldiers were mistreated by white com-
manders and white soldiers in these wars. After fighting wars for
America, Black soldiers had to face White racist discrimination, hostility, and even violence upon returning to America. Blacks have been
one of the greatest supporters of the Democratic Party, but that party
has also been very abusive toward Blacks. Blacks have been told that
their community life is low level and pathological, but if Blacks
sought to organize their community life to improve it, Whites, fearing
any Black collective effort, would seek to interfere with it and to
suppress it.

In *The Souls of Black Folk*, W. E. B. Du Bois spoke of the "double-
consciousness" that Black people developed in America to cope with
and to try to advance their lives, as well as to try to achieve freedom
in the country. In his specific comments, he was rather limited in
expressing his understanding of the situation:

> The Negro is a sort of seventh son, born with a veil, and
> gifted with second-sight in this American world,—a world

which yields him no true self-consciousness, but only lets him see himself through the revelation of the other world. It is a peculiar sensation, this double-consciousness, this sense of always looking at one's self through the eyes of others, of measuring one's soul by the tape of a world that looks on in amused contempt and pity. One ever feels his two-ness,—an American, a Negro.[16]

In his comments, Du Bois made reference to only two sources of Black "double-consciousness," and the two involved contradictions. One was that Blacks had a view of themselves but also had to view themselves through the very negative eyes of others. The other contradiction was Negro and American, with the latter being a contradiction only because, as Du Bois indicated further along in his comments, the American identity was actually white racist American, which was against the Black identity. But Du Bois knew full well the vast number of contradictions that Blacks had to live with and through in America that went into producing the double-consciousness among them. Du Bois described a plethora of these contradictions in *The Souls of Black Folk*, such as the Black artisan trying to develop his skill against the insistence of white racists that Black men and women be hewers of wood and drawers of water or when Black artists captured the "soul-beauty of a race" but then had to face Whites who felt that the black race had no beauty, only ugliness. What Du Bois did not have, conceptually, as part of his understanding of black double-consciousness in *Souls*, and in any of his other writings, was the concept of Black Cognition. But Du Bois knew full well what Black Cognition was, how it fitted into Black double consciousness, how it worked—and how it had been produced by Blacks interacting with the contradictions of their existence in America. Du Bois also knew how white people avoided functioning from a double-consciousness when relating to Black people; understanding that they injected racism into their ideals, beliefs, and thoughts when interacting with Blacks, making all the idealities racist idealities to produce a single racist consciousness. In 1910, for instance, Du Bois wrote that Whites had "injected" into Christianity "a gospel of human hatred and prejudice."[17] And at a later time, he wrote: "But in propaganda against the Negro since emancipation in this land, we face one of the most stupendous efforts the world ever saw to discredit human beings, an effort involving universities, history, science, social life, and religion."[18] Du Bois here was presenting a full picture of how white supremacy/ebonicism was injected into and maintained in all major areas of American society and civilization to make them function as racist entities that inculcated and sustained a single racist consciousness in Whites. Was this saying something about "regimes of truth" or the discursive character and pervasiveness of power in a society? How consciousness was related to "regimes of truth"?

Because of the way they were dominated and controlled in America, Blacks found themselves unable to do to Whites what Whites did to them. Whites could dominate and subordinate Blacks, but Blacks could not do that to them. Whites could exclude or dismiss Blacks, but Blacks could not do that to them. Whites could also segregate Blacks, confine them and isolate them, but Blacks could not do this to Whites. This means that Blacks did not have the experience in America that enabled them to develop—and certainly not to the extent of Whites—the domination-subordination, vertical, and dualistic cognitive systems that Whites utilized. And since Blacks could not overcome the White over Black social relationship in America—and certainly could not reverse it, not even to this day, not even with Blacks having political majorities in many American cities—they could not easily develop and make use of dialectical cognition.

Blacks had to develop a new cognitive system, which had to be developed out of their monointeractive African heritage, their domination-subordination, exclusionary, and segregated (dualistic) interaction with Whites, out of the vast contradictory character of their life in America, and out of their own needs and aspirations in the country. One of the things that Blacks were always concerned with, that Whites made them so concerned about practicing racism against them and holding them as slaves, was their human status, or their humanity—or, as it could also be said, their *wholeness*. As racists, slaveholders, or as supporters of slavery, white people regarded and treated Black people as if they were not human beings or as if they were not full human beings. The United States Constitution even defined most Blacks (Black slaves) as *three-fifths* human beings (meaning that individual Black slaves were counted as three-fifths of a human being, as opposed to a whole human being, in the population of a congressional district that elected a Representative to the U.S. Congress). Over their history in America, many Blacks were encouraged to denounce or reject their blackness, their black racial humanity, which would have made thinking about black or Black wholeness—wholeness as an ethnic group—superfluous. Blacks had often been told to think of themselves as being just "Americans" and nothing else in America, as if they had no other identity nor a larger reality—as if they were not a people of wholeness. In recent years, and this still continues, Blacks have been referred to as "non-Whites." This altogether denied their black humanity, or their Blackness, to say nothing about their wholeness. Albert Murray has expressed his views about Blacks being regarded as non-Whites: "those who are classified as non-white are somehow . . . all too naturally assumed to be non-this, non-that, and the non-the-other."[19] The *culturally deprived* concept means in its continued use the lack of wholeness in black people. The monointeractive cognitive system that continues on in Black Cognition, in the same way that other African retentions continue on in Black culture, as partial or transformed realities, plays a role, as it has from the beginning, in motivating Blacks to seek wholeness in their thoughts and in their lives in America. Another strong, historical, and continuing drive toward wholeness has been the need and determination to deal with contradictions or dichotomies. A third strong, historical, and continuing drive has been the determination on the part of Blacks to be equal to Whites in America, as individuals and as a group of people. All of these quests for wholeness represents the telos of Black history, which continues to function in that history and in Black life, even though the concept *telos* would have no meaning for most Black people. In their historical and continuing quest for wholeness, Blacks also learned that they could not be rigid in their understanding or dealing with reality. They needed all the aid they could muster to survive, make progress, and achieve wholeness. They had to be able to look at reality and to be able to deal with it in a critical manner. This enabled them to see that cooperating with Whites, with American institutions, and even with racists and racism could aid them in their quests. They learned that what might be detrimental might also be helpful, and this process was how they came to view the American Constitution and American law, both of which abused them. They learned that realities that were oppositional were not always oppositional, or that they did not necessarily have to be. They learned that realities that were different might also have some characteristics similar to other realities—that is, they learned that realities that were different were not necessarily oppositional. And they learned to look for similarities in reality, such as

similarities between themselves and Whites, which could be a basis
for understanding or common action. In short, Blacks had to learn
how to be very open and very flexible with reality in America. This
was required to pursue survival, development, and wholeness. This
all led to Blacks, over centuries, consciously and unconsciously, developing a method of cognition that allowed them to perceive and
deal with reality in a flexible, improvisational, and complex manner.
This method emerged and developed as Black Cognition, or what
could also be called diunital cognition, because of the diunital organizational logic associated with this form of cognition.

Black cognition works in the following manner. Its ideational guidance says that all aspects of reality, whether oppositional or not, similar or different, are individual aspects of reality that have their own
properties or dimensions and their own integrity. Even if a given
reality has been formed by a mixture of realities, it still is an individual
manifestation of reality with its own intrinsicness or integrity. All aspects of reality, while individual, are also equal—equal in the sense
that each is individual with its own intrinsic qualities and because all
aspects of reality interact with each other on the basis of their intrinsic
qualities. This is a manifestation of wholeness in Black Cognition, as
realities do not interact with one another except on the basis of their
intrinsic qualities, whatever they happen to be, and what can be
known about them, and the push is to know as much about the
dimensions of a given reality as possible. In Black Cognition, individual realities, owing to ideational and psychological attributes and also
to diunital organizational logic, are juxtaposed to each other and interact with each other on a *horizontal* basis. This means that Black
Cognition is not vertical cognition, because it does not eruct reality.
It is not dualistic cognition because realities interact, and they are not
always necessarily contradictory. It is not domination-subordination
cognition, because the interaction is horizontal and not perpendicular
or hierarchical. And it is not dialectical cognition, because there is no
overcoming, transcending, or hierarchy, as occurs with this form of
cognition. Horizontal interaction of individual realities is the centerpiece of Black Cognition. This keeps individual realities—their intrinsic qualities—in full view. This allows for equal interaction of realities,
which is done on the basis of individual intrinsicness or wholeness.
Blacks and Whites would be horizontally juxtaposed and would interact with each other on a horizontal basis that would allow for the
fullness of interaction. This would also be true with such horizontally

juxtaposed realities as men and women, politics and economics, co-operation and conflict, similarity and difference, evil and good, self-esteem and individual dignity, honesty and goodness, or liberty and equality. Horizontal interaction also functions to enable individual realities to influence or impact each other on the basis of their intrinsic qualities. Aspects of reality interacting with each other on the basis of their fullness help to define each other in a full manner, help to give full meaning to each other, help to augment each other, or help to change each other. But change does not occur by casting out, or by overcoming, or by suppressing and diminishing. It comes about by a process of dissolution, in the same way that two sand bricks would be changed by someone rubbing them against each other. Diunital organizational logic, which forces all realities to interact horizontally with each other, and Black Cognition, generally, give rise to *equi-thinking*, individual aspects of reality interacting with each other on an individual and equal basis to ensure the fullness or completeness of interaction and the full or whole disclosure of reality.

What Black Cognition did for Black people over their history in America was to make them a very *conscious* people. They had contradictions imposed upon them, and they had to be able to see these contradictions fully, or in their fullness. Blacks could not eliminate the contradictions because slavery or White racist power kept them intact and ongoing. So Blacks had to understand the contradictions, to be able to analyze them, or even to be able to use them in ways to benefit themselves. But they had to have the cognitive means to do that, to be able to see and understand reality in its greater complexity or wholeness. This also became the preferred method of cognition. It made it possible to have a more critical perspective on reality, because more of it could be seen and understood and analyzed. There was greater knowledge and greater truth to be had. And from all of this, with Black history and Black culture and social life contributing, Blackcentrism and a Blackcentric Perspective were born. With Black Cognition, Blackcentrism, and the Blackcentric Perspective functioning together in the minds of Blacks, Black people were given more intellectual space, more probing space. These dimensions of Black psychology and the Black mind made Blacks more *open* to reality, more open to learning something new or different, more open to accepting something different or new—and certainly as opposed to Whites, functioning from vertical, dualistic, domination-subordination, and dialectical cognition, which all sought to narrow the intellectual and probing space, and the context or content of reality. Blacks were less aggressive toward reality; not out to dominate it, or to subdue it, or to control it—and certainly not like Whites. Blacks, owing to their method of cognition and other attributes, such as Blackcentrism and the Blackcentric Perspective, were inclined to let reality, to let people, *reveal* themselves. Thus, quick judgments were not to be made about reality or about people. It was necessary to draw out as much information as possible and let things, or people, be revealed. Blacks have always been *revelationists* in America. This helped to inculcate a patience in them, with regard to realities and with people, and especially white people—and with America.

There have been many people over the history of Black people in America who have perceived the Black method of cognition, but who had no name for it. There have even been white people who have perceived it, but who saw it to be so different from the way in which they thought and perceived that they were inclined to believe that Blacks did not think in as logical a manner as they did. Mary White Ovington, one of the founders of the NAACP, was one of these white individuals. In a book she published in 1911 called *Half a Man*, a study of Blacks in New York, she made the following remark: "few, if any, Negroes hold logically to one ideal wholly to the exclusion of the other. They cannot be logical and live."[20] White regarded logic as having an either-or structure, not a diunital structure. Black thinking was "prelogical" or "unlogical" to her, perhaps even mystical to her. Black historian Lerone Bennett, Jr., showed his understanding of Black Cognition without having a formal name for it, but seeing logic in it. He reflected his understanding at a point in his book, *The Negro Mood*, in which he criticized Whites for trying to understand Black culture with either-or cognition: "The creators of this great tradition respected the cutting edge of life; they understood that good and evil, creative and destructive, wise and foolish, up and down, were inseparable polarities of existence." He further remarked that "What is lacking in most white interpretations of Negro reality is a full-bodied evocation of the entire spectrum. By seizing on one element to the exclusion of the other white interpreters and white imitators of the Negro deform themselves and the total ensemble of the Negro tradition which stands or falls as a bloc."[21] Black psychologist Joseph White, Jr., recognized Black Cognition without a formal name. Addressing other Black psychologists in an article, he said, "We should also recognize that black people have a great tolerance for ambiguity and uncertainty, for living with seemingly contradictory alternatives. As practitioners, then, we must eliminate the tendency to think in either-or terms, with respect to the black experience."[22] About the same time, Black and black scholars at Princeton University gave Black Cognition a formal name, *diunital cognition*, in their book *Beyond Black or White*, edited by Vernon Dixon and Badi Foster. Recently, Toni Morrison reflected her understanding and use of Black Cognition, when she remarked, "Black women seem able to combine the nest and the adventure. . . . They are both safe harbor and ship; they are both inn and trail. We, black women, do both. We don't find these places, these rules, mutually exclusive."[23] But it was Du Bois who captured in a clear and pure way, Black Cognition and the way it functioned, although not with a formal name. But in *The Souls of Black Folk* he wrote:

> The history of the American Negro is the history of this strife,—this longing to attain self conscious manhood, to merge this double self into a better and truer self. In this merging he wishes neither of the older selves to be lost. He would not Africanize America, for America has too much to teach the world and Africa. He would not bleach his Negro soul in a flood of white Americanism, for he knows that Negro blood has a message for the world. He simply wishes to make it possible for a man to be both a Negro and an American, without being cursed and spit upon by his fellows, without having the doors of Opportunity closed roughly in his face.[24]

Du Bois, in the above comments, not only indicated how diunital cognition worked, but how it was the culturally preferred method of cognition among Blacks. There was the horizontal interaction between *Negro* and *American*, with the two realities (identities) interacting on the basis of their integrity and fullness. This aided each element of reality to identify and affirm itself. The horizontal or diunital interaction of Negro and American led to the full or whole identity of Negro American, which is to be translated Black American. Du Bois, as seen, rejected the idea that Blacks were Africans, and also the idea that they should give up being Black and become just white people with black skins. The full Black American identity, as Du Bois saw it, gave Blacks "balance" in their identity and sense of who they were. This balance extended further, as implied in Du Bois's remarks, by Blacks being balanced between Euro-America and Africa and also the slave experience, which was also implied in Du Bois's remarks and which were, as he knew, the three elements that formed the historical foundation of Blacks and their Black identity in America.

Those Black intellectuals and other Blacks who call Black people in America *Africans* are engaged in White either-or cognition and are also rejecting both Blackcentric knowledge and the Blackcentric Perspective. Those black intellectuals and other Blacks who call Black people *African-Americans* are employing diunital cognition, when they see these two identities as individual and equal. But they are employing Black Cognition to accept a fantasy (African), rather than an actuality (Black), and they are also rejecting Blackcentric knowledge and a Blackcentric Perspective in favor of Africancentrism and an Africancentric Perspective, which appropriately belong to black Africans, but which can reach out to other black people in the world with limitations.

There are Black intellectuals and other Black people who engage in either-or or domination-subordination cognition when interpreting Black history, Black culture, or Black social reality; they look at these realities with White cognitive methods. This is true of those Black intellectuals who dichotomize the Black middle class and the Black lower class as either-or realities or as more-than realities, that is, the Black middle class more than the Black lower class or vice versa. Historically there have been Black clergy who have been against materialism among Blacks and have accepted only religious or spiritual values among them. There have been Black intellectuals and other Blacks who have accepted separation among Blacks and who have rejected integration. And there have been Black intellectuals and other Blacks who have gone the other way with these concepts and realities. Any time that Black people look at themselves or their history, culture, or social life from White cognition, they will see themselves in a partial and even distorted manner and will advocate partial or ineffective actions or solutions. Black people are a people who have to be seen whole, and their diunital cognition makes this possible. This same diunital cognition calls for holistic efforts to help Blacks develop and achieve freedom in America. It cannot be one form of help or one form more than another. It has to be many forms of aid—political, economic, educational, and artistic—and all in diunital interaction to pursue full development and full freedom.

In the 1920s, Alain Locke made the following observation about how Blacks should evolve in America, reflecting his diunital thinking:

> It is obvious . . . that the main line of Negro development must necessarily be artistic, cultural, moral and spiritual . . . in contrast with the predominantly practical, and scientific trend of the nation. . . . Although he must qualify in all the branches of American life and activity, the Negro can be of more general good in supplementing Nordic civilization than through merely competitively imitating or extending it along lines in which it is at present successful and pre-eminent.[25]

Locke was here doing some faulty thinking. American civilization was not just a white civilization or a "Nordic civilization" (and Locke knew this and said so in other writings). Blacks had made enormous cultural contributions to America to help to give it its distinctive characteristics and its distinctive civilization. Blacks had to engage in the "practical" and "scientific" pursuits as much as white people did. This was where great power and great wealth were, and Blacks would be left out of both, or diminished in their ability to attain and exercise both, if they did not pursue practical and scientific things with the same zeal as Whites. This was also another way to protect the "artistic, cultural, moral and spiritual" existence of Blacks in America; to attain and reflect (aided by wealth) a full ethnicity of ideational and moral and practical and scientific qualities when interacting in a diunital fashion with Whites in America. Locke, in his comments, was indirectly criticizing what he understood to be modernity in American life, which made it technological, materialistic, mechanistic, and crass, and often devoid of morality and spirituality. He wanted Blacks to counter modernity in America or to interact with it in a diunital manner that would prevent it from being so dominant in American life. Many black intellectuals in the past had spoken on modernity or modern life, and in a critical manner, and for and against. There are Black intellectuals now, especially Black literary elements, who are caught up in what is called the postmodern stance, which has had a great impact on their literary efforts. These Black intellectuals and others have joined white intellectuals in attacking modernity. In the next chapter I will look at modernity and postmodernity, as they have been labeled in American and Western life, with a view toward showing the false character of both and the inadequacy and destructiveness of the latter.

4.

The Modernity and Postmodernity Deceptions

Modernity and postmodernity, as subjects of context, analytical capabilities, and modes of expression, have been at the focus of Western intellectual activity for the past few decades. The reason that modernity has come in for so much attention during these decades is because of postmodernity. Postmodernists claim that modernity has come to an end and that what now exists, in the Western world at least, is the period of postmodernity. A thing that has made postmodernity itself so prominent and consuming over the past few decades has been the confusion of postmodernists as to who they are, what they stand for, and where postmodernity might be heading. As Jon Snyder wrote in the introduction to Gianni Vattimo's book *The End of Modernity*:

> The idea of 'post-modernity' lies at the centre of contemporary intellectual debate in the West. The critics and supporters of postmodernity have engaged in often heated exchanges over the course of the past decade, particularly regarding painting, architecture, ballet, theatre, cinema, literature and philosophy. There is a widely shared sense that Western ways of seeing, knowing and representing have irreversibly altered in recent times; but there is little con-

sensus over what this might mean or what direction Western culture is now taking.[1]

But these are not the only quandaries facing postmodernists and
postmodernity. While postmodernists claim that modernity is over, it
is not always clear from their writings what is meant by *modernity*
and, therefore, what has ended. Postmodernists also evidence lack of
unity as to when modernity itself began. Some say the seventeenth
century, with the European Age of Reason, and René Descartes's
philosophical innovations. Others say the eighteenth century, with
the European Enlightment, with its emphasis on rationality, the
scientific method, the domination and uses of nature, and the progressive and even redemptive character of history. Still other postmodernists see modernity as having begun in the latter nineteenth
century with industrialization and the transformation of Western civilization from a rural to an urban civilization, which gave a great boost
to the development of technology and science, and later bureaucracy,
which became the primary means to build and sustain the modern,
Western urban civilization.

Postmodernists, not agreeing on the beginning of modernity, are
not in agreement as to when it ended. Some mark the end of modernity in the late nineteenth century, when Friedrich Nietzsche put
its paradigm under wrenching criticism that in the minds of some
postmodernists inaugurated postmodernity. Some postmodernists
have put the American pragmatic philosophers of the late nineteenth
century, such as William James and John Dewey (although not with
the same sanguinity as with James) in the same category as Nietzsche,
as signals that modernity was over and as initiators of postmodernity.
Then there are those postmodernists who claim that modernity ended
with the end of the Victorian age, which had begun in 1830 and
ended in the early 1900s. At this point (or a little earlier), what has
been called *modernism* in art, sometimes, *modern art*, emerged, ending Victorianism and modernity and inaugurating postmodernity. But
for others, postmodernity is a phenomenon of the 1960s and
thereafter, with a number of early precursors from Nietzsche on up
to the 1960s, with Martin Heidegger a seminal figure along the
route. If postmodernity commenced in the 1960s, then that decade
had to mark the end of modernity. This was Steven Best and Douglas
Kellner's view in *Postmodern Theory*.

During the 1960s, sociopolitical movements, new intellectual currents, and the cultural revolts throughout the West against the stifling conformity of the postwar celebration of the "affluent society" produced a sense that a widespread rebellion was occurring against a rigid and oppressive modern society. Sixties radicalism put in question modern social structures and practices, culture, and modes of thought. While the radical political movements of the era eventually dispersed and failed to carry through the revolution that many thought would follow the tumultuous events of 1968, a series of socioeconomic and cultural transformations in the 1970s and 1980s suggested that a break with the previous society had indeed taken place. An explosion of media, computers and new technologies, a restructuring of capitalism, political shifts and upheavals, novel cultural forms, and new experiences of space and time produced a sense that dramatic developments have occurred throughout culture and society. The contemporary postmodern controversies can therefore be explained in part by an ongoing and intense series of crises concerned with the breaking up of the "modern" modes of social organization and the advent of a new, as yet barely charted, "postmodern" terrain.[2]

It is not clear to this writer why such things as "an explosion of media, computers and new technologies, a restructuring of capitalism" are not part of what is called *modernity* rather than *postmodernity*. In the nineteenth century in America, there was an explosion of newspapers, magazines, and journals and various public speaking forums. And the same happened in Western Europe. But this explosion of media, representing change and transformation, occurred in what postmodernists call the modern period or modernity. From the late eighteenth century and throughout the nineteenth century in the Western world there were many new technologies, from the cotton gin to things like the refinement of sugar, the electric telegraph, the cylindrical press, the lasting of shoes, the lubrication of railroad cars in motion, the steel plow, the steel-toothed reaper, the electric light, and assembly line production, which changed and transformed the Western world, but which postmodernists would place within Western modernity. The capitalistic system was transformed in the Western world in the nineteenth century, in a very distinguishable manner, from private enterprise to corporate enterprise, which Marx, studying its initial phases, called "modern" capitalism, not postmodern capitalism. So what makes something modern, as opposed to being postmodern?

In 1990, sociologist Anthony Giddens published *The Consequences of Modernity*, in which he was critical of the postmodernists for contending that modernity had ended. He argued that they had not fully understood modernity itself which was continuing on in time, or history, and, indeed, on a global basis: "we have to look again at the nature of modernity itself which, for certain fairly specific reasons, has been poorly grasped in the social sciences hitherto." Rather than the end of modernity and moving into postmodernity, Giddens asserted that "we are moving into one [a period] in which the consequences of modernity are becoming more radicalised and universalised than before. Beyond modernity, I shall claim, we can perceive the contours of a new and different order, which is "post-modern"; but this is quite distinct from what is at the moment called by many "postmodernity.""[3]

Giddens, as can be seen, was saying that postmodernity did not even exist, and could not exist, because modernity was still functioning in the Western world and beyond. Institutional and other aspects of Western modernity had moved into other parts of the world, globalizing modernity, with its consequences on other local societies, such as separating time and space in human thought and perception in a profound, unheard-of manner, by placing thought, or "reflexive activity," at the service of endless cultural and social change, and by the universalizing or globalizing dimension of modernity that make local communities and local life anachronisms. These things, Giddens argued in his work, so-called postmodern thinkers had not thought about or grasped as yet.

But Giddens takes away from the logic and cogency of his own argument, when he, contradictorily, acknowledges the existence of those claiming to be postmodernists, as well as their body of thought: "Post-modernism, if it means anything, is best kept to refer to styles or movements within literature, painting, the plastic arts, and architecture. It concerns aspects of *aesthetic reflection* upon the nature of modernity."[4] If Giddens believed that postmodernity had not yet come into existence, he should have said, to be logical with his own argument, that what is called and understood to be postmodern should be referred to by some other name. Of course, he would have been criticized for doing that. But on the other hand, for his own study and position to make sense, he should have done this. Despite his intentions or feelings, he has indicated that there are two post-modernities: the one that presently exists, even if aesthetic, and the one that will exist, in time. But if a postmodernity already exists, then that has to mean, does it not, that modernity is over?

There are those Western thinkers who are not interested in seeing modernity die and are doing their best to hold onto it, in some of its originality, mainly by reevaluating it and extracting what is still vital and useful in it. This has been the project of the German philosopher Jürgen Habermas. Agnes Heller has made this her project as well, as reflected in various writings and as recently as *Can Modernity Survive?* In this writing, Heller argued that modernist thinkers did not always see the larger dimensions of their own reflections or perceptions. She said that such thinkers were often not modern enough: "The great narratives of philosophy of history have lost their appeal not because they were too modern, but because they were not modern enough."[5] Or, as she also said: "The problem with philosophies of histories is not foundationalism, but the way they practice it." Heller even thinks, and hopes, that philosophies of histories will return to Western discourse. After all, the postmodernists assert, she says, that there can be and should be a "plurality of interpretations," which leaves the door open to the grand narrative as one of the plural interpretations. Indeed, and what is the tilt of Heller's position is that she accepts postmodernity, as Giddens does, although somewhat differently, as a part of modernity. "Postmodernity cannot be interpreted as *post-histoire*, as a new period that comes after modernity and that cancels history as such together with modernity. At any rate, our life experiences do not bear out this proposition." Heller offered a recommendation to those who regarded themselves as modernist and postmodern thinkers:

> I recommend, therefore, that the term post-modernity be understood as equivalent to the contemporary historical consciousness of the modern age. Post-modern is not what follows after the modern age, but what follows after the unfolding of modernity. Once the main categories of modernity have emerged, the historical tempo slows down and the real work on the possibilities begins.[6]

So, for Agnes Heller, postmodernity is the reflective stage of modernity, when postmodern thinkers, by having a chance to look at modernity in the way the creators of it could not, or did not, can carry modernity to greater fruition. Philosopher Stanley Rosen wants to save what is vital in modernity, which he feels continues on, but is in serious crisis, as reflected in things like "post-modernism, anti-platonism, post-philosophy, and deconstruction." Rosen feels the way to save what is vital and useful in modernity is for modernists to turn to ancient Greek thought and have a dialogue with it. After all, according to Rosen, it is to ancient Greek thought that modernity can be traced. A retracing might lead to things not previously seen, understood, or understood well about modernity and its parameters and intentions.[7]

Intellectuals and others in the Western world have been talking about the latter in terms of modernity for a long time—indeed, for centuries, in such phrases and discussion as *modern history, modern culture, modern social life, modern thought, modern technology,* and *modern warfare.* Only the word *modernity,* which seems to be of recent vintage, was missing from these conceptualizations and discussions, coming out of postmodern thought and postmodernity itself. Many, if not most, postmodernists show hostility toward, or contempt for, what they call *modernity.* They do not see themselves salvaging anything from it, but rather see themselves bringing it to a close that they argue modernity itself initiated by going against itself; when reason or rationality turned against itself and became the opposite of itself, as an instrument of oppression, destruction, and control, and when reason or rationality could no longer stand as the foundation for establishing and maintaining morality. As philosopher Ross Poole has recently written, "Modernity has called into play a dominant conception of what it is to have reason to act; this conception has the consequence that the dictates of morality have little purchase on the motivations of those to whom they are addressed. Modernity has constructed a conception of knowledge which excludes the possibility of moral knowledge; morality becomes, not a matter of rational belief, but subjective opinion."[8] Many, if not most, postmodernists see themselves, intellectually, bringing modernity to a close, putting, as it were, finishing touches on the situation.

Postmodernists generally view postmodernity to be intellectually (and as they hope, as time goes on, and stimulated by the new thought, practically) different from modernity and to have a life of its own, although they are not in any consensual agreement as to what that life is, what it means, or where it is going. And there are postmodernists who add to this tension and even confusion by saying there are not to be any certainties about these things, because post-modernity by definition rejects such things, as it rejects absolutes and grand narratives and any kind of ranking or privileging. But there are postmodernists who talk, rather strangely, about a "crisis" in post-modern thought, or a "crisis" in postmodernity, as Cornel West did in *Prophetic Thought in Postmodern Times*.[9] For modernist thinkers, this would not make any sense, because they see modernity contin-uing on; if there were any crisis, it would have to be in modernity itself. If postmodernity is new and ongoing, with no clear view of its direction and end, and still less with manifestations that can be de-termined to be decisive, discontinuous, or transformative, that threaten or clash with existing reality, that augur new potentials or a new direction, how does one speak of crisis? If modernity was con-sidered to be over, then it would be possible, in assessing it, having the long view of it, to talk about the crises of modernity with some certainty. This would even be possible if modernity were still ongo-ing, because it has been in existence for centuries; looking back on it, crises could be discerned and discussed. But there are modernists, still functioning and still enthused with and supportive of modernity, who would say that there could not be a crisis in postmodernity be-cause the latter itself has come to an end. Focusing on critics of post-modernity, such as Dario Fo, Felix Guartari, Andrew Britton, and Jürgen Habermas, Best and Kellner have written: "Critics of the post-modern turn argued that it was either a passing fad . . . a specious invention of intellectuals in search of a new discourse and source of cultural capital . . . or yet another conservative ideology attempting to devalue emancipatory modern theories and values."[10] But post-modernists would reject this assessment and also the contention that postmodernity had come to an end, that it had been a passing fancy, or that it had spent itself as a counter to modernity but had not been able to effectively counter it.

I think that the word *crisis* is not only overly used, but grossly misused in the present day, with intellectuals and political leaders being the principal misusers. This is a word that seems to pump up intellectuals and political leaders, seeming to give them a purpose or meaning or indicating that there is an important or indispensable place for them in a situation or in society or an important or indispensable role they can play or service they can perform in a situation or for society. Postmodernists have made the comment on more than one occasion that postmodernity has cast a heavy shadow over the intellectual, and has raised serious questions about the usefulness of intellectuals, inasmuch as there is no longer a pursuit of absolutes, grand narratives, or truth when the individual author is devalued or cast aside and when no point of view carries any more weight than any other. One might be tempted to talk of a crisis of intellectuals in Western civilization. But then what would constitute the crisis, when it is known that intellectuals still exist in large numbers, functioning in colleges and universities, as public and private schoolteachers, as clergypersons, as journalists, editors, and various kinds of literary elements, such as poets, fiction writers, dramatists, or literary critics, and as scientists, researchers, and in think tanks? What is the crisis among intellectuals that one would be able to identify? Are intellectuals sometimes arrogant or egotistical enough to believe that their own personal crisis, intellectual, psychological, or social, reflects a historical, cultural, or social crisis? The answer to that question would be yes, and individuals like Johann Fichte, Friedrich Nietzsche, and Martin Heidegger are individuals who can be named as fitting this bill.[11] And it seems that some postmodernist thinkers fit that bill as well, such as Jean-François Lyotard and Jean Baudrillard.

But what I find as the greatest abuse of the word *crisis*, which is the same as the greatest abuse of the phrase *postmodern*, is the way they are used to cover up reality and to promote a great *silence* about reality, or the present world. Michel Foucault is the postmodern thinker who has alerted other postmodern thinkers about the silence, and even silences that can be found in public discourse; a silence or silences about things, that alone make it possible to talk about something, or in a certain way, that would not be possible if the silence or silences were broken and what was hidden or obscured was brought into the discussion:

> Silence itself—the thing that one declines to say, or is forbidden to name, the discretion that is required between different speakers—is less the absolute limit of discourse, the other side from which it is separated by a strict boundary, than an element that functions alongside the things said, with them and in relation to them within overall strategies. There is no binary division made between what one

says and what one does not say; we must try and determine the different ways of not saying things, how those who can and those who cannot speak of them are distributed, which type of discourse is authorised, or which form of discretion is required in either case. There is not one but many silences, and they are an integral part of the strategies that underlie and permeate discourses.[12]

Foucault made these remarks in 1984 in the first volume of his *History of Sexuality.* This was an astute observation by Foucault, but it was not an insight that commenced with him or with postmodernity. Black people have lived in a country where silence about them has been a cardinal rule. White people have historically denied the presence and reality of Blacks in America. White people have historically talked about America as if Black people have never existed. The only way that white people could talk about America being in a universal sense, the "land of liberty," or the "land of equality," or "opportunity," or "justice," was to be silent about racism, slavery, racist exclusion, or racist segregation. And the silence could also occur in another way, by lying about Black people and their history in America, which would prevent white people, and even Black people from knowing about both, or much about both. Lying and distorting facts or information were ways to keep realities from being known, to maintain a silence about them. And black people themselves, over the course of their history, have participated in the silence thrown over their existence in America. Booker T. Washington, for instance, felt that the only way that Blacks would be able to get assistance from Whites for education and economic development was to keep publicly silent, and this he often did about the White violence and atrocities against Blacks in his day, which were the height of White racism in America. Blacks have historically also maintained a general silence about how racism has affected Whites in this country as a people, intellectually, psychologically, morally, and spiritually. When Black intellectuals or political leaders talk about racism, predicated on race, they invariably talk about Black people and invariably their victimization but rarely talk about white people as the racists and as victims of their own racism or about how the racism of Whites has affected American history, culture, and social life. Whites in America carry the incredible view that they have not been affected by their own racist beliefs and social practices. And one of the reasons they carry it is that Blacks have not told them, and certainly not often enough, extensively enough, or clearly enough how their racist beliefs and practices have affected them. But Blacks do know, even when they do not or cannot put things in an analytical or conceptual mode. But there have been Black intellectuals who have made remarks about the way Whites have been affected by their own racism. Frederick Douglass made the following comments on one occasion: "self-deception is a chronic disease of the American mind and character. The crooked way is ever preferred to the straight in all . . . mental processes, and in all . . . studied actions . . . [Americans] are masters in the art of substituting a pleasant falsehood for an ugly disagreeable truth, and of clinging to a fascinating delusion while rejecting a palpable reality."[13]

And Du Bois made the following remarks at a later time about white racism's impact on white people: "We have the somewhat inchoate idea that we are not destined to be harassed with great social questions, and that even if we are, and fail to answer them, the fault is with the question and not with us. Consequently we often congratulate ourselves more on getting rid of a problem rather than on solving it."[14]

In the early 1970s, Black psychiatrist James Comer wrote about what he called a "secret pact" between Whites and Blacks, which called for Blacks to be silent about Whites, as to who they were and what they had done and were doing in America, as racists, in return for some gains for Blacks. In *Beyond Black and White*, he wrote: "Blacks and whites have had a kind of secret pact over the years which has helped whites minimize their guilt and anxiety. Whites have said, 'Don't show me my white mind. Don't break down my defenses. Don't challenge the structure on which I base my identity. If you don't, I shall approve of you, I shall even open up a few token opportunities to you.' "[15] Here was Comer saying how silence played a critical role in Black oppression in America and also how Blacks, out of pressure and necessity, collaborated with the silence and how they also collaborated with their own oppression. One of the reasons that there are white intellectuals who do not want to admit the general blackness of ancient Egyptian civilization is that they want to maintain the silence about the intellectual and cultural achievements of some black people. One of the reasons that many white intellectuals are against the Africancentric Perspective and Africancentrism is that they are afraid that they will reveal the general blackness of ancient Egypt and the achievements of black people. That is, this perspective and this body of knowledge will break the long White-imposed silence on ancient Egypt. Does all of this not say something about how silence itself plays a critical role in establishing and maintaining a "regime of truth," to borrow a phrase from Foucault?

Two regimes of truth that Foucault and other postmodernists seem not to perceive and the role that silence plays in their projection and maintenance are the regimes of truth of modernity and postmodernity. Both of these things are fantasies and deceptions, despite all the writing that has been done on them and all the explanations given. But the explanation not given, which reflects the method and role of *cultural silence*, to coin a phrase, is that neither modernity nor postmodernity has ever existed, except in language and in fact, as regimes of falsehood.[16]

To be able to make this point, initially, I want to turn to a word that once had considerable currency, and that is *modernization*. Postmodernists have been quick to indicate that modernization and modernity are not the same. And they are not. Modernization refers to the process and methods of modernizing a culture or a society. Modernization is something that can occur intermittently, or over a long, sustained period. Modernizing is different from modernization. It is something that happens individually, as when an aspect of culture, such as science, bookkeeping, printing, or ship building, is modernized. Modernizing can occur intermittently or continuously, and it occurs in an uneven manner. Modernization involves modernizing, of course, but modernizing can occur without modernization. America underwent modernization intermittently over its centuries of life and modernized continuously. Today, America looks a lot different from the America of the seventeenth century. America two thousand years from now will doubtlessly look different from the way it looks now and will be more modern than it is now. And two thousand years beyond that will reflect an America that is even more modern.

With the concepts of modernization and modernizing it is possible to see that any people, anywhere in the world, at any point in time, can modernize their culture, their institutions, and themselves, that what is modern is not confined to the creative efforts, or "creative genius" of any given people, nor is it the sole or exclusive activity of any given country, or any given civilization. But this is the precise false view of modern, the precise regime of falsehood, that Whites/ Europeans have perpetrated. Because the word *modernity*, especially, gives the impression, and deliberately (but also unconsciously, as a matter of cultural rote) that modern or a modern life has appeared in history only once, among only one group of people, and in only one place in the world. In short, what is modern is associated with Whites/Western Europeans. The word *modernity*, constructed by these people, makes *modern* inclusive and confined to Whites/Western Europeans who, as the argument goes, have spread modernity and modern life to other parts of the world, with this spread continuing. This position is fully a *White racist position.*[17] But the racism is obsured by language or discourse and is thus buried in silence. Modernity is often, if not usually, discussed as if people are not involved in constructing it or implementing it. This maintains the silence about white people and obscures the racism in which the concept of modernity is rooted.

What history shows is that there is modernization and modernizing, and not modernity. And, of course, if there is no modernity, there can be no postmodernity or postmodernism. Modern cannot have a *post*, because it is something that continues on in time, even if on an intermittent basis. Western Europe four thousand years from now will be a lot different and more modern than it presently is. But this will also be true of other parts of the world. And it will be undoubtedly true that people other than Whites/Western Europeans or Whites/Americans will be innovators in modernizing and in producing and promoting what is modern. Postmodernists are the creators of the fiction and regime of falsehood of modernity, and they sustain it by their own fiction and regime of falsehood of postmodernity; and by the racism in which they have their feet planted, and which they have yet to detect, and which swarms through much of postmodern thought.

These are some harsh comments, I realize, and also they are resented. That is to be expected. But postmodernists claim, following Foucault, that regimes of truth must be analyzed and that postmodernists accept, and accept only, pluralistic interpretations. This is one of those pluralistic interpretations. And to get on with it, I want to focus on racism, mainly white supremacy/ebonicism, and how it initially became associated with what is called modernity and how the latter became rooted in the former and which would also pass into what is called postmodernity, again, as foundationalism.

One turns to Du Bois to pinpoint these beginnings. Du Bois, like other black intellectuals of the late nineteenth century and throughout this century, accepted the idea and even the reality of European or Western modernity. The paradigm was inescapable and had to be related to. Du Bois related to it critically, without reacting critically to its premises; that is, he did not react to it fully critically. This was also true of other Black intellectuals of his day and continues to be true about Black intellectuals, as well as about white and other intellectuals in America, Europe, and elsewhere in the world.

But what Du Bois noted, which was of importance, and which he noted in the late nineteenth and very early twentieth centuries, was that White racism (i.e., white supremacy/ebonicism) came together with European or Western modernity at its outset. The development of modern Europe and European modernity were connected to the African slave trade, which helped to produce the white supremacy/ebonicism that also was connected to European modernity at its outset, as an integral part and driving force of it. In *The Negro*, published in 1915, Du Bois stated the case of the beginnings:

> These were not days of decadence, but a period that gave the world Shakespeare, Martin Luther, and Raphael, Horoun-al-Raschid and Abraham Lincoln. It was the day of the greatest expansion of two of the world's most pretentious religions and of the beginning of the modern organization of industry. In the midst of this advance and uplift this slave trade and slavery spread more human misery, inculcated more disrespect for and neglect of humanity, a greater callousness to suffering, and more petty cruel, human hatred than can well be calculated. We may excuse and palliate it, and write history so as to let men forget it; it remains the most inexcusable and despicable blot on modern human history.[18]

One can see at the tail end of Du Bois's comments, the reference, without conceptualization, to what I call, cultural silence. He indicated how historians played a role in promoting cultural silence. It can also be seen that Du Bois dates European or Western modernity to the sixteenth century (Shakespeare), which was when the African slave trade went into high gear, and when, as he indicates, white supremacy/ebonicism was produced to help drive it. Du Bois's comments also show another understanding of his, which was the understanding of the sociologist, and even historical sociologist, that he was. He noted how European modernity, integrally associated with racism and slavery and drawing off both to flourish, inculcated a profound dichotomization between white and black people, a profound social distancing between white and black people. And what made the division and distancing so profound is that both were predicated on the assumption that black people were not people, or not full human beings. The division and social distancing could not have been greater. Sociologists today talk about social distancing but see it as a reality of the twentieth century, and as a consequence of European modernity gone berserk. But Du Bois saw this social distancing occurring much earlier, and he saw the situation in a very special manner. In the eighteenth century, Immanuel Kant had philosophically separated morality from politics, with all the implications that that would have for Western politics, or modern politics. What Du Bois gleaned from his observation of the inauguration of European modernity was the way Whites/Europeans separated morality from social life: "this slave trade and slavery spread more human misery, inculcated more disrespect for and neglect of humanity, a greater callousness to suffering, and more petty cruel, human hatred than can well be calculated." Then he said, that history would have to be written to remove memory and guilt from Whites so that they would not be troubled by their own behavior, to make certain that they would not have to confront their history and their own minds and personalities where they all connected in gross inhumanity. Indeed, as Du Bois knew, and would say on many occasions, even in this early period of his writing, white supremacy/ebonicism played the primary role in erasing memory and guilt. It reduced black people to the status of nonhuman or subhuman, which removed them from a human status, from human morality, and, therefore, removed white people from any guilt for the way they related to and treated black people. Because guilt was associated only with morality and with people.

This also all meant the following: European modernity was associated with removing the *author*—in this case, the author of historical and social crimes; indeed, crimes against humanity. Whites/Europeans made their modernity an instrument to produce holocausts, namely, the African and Native American holocausts, and these were other realities that were part of the launching of Western or European modernity, as integral parts of it, and as driving forces of it. And white historians, as John Henrik Clarke said in *Christopher Columbus & the*

Afrikan Holocaust, went through elaborate pains, using many cultural devices to cover up the African and Indian holocausts, to maintain a historical and civilizational silence about them.

At the outset of European modernity, the latter got locked at the hip with racism and slavery and gross assaults against humanity. This means that the rationality of European modernity got joined at the hip with racist irrationality. Michel Foucault would later say in one of his writings that European rationality reached its boundaries or limits with the establishment of the asylum and the category of insanity in the seventeenth century. Du Bois argued, differently and much earlier, that the rationality of Whites and European modernity reached their limits with racist irrationality and racist inhumanity. When Western modernity moved across the world, it took White racism with it, which actually turned out to be a number of White racisms, because white people devised different racist beliefs for different groups of people of color. But Western modernity and Western civilization functioned from a profound and deep racist foundation, which I call *racist foundationalism*. This is not a term to be found in the literature on racism or race (which, in the literature is invariably, and erroneously, depicted as the same thing). I devised this term to take the discussion of racism well beyond where it usually goes, to those other dimensions of it that are usually not seen, because racism, as such, is rarely ever investigated. My investigation over the years has indicated to me that racism not only exhibits beliefs and values but also a metaphysic, or ontology, that is, essentialist racist beliefs that purport to present absolute and transcendental knowledge, truth, and understanding about people, and function as a grand narrative about them—all of this being predicated on a racist epistemology. Racism bends or utilizes forms of thought for its own purposes, creating various forms of *racist scholasticism*. There is also a racist psychology—actually, psychologies—as racists fall into psychological types, depending on the extent and intensity of their racism. Racism is also characterized by pathology, irrationality, and immorality. And it is also possible to talk about racist cultural and social practices. All of what I have just mentioned, which is all that can be done in this essay, constitutes racist foundationalism. This is what Whites/Europeans, acting as racists, put at the foundation of Western civilization, where it has existed for centuries and where it still exists. And functioning as the foundation of Western civilization, racism has always intruded into the lives of white people and into all the major areas of Western civilization: its politics, economics, science and technology and in its philosophy, literature, and art. This kind of intrusion has been especially strong in the United States, where white supremacy/ ebonicism has interpenetrated American liberal, democratic, and Christian ideals, turning them into racist ideals when Whites inter- acted with Blacks. When Whites/Europeans interacted with people of color in their colonies, their racisms interpenetrated their thought and colonial institutions, making them both function as racist entities when white Europeans related to their colonized people of color. And then there could be very violent intrusions of racist foundationalism into the lives of Whites/Westerners and Western civilization, as oc- curred in America in the late nineteenth and early twentieth centuries and in Nazi Germany in the 1930s and 1940s. The racist intrusion here was Aryanism/anti-Jewism. Anti-Jewism was, as it had been for centuries, the centerpiece of racist foundationalism in Europe. White supremacy, ebonicism, racism, and xanthicism were added to this foundationalism when Whites/Westerners started making their march to world denomination. Hitler and the Nazis drew on several forms of racism to promote their activities; that is, they drew on the broad expanse of Western racist foundationalism and intruded it grotesquely into Western history and Western life.

When Nietzsche was attacking theological and philosophical ab- solutism and transcendence and the metaphysical foundationalism of Western modernity, he was totally ignorant of or at least ignored the racist foundationalism of Western modernity, in which the theological and philosophical absolutism and transcendence and metaphysical foundationalism were rooted. Max Weber, in the twentieth century, in *The Protestant Ethic and the Spirit of Capitalism*[19] and other writ- ings, spoke of the destruction of medieval romanticism, mysticism, superstition, and other affective and subjective realities, which he la- beled, collectively, European *enchantment.* He was essentially obliv- ious to the *racist enchantment* that was deeply rooted in Western civilization and in Western modernity and which was making bois- terous noises all around him and which was strongly driving these structures. Zygmunt Bauman recently argued that racism and mo- dernity came together to produce the Jewish Holocaust.[20] But as Du Bois had shown, and as other black or Black writers have shown, racism and modernity had come together at a much earlier time and had produced a slave trade, slavery, and African, Indian, and African-

Black holocausts, and all lasting for centuries, and predating by centuries the Jewish and Slavic holocausts of the twentieth century.[21]

There was a long historical silence about the union of racism and European modernity, because the combination was implemented against black people and other people of color. When the combination was implemented against white people, Jews and others, the silence with respect to the other combinations and people of color continued, because the focus was on present white victims of holocaustic experiences. In the 1950s and 1960s, Black people broke the silence about the crimes that white people had committed against their humanity. And black Africans and Asians did the same. This is not a silence to which there will be a return, and it can be predicted that the silence will be broken more loudly as time goes on. This will lead in America, most likely, to a breaking of the silence about how racism has affected white people, and through them, how it has affected American history, culture, and social life and even America's relationship with the world.

Modernity has never been real, but modernizing and modernization have been realities. Whites/Europeans had a long period of modernizing, a period of centuries, and this modernizing has not ended, and it has also impacted the world and will continue to do so. And in time, modernizing in other parts of the world will have a profound impact on Whites/Europeans and others in the Western world, as had occurred at earlier times in Western history.

Here is where postmodernists carry out another deception: the intellectual origins of Western modernity, which they trace to the ancient Greeks. This can only be done if there is a silence maintained about the ancient Egyptians and their impact on the ancient Greeks, particularly in terms of thought, mathematics, and science. Something that so many white intellectuals cannot bring themselves to accept is the idea that white people could learn abstract thought, mathematics, and science from black people. There was a time when white scholars and other intellectuals admitted that they learned these things from black Egyptians or black people. At that time the color of the ancient Egyptians did not make much difference to them. But in the late eighteenth and early nineteenth centuries and thereafter, the color and race of Egyptians became acutely important, because White racism—white supremacy/ebonicism—became acutely important. It tried to prove that black people were related to monkeys, orangutans, and gorillas and that they were severely arrested in their physical and cerebral development. In this racist view, black people did not have the intellectual, moral, or psychological capacity to construct a sophisticated culture, let alone a sophisticated civilization. This meant that the ancient Egyptian civilization could not have been a black civilization. But even when this position was being taken, there were white scholars who knew and accepted that the ancient Egyptians were black people or mainly that. Their racism then led them, as Martin Bernal said in *Black Athena*, to ridicule ancient Egyptian civilization. These were both manifestations of racism and racist power and the desiccation of scholarship.

It was during the eighteenth-century European Enlightenment that white intellectuals turned to ancient Greek thought that would help them construct the ideological orientation and guidelines for European modernizing activities and a new phase of European modernization. This was mainly being done by Western European intellectuals who were greatly concerned to increase the secularization of Western Europe, which, it was believed, would help Europeans to engage in extensive modernization.

A number of ancient Greek intellectuals studied in ancient Egypt. Bertrand Russell wrote in his *History of Western Philosophy* that "nothing is so surprising or difficult to account for as the sudden rise of civilization in Greece." And then he went on to say that the ancient Greeks "invented mathematics and science and philosophy."[22] Russell also admitted that there had been civilizations in Mesopotamia and Egypt thousands of years before civilization occurred in Greece. But he could not account for that "sudden rise of civilization in Greece." The truth was, it was not sudden. It took centuries for Greek civilization to evolve, and it did so by taking in culture from Mesopotamia, especially Phoenicia and Babylon, but particularly from Egypt. During the late Archaic period, and during what is called the Classical period in ancient Greek history, a number of Greeks studied in Egypt or studied with Greeks who had studied in Egypt. What Russell did not seem to know, George Sarton did. He wrote in the 1950s, and a decade before Russell's work appeared: "The Egyptian invention of mathematical and physical sciences is implied in many of the Greek fragments referring to the Ionian philosophers. . . . Egypt was generally considered by early Greek writers as the cradle of science, and the Greeks who had intellectual ambitions would try to visit that country and to spend as long a time as possible interrogating the men of learning and the priests."[23]

Pythagoras studied in Egypt for twenty-two years and brought Egyptian philosophy and mathematics to the Greeks. Pythagoras also came back to Greece with an understanding that music could be understood and composed mathematically. This was not an understanding he could have gained from Greek culture, because such an association between math and music was not understood there. Joan Erikson wrote the following about Greek music that predated Pythagoras's studying in Egypt: "There is little recorded in the early Greek myths and legends about music, song, and dance, except as elements of religious ceremony."[24] The Egyptians had an understanding of the relationship between mathematics and music that existed before Pythagoras studied in the country, and that was very old knowledge. As Ivan Van Sertima has written: "Experiments in ancient Egypt with a music notation system and the establishments of schools of music that not only taught vocal and instrumental performance but also theory and chirenomy (the art of notation by means of gesture) made Egypt the first civilization to do so."[25] Whatever contribution Pythagoras made to the mathematical understanding of music was predicated on what he had learned in Egypt.

Thales was one of the earlier Greeks who had studied in Egypt, going there even before Pythagoras. He studied philosophy as well as geometry and astronomy there and came away with knowledge about eclipses of the sun and also with the view that water was the first substance of the universe. Mary Lefkowitz, an extreme Eurocentric, has recently denied that Thales acquired this knowledge in Egypt. She wrote in *Not Out of Africa*: "Why insist that it was in *Egypt* that Thales . . . learned about the importance of water, when the idea is inherent also in Babylonian mythology?"[26] The people of India also believed in this principle, which was expressed in their oral Vedas literature, which dated back to about 1200 to 1500 B.C., and long before the Vedas were written down, which was about the time Thales studied in Egypt. But the Egyptian belief in the primeval water predated that belief in India by nearly 1500 years. Babylon emerged in history, in Mesopotamia, about fifteen hundred years after the establishment of Egypt, and long after the Egyptians had established their Heliopolitan Theology, which had occurred by 2500 B.C., as reflected in the Pyramid Texts, but which Egyptologists believe is much older. In the Heliopolitan Theology, the primeval water is the goddess Nun, out of which emerged the creator god, Ra or Atum, who was also known as Ra-Atum-Khepri, with the latter name meaning "he who comes into being," or "he who brings into being."[27] In the Memphite Theology of Egypt, Ptah is the primeval water and the creator god. Thus, it is logical to believe that Thales learned about the primeval water in Egypt, inasmuch as he studied there, and it was a very developed idea there. Democritis, according to the ancient Greek writer Diodorus, spent five years studying in Egypt. He went there to study geometry, astronomy and, according to Diodorus, also astrology. Mary Lefkowitz denied that Democritis even studied in Egypt (she denied that any other Greeks did). Democritis has been accredited with discovering the atom, and that it was the primeval material of the universe, and not the elements of water, fire, air, and earth, as the Egyptians had said. The Egyptians believed that reality was whole or one, but that it was also plural. They also spoke of monads. The Egyptians also held the view that reality was always changing, even though it also had stability and remained the same. One can see how this kind of naturalistic philosophical thinking would influence Democritis's theorizing about the atom. This thinking is at least preatomistic. Lefkowitz obviously did not want to believe—or could not accept—believing that Democritis's thinking could have been influenced by his Egyptian instruction. Like the extreme Eurocentric Bertrand Russell, Mary Lefkowitz wished to hold onto the fanciful notion of a "Greek Miracle"—some kind of "Immaculate Conception in the Peloponnesus"—with Greeks out of nowhere, suddenly creating—nay, inventing—"mathematics, and science and philosophy," and other aspects of culture. She attempted to discredit Diodorus's testimony and to deny that Democritis had studied in Egypt by the following comment: "This connection seems particularly tenuous, because in fact the Egyptians were interested in astronomy, that is, the motion of the stars, and not in astrology, the predictions about human fate that might be derived from astronomical observation."[28] She also said a little later on: "Diodorus reports that the fourth-century Greek philosopher Eudoxus of Cnidus, like Democritis, learned astrology from the Egyptian priests, even though it was the Alexandrian Greeks and not the Egyptians who were interested in that subject."[29] What Mary Lefkowitz, a Western classicist, proved is that she simply did not know much about ancient Egyptian history or culture. She asserted that the Egyptians could not have engaged in philosophy or initiated that form of human activity, because there were no extant Egyptian philosophical treatises. This view is wholly absurd. Philosophy can be articulated orally, can be reflected in art work, or can be encased in architecture or even in myth or religion. Karl Marx did not write a philosophical treatise, but he was, as many people recognize, a materialist philosopher. And as to the Egyptians and astrology, it seems that they in fact invented it.[30] As Egyptologist Dr. Charles Finch III has written:

> For uncounted generations lost in the dim mists of pre-historic antiquity, the Kamite (Egyptian) astronomer-priests painstakingly mapped out all of the visible sky. They used typological nature symbols to create markers to help them chart the heavens. One product of this careful labor is the Zodiac which the modern world inherited from the priests of Kemit.[31]

A couple of other remarks have to be made about the mathematical knowledge of ancient Egyptians, which so many Western writers wish to discredit. One wonders why they must discredit it. If it were not as advanced, in some respects, as that of the Greeks or Babylonians, so what? Why do their achievements have to be discredited? No one seeks to discredit Greek mathematics, which could be done by comparing them to today's mathematics. The Greeks got involved in mathematics and science twenty-five hundred and more years after the Egyptians. They learned from the Egyptians and improved upon what they learned. That was to their credit. But it does not follow from this that Egyptian achievements in mathematics have to be put down. After all, they built the pyramids and temples with these mathematics, and these achievements never cease to be praised. The mathematician Otto Neugebauer argued that Egyptian mathematical calculations were "childish." It seems clear that "childish" mathematics could never construct the pyramids (or the Egyptian temples). Some Japanese engineers and other personnel, with the permission of the Egyptian government, discovered that it was not easy to build an Egyptian pyramid, not even on a small scale. These Japanese made the effort in 1978, and it was a miserable failure. They found it incredibly difficult to transport the heavy stones and construct them in the form of a pyramid. "Finally, adding insult to injury, the great numbers of men that they had amassed, could not lift the blocks by pulley, levers, nor ropes, and as a result, power cranes plus helicopters were contracted to do the job. *Even then*, employing the use of today's most powerful lifting machines, those blocks set in place were greatly out of alignment, and many (if not most) were broken, chipped, and badly scratched, due to improper handling. . . . The project was terminated and the pyramid, what little was intact, was dismantled."[32] In describing Egyptian mathematical calculations, art historian/mathematician Gay Robins has written: "It seems that when Egyptians sought the answer to a calculation, a deliberate choice was made not to repeat the same unit fraction; to have repeated one would have been equivalent to using numerators greater than their unity. . . . One should therefore be cautious [e.g., Neugebauer] in claiming that unit fractions were an impediment to mathematical advance."[33] Robins also said the Egyptians "could . . . handle arithmetical and geometrical progressions . . . using methods similar to those employed today."[34] Mathematician Beatrice Lumpkin recently indicated that the Egyptians had invented pi (π, which was an important step in mathematics, achieving a measurement of "3.16, compared to the modern 3.14 and the Biblical [and also Babylonian] value of 3."[35] In *Black Athena Revisited*, mathematician Robert Palter, who, like Neugebauer, played down the mathematical achievements of the pyramids, nevertheless said the following about the Egyptian achievement with pi: "the Egyptians estimated π to within 0.6 percent of its actual value and . . . they could in fact calculate square roots of perfect squares (and possibly even estimate square roots for numbers that are not perfect squares)."[36] The Egyptians also invented phi "the Golden Section, the ratio 1.6180339 . . . , arrived at by dividing a line in such a way that the smaller portion is to the larger as the larger is to the whole."[37] And the Egyptian ability in analogical thinking, and their understanding of the symbolic connection between mathematics, astronomy, and astrology were greatly developed.

Palter repeated the traditional Eurocentric view that Pythagoras invented the theorem associated with his name—that "the sum of the squares of the sides of a right triangle is equal to the square on the hypotenuse"—and denied that the Egyptians knew or invented that theorem. He even argued that the Babylonians invented it, saying in his article that it was "perhaps their greatest mathematical achievement . . . (ca. 1700 B.C.E.)." If the Babylonians discovered the right triangle theory, then why do Western scholars like Palter keep attributing this theorem to Pythagoras, who did his "discovering" twelve hundred years after the Babylonians were supposed to have discovered the theorem? Is this saying something about how the "Greek

Miracle" was created? Palter did not perceive his own glaring testimony. Instead, he continued on in his article holding onto his contradiction, praising the Babylonians, and putting down the Egyptians, not even willing to admit or acknowledge that Pythagoras might have learned something from the Egyptians with whom he studied for twenty-two years. He said, at best, that whatever knowledge the Egyptians had about triangles and right angles was achieved by accident, by trial and error, not by theorizing. "Perhaps ancient Egyptian builders had determined by trial and error what they took to be a fixed relation between 3:4:5 triangles and right angles; they need not have known the Pythagorean theorem or any other set of integers satisfying the theorem."[38] Palter went on to praise the Babylonians some more. He said, and again contradictorily, that they had not only discovered the Pythagorean theorem but also "a general procedure for finding so-called Pythagorean triples (which should be Babylonian triples), that is, sets of integers such that the sum of the squares of two of them is equal to the square of the third."[39] Palter was aware of Gay Robins's views about the Pythagorean theorem and the pyramids and also about her view that the Egyptians could well have known about triples. But he only partially disclosed her views in his article and even misrepresented her position. He wrote: "The important thing to note is that Robins . . . (like me) see(s) no reason to attribute any knowledge of other Pythagorean triples or of the Pythagorean theorem to the Egyptian builders."[40] Here is what Robins said in the article referred to earlier:

> A subject that has been hotly debated is the extent of the Egyptians' knowledge of the properties of right-angle triangles, including the theorem attributed to Pythagoras. It seems almost certain that the triangle whose sides have the ratio 3:4:5 must have been known during the Old Kingdom, since it can be found in the proportions of the half-base, height, and apothem of the sides in the pyramid of Chephren (Khafre, Rekhaef) at Giza and in all surviving pyramids of the Sixth Dynasty. "Half-base" is half the length of the side of the base; "apothem" is the name given to a line joining the apex of the triangle forming a face of the pyramid to the mid-point of its base. It is hypothesized that the adoption of these proportions would have facilitated the cutting of the casing stones. The 3:4:5 ratio can

also be found in Problem 1 of Papyrus Berlin 6619 concerned with the areas of squares and, later (the third century B.C.E.), in some sloping problems contained in a
demotic Cairo papyrus.

The numbers 3, 4, 5 are the simplest example of the so-
called Pythagorean triple, in which the square of the largest
number is equal to the sum of the squares of the other
two. . . . Whether the Egyptians knew of the generating
method is unknown, but it is worth reiterating that they
were very familiar with reciprocals, so that they could have
obtained the 3, 4, 5 triple from the simplest reciprocal pair
of all, namely 2 and $\overline{2}$. . . . The method, once discovered,
could yield other triples, such as 5, 12, 13. . . . Alterna-
tively, such triples could have been worked out from tables
of squares.[41]

Robins held out the strong possibility that the Pharaonic Egyptians
had knowledge of the so-called Pythagorean theorem or had the
mathematical knowledge to work it out. Lost papyri keeps the matter
controversial. But the 3, 4, 5 ratio appearing in another papyrus and
the construction of the pyramids of Giza and other pyramids and the
fact that the Egyptians could, as Palter said, calculate square roots of
squares, and knew about phi, rectangular coordinates, second degree
equations and so on leaves less room for controversy or doubt that
the ancient Egyptians had enough knowledge of triangles, right-angle
triangles, and triples to have imparted at least some knowledge to
Pythagorus when he studied in Egypt, before going on later to study
in Babylon. (Given that the Babylonians knew about those pyramids,
too, is it possible that they learned something, directly or indirectly,
about right-angle triangles and triples from Egyptians? Western scholars are loath to look at matters this way).

There is evidence that the ancient Greeks learned *at least something*
about philosophy, mathematics, astronomy, and even astrology from
ancient Egyptians, who had been involved heavily in all of these subjects thousands of years before there was even a Greek civilization in
the Peloponnesus. The Egyptians taught more to the Greeks, such as
things about medicine and architecture. Writing about ancient Greek
medicine, historian W. G. Hardy wrote: "Surgery . . . was excellent.
Egyptian doctors could remove a piece of the skull so skilfully that
the patient lived, and for such a delicate operation to have been suc-

cessful they must have used some sort of anesthetic."[42] Adolph Erman wrote the following in his study of 1927, reissued and retitled *The Wisdom of Ancient Egypt* in 1993 under the editorship and translation of Joseph Kaster: "An extremely important factor in human history was the discovery and extensive development of the principles of medicine and pharmacology; our earliest pharmacopoeias and medical treatises come from ancient Egypt."[43] Robert Palter had to admit that there was at least some Egyptian influence on Greek medicine. He did so very grudgingly. His concern was always primarily to show how Greek medical practices were different and more advanced. In his extended writing in *Black Athena Revisited*, he wrote that there were two medical practices in which the Greek physicians engaged that "would have been unthinkable to Egyptian physicians." . . .

> The two practices are public competition between wise men, and open acknowledgment of uncertainty and error by wise men. Each of these practices has its exemplification in the field of medicine. Thus, "Galen several times refers to competitive public anatomical dissections in front of an audience quick to ridicule failure," and "[I]n some Hippocratic texts . . . the author explicitly acknowledges that he was himself mistaken." . . . Either of these practices would have been unthinkable to Egyptian physicians.[44]

A matter that should be clarified at once is that scholars now have great doubts that Hippocrates wrote any of the medical treatises ascribed to him or that he was even the author of the Hippocratic Oath. Galen was a Greek physician during the Ptolemaic dynasty and Greek domination of Egypt and when all of Egypt's medical and other kinds of learning were fully available to the Greeks. Historians have said that Galen learned his medicine considerably from the Hippocratic school and built upon it. P. Ghalioungui indicated in *The House of Life: Magic and Medical Science in Ancient Egypt*[45] that Greek physicians, including Hippocrates, learned much of their medicine from the Egyptians; Galen is also included among them. After all, Galen studied in the medical library at Memphis, where Egyptian medical papyri were housed. And it was the argument of Charles Finch, who is not only an Egyptologist, but a medical doctor and even a health official, that the Egyptians had devised clinical practice and had worked from case studies long before Hippocrateans and other Greek physicians did so. Finch even wrote: "In fact in some ways, Hippocrates had not even advanced as far as the ancient Egyptians before him. He never mentions pulse-taking and considered the brain to have been a gland. To cite but two examples in therapeutics, the Hippocratic methods of setting clavicular fractures and reducing a dislocated mandible are almost exactly as described in the Edwin Smith Papyrus . . . There are many more examples that could be cited of the pronounced similarity of important facets of Hippocratic medicine to ancient Egyptian medicine."[46]

To get back to Palter: he made a great point of the fact that Galen engaged in dissection in public. That does not seem to have been the style of Egyptian physicians, but that certainly does not mean that they did not practice, or were not careful in, their dissecting activities, which they did in private. After all, they were doctors and were trying to aid their patients. H. W. F. Saggs has written that the Egyptian physicians were engaged in dissection in the third millennium B.C. He referred to one rather significant example:

> A case in point is total paralysis resulting from a fall on the head, which the Egyptian surgeon attributed to a crushed vertebra in the neck. He can only have discovered the pathological cause of the symptoms by carrying out a post-mortem dissection of a patient who had died from such injuries. In view of this and other instances, there can be no doubt that at least one third-millennium Egyptian surgeon practiced dissection to further his understanding of the human body and the nature of such injuries.
>
> The practice of dissection is not the only indication of the third-millennium surgeon's scientific approach. As the first editor of the *Edwin Smith Papyrus* pointed out, the careful detailed study of cases of the type which the surgeon-author admitted—in the verdict "an ailment not to be treated"—were beyond his power to assist, shows that he was concerned not only with alleviating suffering but also with an understanding of the underlying nature of the injuries which produced certain symptoms.[47]

Here was a surgeon not admitting publicly to error, but indicating in a writing to be read by others that critical judgment should be used in treating patients. Kent Weeks has recently written that what impresses about ancient Egyptian medical practice is that prescription and treatment followed diagnosis. And if the diagnosis suggested that the patient could not be treated effectively, caution was entered not to try to do so. "Egyptian medicine was more than prescriptions. It was a set of systematic procedures, generally cautious—rare and precious attributes."[48] Weeks also pointed out that neither Greek nor Arab physicans made use of these Egyptian practices, as often or as diligently as they should have. "Indeed, it would be more than two thousand years before medical practitioners would again hold an opinion of themselves and their art as wholesome as that of ancient Egypt."[49]

Writers like Denesh D'souza, who labor hard, as D'souza did in *The End of Racism*, to discredit Africancentric claims about ancient Egypt, mainly by simply denying them with no evidentiary proof to the contrary, or by quoting Egyptologists or others who desire to deny the primary blackness of Egyptians, and the achievements of black people,[50] ignore what white Egyptologists and archeologists have said about such achievements, when they were calling ancient Egypt a white civilization or a civilization of "dark Caucasians." Fred Gladstone Bratton was one of these archeologists and in 1968 wrote the following:

> In no other place can one see such evidence of high culture, such splendid examples of technical skill and artistry. Greece, the only rival, reckons her cultural history in centuries but Egypt reckons hers in millennia. The Greeks, and later the Romans, looked to Egypt as the source of all wisdom and transmitted that wisdom to posterity. To Egypt we owe our system of dividing time into twenty-four hours to the day, twelve months and 365 days to the year. The Egyptians invented the clock. They were the first to record historical events and the first to use practical writing materials.[51]

Gladstone also wrote the following:

> No Sumerian, Babylonian or Persian sculpture can compare with the Egyptian in draftsmanship, mastery of form or sense of proportion. No ancient sculpture except possibly the Greek has such a universal appeal. Goethe recognized

the classical nature of the Egyptian sculpture in his com-
parison of the "black basalt" figures with the Greek "white
marble." What titanic labour and ingenuity were needed
to erect those colossal columns at Karnak. . . .

Where in all antiquity can be found anything more grace-
ful than the Isis temple at Philae. . . . Standing before the
magnificent funerary temple of Hatshepsut at Deir el Bahri
makes one almost forget the Parthenon, for no building in
all history excels this masterpiece of the architect Senmut
in symmetry, proportion, and artistic use of the exterior
colonnade. . . . [52]

And just one more reference, because of its corrective and illumi-
nating character, and that derived from the Egyptian ideal of Maat,
which meant right, truth, moderation, harmony, justice, and order.
Adolf Erman wrote in his reissued book: "Evidently the Egyptians
felt that they did not need codifications of the law, that man had a
vivid awareness of his inner sense of human justice. It was not until
a relatively late stage in the development of the culture of the ancient
world that this humanistic ethic was formulated by Socrates, after the
Egyptians had been governing themselves by its principles for over
two thousand years."[53] It cannot be argued that the Egyptians
learned this from Socrates. But it could be suggested that Socrates
imbibed it from the Egyptians.

All that I have said over several pages was not said to diminish the
achievements that the ancient Greeks had taking these subjects and
going further with them or in different directions (although neither
is easily discerned, because ancient Greek thinkers were notorious in
not saying specifically what they had learned from Egyptian priests or
others), but to counter the racist notion—and that is all it is—that
the ancient Egyptians—mainly black people—were not capable of significant intellectual achievement, including abstract philosophical,
theological, and theoretical thinking. And that they passed these
forms of thinking onto the ancient Greeks. Bika Reed translated the
Berlin Papyrus 3024, housed in the Berlin Museum and dated 2500–
1991 B.C. and made the following remarks: "While translating the
Berlin Papyrus 3024 and reviewing earlier interpretations, I experi-
enced awe at encountering [the most] philosophical language ever
conceived by man, and at the same time felt sorrow at witnessing its
debasement." The latter, as Reed indicated, was done by white West-

ern Egyptologists. "Can somebody who believes that Ancient Egypt was a primitive society, incapable of abstract thought, transmit . . . its wisdom? . . . It is as if a sleepwalker were placed as judge over the awake."[54] In 1970, Hans Goedicke published a study of the Papyrus Berlin 3024 which carried the title *The Report About the Dispute of a Man with His Ba*. The word *Ba* meant "self." Goedicke argued that the manuscript was a text that reflected "on the human position and is thus speculative in its nature and philosophical in its tendencies."[55] Goedicke also indicated that *The Report* employed a dialogue philosophical method to discuss such things as the relationship between the body and self, the spiritual and the material, and good and evil. If the date 2500 B.C. is accepted as the original publishing date of *The Report*, this means that the ancient Egyptians had been engaged in philosophical speculation and reflection almost a thousand years before the ancient Greeks ever moved into the Aegean and Peloponnesus. It also makes it clear that the dialogue method of philosophical discourse originated with the ancient Egyptians and not the ancient Greeks, as did the quest for self-knowledge, or knowing thyself, and the idea of rational inquiry to obtain knowledge to know thyself.

There were two aspects of ancient Egyptian thought that had a great impact on the ancient Greeks and which would find their way into Enlightenment thought of the eighteenth century, by way of studying the ancient Greeks, and that would become a large part of the intellectual orientation to guide and to engage in modernizing activities. The ancient Egyptians believed, philosophically, in absolutism, namely, ontology, transcendance, permanence, and foundationalism. The ancient Egyptians also, as seen earlier, believed in the life force, the universal reality, the unceasing movement, changing, and becoming of reality (God). Thales took this thinking away from Egypt when he took from it the idea that water was the basic element of the universe and implied that it constituted the "first principle" of the universe. He said that elements of nature were regulated by a driving force that the elements did not control. Anaximander declared that there was an "all-steering" provider (Maat, Ptah, or Thoth in Egyptian thought) of the natural order. Pythagoras accepted and made use of the four elements of Egyptian philosophy but also argued that the four were regulated by a fifth element: the "Whole," which produced the harmony of the parts. Heraclitus asserted that it was the universal force of *logos* (initially associated with Ptah) that organized the world. Plato argued that order and valid knowledge were based on universal principles that pervaded nature (i.e., Maat). Aristotle asserted that life had a universal, driving force, which he called *telos*, that was disassociated from any kind of interpretation. Through the ancient Greeks, the ancient Egyptian dialectic (which was part of Egyptian monointeractive cognition) and the notion of "becoming" would find their way into Georg Hegel's rationalist and metaphysical philosophy and his emphasis on the universal reason. Edmund Husserl was to write that all knowledge was "intentional," and that "consciousness" was a universal principle that permeated all reality, and what he called the "life-world." Ancient Egyptian thought about existence and universality would, via ancient Greeks, find its way into Heidegger's ideas of "Being," and "being there" and "existence."[56]

The Enlightenment thinkers, of course, were also utilizing and building upon Descartes's philosophy of the seventeenth century, which was rationalistic and metaphysical and stressed the absolute and transcendental and the epistemological view of the individual human subject using reasoning powers and being the source of knowledge. Descartes was altering and building upon medieval thought, which had been strongly influenced by Aristotle's and other Greeks' thinking; this in turn had been influenced by ancient Egyptian thinking.

The philosophical basis for guiding and justifying modernization and modernizing in Europe, which would later be described as the philosophical basis for European modernity, was constructed in the seventeenth and eighteenth centuries. A silence was maintained about an ancient Egyptian input by cultural borrowing. But this philosophical or ideological basis for the alleged European modernity was also silent about the racism that was an integral part of its structure, especially white supremacy/ebonicism. It was in the seventeenth and eighteenth centuries that Western thinkers, publicly declaring the natural physical and, especially, cerebral superiority of white people over black people and other people of color as well, developed the racism to rationalize and justify the African slave trade, slavery, the extermination of Indians, colonialism, and imperialism, which were all associated with European modernizing or European modernity.

White Western intellectuals began to launch their attack against modernity in the late nineteenth century that carried over into the twentieth century, which ultimately gave rise, as the story goes, to postmodern thought and postmodernity. But here is where I wish to speak of a crisis, and not about modernity or postmodernity, but about Western civilization. Postmodern thought actually reflects this crisis. This crisis is: *what does Western civilization offer the world, or what can it offer the world, after it has produced Hitler and the Nazis, the fascists, communists, totalitarians, gulags and death camps, horrendously destructive wars, and a civilization that has been extensively divested of its morality and spirituality?* This crisis is also the crisis of white people and also of white intellectuals. What do they have to offer the world, given these past events, which were events that they primarily created and are primarily responsible for? Postmodern thinkers deceive themselves thinking that their primary target of critical analysis should be the alleged modernity, not themselves and other white people, and the way both engage in cognition and behave, and the peculiar psychological traits of both and Western civilization. We have come to the fin-de-siècle of the Western White Voice, which is really the voice of the Western White Male. This is a Voice that does not impress intellectually anymore, and certainly not like it used to. And it does not carry much, if any moral weight, not even among white people, let alone people of color. It cannot be said that white postmodern thinkers are marking time trying to figure out what to say or what to do. They actually believe that they have said very important, if not profound things already—about modernity and about such things as philosophy, literature, art, truth, representation, interpretation, language, epistemology, morality, and a host of other things. Postmodern thinkers disagree with each other on all of these subjects. What is equally astounding is that they take pride in not agreeing with each other, or arriving at some kind of consensus on specific things. Of course, they eschew any kind of grand narrative that would provide a unity of thought and that could provide a general intellectual and moral direction. Postmodern thinkers are cut adrift at sea, but they think they occupy dry land. But if we conceded their assumption, what does this dry land look like or amount to? Not something that postmodernists would want to hear. The dry land is not so dry and is considerably racist muck, or racist marsh. White postmodern thinkers, especially, have yet to realize the racist premise, the racist foundationalism, from or out of which they considerably function. Such thinkers are against privileging, but they privilege White racism. When they say *modernity,* and the way they use that term, privileges white people. They are attacking modernity on the one hand and privileging it on the other. They are attacking white people but privileging them at the same time, although this privileging is done in silence, because white postmodernists rarely talk about racism, or race, for that matter. But who would such people be talking about, if they were engaged in a discussion of modernity? And which people are they talking about when they use the phrases *postmodernity* or *postmodern*? This is racism interpenetrating postmodern thought, but in silence and unseen and undetected—by most white postmodern thinkers.

Just as white supremacy and other forms of racism interpenetrated what has been termed modernity, so does it interpenetrate postmodernity. There are several examples that reflect this, and I want to discuss a few of them. One of them is the cognitive systems that white postmodern thinkers use, which are the cognitive systems of white people generally in the Western world. These cognitive systems functioned during modernity, and they continue on in postmodernity. It is another example of the deception in which postmodern thinkers are engaged, as to who they are and what they are doing. The four cognitive systems that white people function with do not necessarily or logically have to be associated with racism, but they have been, and for the past several centuries and, thus, have been an integral part of racist foundationalism. With racist beliefs, values, attitudes, emotions, and so on, as part of cognitive systems, the latter have steered Whites into dominating, subordinating, segregating and excluding people of color, whether it has been done at home or abroad. Racism(s) and White cognitive systems have been laminated together, and the two have not as yet been pried apart. Postmodernists claim they are against hierarchy, which would be domination-subordination cognition, but they privilege modernity, postmodernity, and white people, meaning these things are ascendant, and other things are subordinate or secondary. In *Post-Modernism and the Social Sciences*, Pauline Rosenau wrote: "Post-modern art, therefore, emphasizes the aesthetic over the functional. . . . Appearance and image have priority over the technical, practical, and efficient. . . . In philosophy . . . renewed respect for the subjective and increased suspicion of reason and objectivity."[57] What is all of this if it is not privileging several things, domination-subordination organizational logic, and hierarchical thinking? Many postmodern thinkers accept the subjective and reject the objective, accept indeterminacy and reject determinism, accept the individual and reject the group, accept the unique and reject the general, accept the relative and reject the universal, accept diversity and reject unity, or accept plurality, but reject universality. What is this except vertical cognition and either-or thinking? And is it not, as well, absolutist foundational thinking? When postmodern thinkers eliminate the author from the novel or text, this is either-or cognition at work. Or it is domination-subordination cognition at work, when the author is subordinated to the text or the reading audience. When postmodern thinkers say, "there is nothing outside the text," or "nothing outside language," or "nothing outside interpretation," they are engaging in vertical cognition and either-or thinking. When postmodern thinkers are against binaries and seek to synthesize binaries into a monism, this is dialectical cognition and transcendental thinking. The latter is also reflected in the following comments by Jon Snyder, even if not in full regalia: "When deprived of the hierarchical order established by the highest value, in other words, the system of values itself becomes an infinite process of transformation, in which no value can appear to be 'higher' or more 'authentic' than any other."[58] There are a number of postmodern thinkers who employ dualistic cognition, not to establish dualisms, but to be able to establish individual realities that remain separate or distanced from each other, to be evaluated individually. This enables these thinkers to put an emphasis on multiplicities and differences. Some of the thinkers who use this kind of cognition are Jacques Derrida, Gilles Deleuze, and also Michel Foucault. These particular thinkers also employ vertical cognition. Sometimes postmodern thinkers employ dualistic and vertical cognition together. This is reflected, for instance, in the following comments by Sven Birkerts: "One of the many consequences is that formerly freestanding disciplines like philosophy, history, sociology, and so on, cede their autonomy, becoming part of a larger unstructured entity known simply as 'theory.' "[59] This is setting up different points of reality, keeping them separate from each other, as the different names of the academic disciplines indicate, and then diminishing them by eliminating the theory associated with them, and which also establishes the boundaries around them and invests them with a strict autonomy. Specific theories are thrown away to establish a general, or single, or monotheory that encompasses all the academic disciplines. This seems to move toward the area of the grand theory or the grand narrative, which so many other postmodern thinkers rant against.[60] Dualistic cognition is used when irony is used by some postmodern thinkers the way they do so, namely, the way postmodern literary critics use it. These individuals see themselves replacing philosophers and literary criticism replacing philosophy. These individuals seek irony in literary and other texts. Irony establishes something that is not supposed to be in the text but is there standing next to something that is supposed to be there.[61] So a dualism is created. Ironists feel this is a radical approach to literary analysis, an innovation by postmodernists. But the approach reflects dualistic cognition, which was found in the alleged modernity as well, even in the so-called modern novel. And then it has to be said that there are postmodernists who see themselves as Left postmodernists and those postmodernists who see themselves as conservative or Right postmodernists; this reflects vertical cognition and absolutism and foundationalism.

What postmodernists do, and they do not realize that they do, is attack or assault reality just as the alleged modernists did. And in this attack or assault they take the same form of looking at reality in essentially a negative way, thinking that negativity is the same as being critical. And propelled by this negativity, and employing vertical, domination-subordination, dualistic, and dialectical logic, they proceed to slice reality into many fragments. They do this even more than the modernists did. And unlike the latter not many of them have any interest to bring any structure or order to all this fragmentation or any interest to end the fragmentation. But in reality, they do bring about some structure and order because the cognitive systems they are using do that. These systems also promote foundationalism. Accepting subjectivity and rejecting objectivity as a basis for thought— this either-or activity simply replaces one form of foundationalism with another.

A great irony is that postmodern thinkers do not think that they establish structure, organization, or foundationalism with their thought and discussions. Consciously, and in their discussions, they reject such things. They also reject consensus, universality, grand theory, and the grand narrative, and also the philosophy of history— things which would give them a sense of where they, their thought, and Western civilization are heading. It means that postmodernists are very confused in their thinking. It also means that they have not moved and cannot move away from the modernist notion of time, place, structure, or order as long as racism and traditional White cognitive systems guide their thinking and social actions.

Let's look at some other examples of racism that are reflected in postmodern thought. Today, that racism will be more subtle, as it has to be. The United States is a haven for subtle racism, but it can be found in Europe, too, although it is very blatant in some places in Europe. Subtle racism is characterized by investing racism in ideals, ideas, beliefs, values, concepts, analyses, theories, or even social institutions, and then speaking of these things, or employing them, as if they had no racist content. This is where postmodern thinkers fail to see the fullness of the textuality, or contextuality that they like to talk about. There is racism in that textuality or contextuality; it is subtle, and they consciously or unconsciously employ and also hide behind it. But people who have been victims of White racism, or maleist-sexist racism, for centuries are not likely to be fooled by the changes in racist behavior, which has a logic and structure and also a telos of its own.

When postmodernity became a rage in the 1960s and thereafter, there was the concept of *decentering*. This followed from the rejection of theological, but especially philosophical absolutism, transcendence, foundationalism, and the individual human subject as the source of all knowledge. The individual human subject had to be decentered, because it was now said that there were other sources of knowledge, and other ways of acquiring and learning knowledge. New concepts like *desituating, situating, situated,* or *social epistemology* appeared. But the initial strong advocates of decentering backed off of that concept. The reason was simple. When they began to think about who the real human subject was that was the source of knowledge, which mirrored the philosophical construction, they realized they were talking about the white male; that is, they were talking about themselves and assaulting themselves and their own presumed genius and infallibility. They were voluntarily, philosophically, assaulting and displacing themselves from their traditional dominant and privileged status in Western civilization. They were attacking white male hegemony, the epitome of racism in Western civilization. They had opened up a Pandora's box, and some people, and especially, white women, but also some Black women, and other women of color, began peering in. White men were afraid of what they would see. And what they would see would be white male power, white male affirmative action, white male entitlements, large white male quotas, and white male wealth that had historically been promoted in Western civilization. The Pandora's box had to be closed, or other postmodernists, those who had smelled or tasted blood, had to be steered away from it. This could be done by deemphasizing decentering. It could also be done by supporting the concepts of desituating, situating, situated, or social epistemology, and encouraging others to use them, those with blood in their nostrils or on their tongues, which would have them focusing on themselves and their circumstances, or victimizations, or their own aspirations. And the white male–owned, controlled, or heavily influenced media could keep them locked in that posture, even going so far as to subsidize it with scholarships, research grants, publications, and academic promotions.

A favorite device of a number of white male postmodern thinkers to divert white, Black, and other women, or even white or Black, or other males from focusing on the continuing white male hegemony in Western culture is the concept of *dissemination*, which conjures up other concepts, such as pluralism, multiplicities, many voices, many interpretations, and the like. Dissemination, a term apparently devised by Jacques Derrida, denotes the intellectual activity of proliferating things, spreading things out, and creating endless fragmentation, endless voices, and endless signification. But the hard-nosed truth is that dissemination and all its by-products, such as pluralism, multiplicities, and many voices are not the same as inclusion or significant or effective participation. In the early 1970s Black historian Nathan Huggins noted how white historians and white publishers were including more of Black history in American history textbooks. But he noticed that it was done in a peculiar manner:

> Except for the necessary discussion of Afro-Americans in slavery . . . the taught history of the United States has been that of Anglo-Saxons and Northern Europeans. Even the current consciousness of Negro history on the part of textbook publishers, though it has resulted in efforts to improve the nonwhite's image, has made no fundamental changes in the character of the history. It is now more likely that Negroes will be mentioned as participants in the development of the country; heroes, achievements, inventions, are duly recorded. But in very important ways, the history has remained untouched; the ethnic conception of American history persists.[62]

The Anglo-Saxons and Northern Europeans were white people, so Huggins could have said that the "White racist conception of American history persists." He was silent on that point, but was not in his other writings.

What this example shows is that dissemination and pluralities and multiplicities do not necessarily lead to inclusion, or effective inclusion and participation. They do not necessarily lead to the inclusion of a new voice or new voices or a new interpretation or new interpretations. And new voices and new interpretations could be kept subordinate to (domination-subordination cognition) or at a distance from (dualistic cognition) the main view. Which all keeps the main view intact, undisturbed, and able to hide behind concepts and practices of dissemination, plurality, inclusion, and participation—all inundated with racism and carried by racist inundated cognitive systems that prevent or diminish proffered possibilities.

Postmodern literary elements, particularly literary critics, have eructed, decentered, or subordinated the author in literary texts. There are postmodern social scientists who have done the same with social science texts. The author represents a human being, humanity. The practices of eructing, decentering, and subordinating a human being and humanity are clearly racist practices. They follow the racist practice of social scientists of the late nineteenth, but especially the early twentieth century, which modernists say was part of the period of modernity, who sought to devise social sciences that would have the same attributes as the physical sciences. The physical sciences dealt with things, or inanimate objects, or with what some physical scientists, so obviously racist, thought were nonhumans or subhumans, namely Black people, or Indians, or other people of color. This kind of use of science was so obviously inundated by racism and was used by racists.

The social sciences could also be used in a clear racist manner, which was how white social scientists used them in studying Blacks in the United States in the late nineteenth and early twentieth centuries. But there was a more subtle racist motivation, and a more subtle use of racism in the social sciences—subtle, because it was not necessarily conscious and could not be seen clearly—indeed, would not have been seen clearly by the social scientists, who were overwhelmingly white and overwhelmingly racist. The subtlety involved the silent, but gross, behavior of dehumanizing people and turning them into things or inanimate objects to study them scientifically. It was decided that all about human beings could not be studied scientifically, such as their mental processes, their consciousness, their feelings, or emotions. What was to be studied scientifically was what could be directly observed, namely, their overt behavior, which was then labeled *objective* behavior. The *objectivity* of the social sciences, which could match the presumed objectivity of the physical sciences, was presumed. Objectivity equaled rationality, knowledge, truth, and understanding. Subjectivity, on the other hand, equaled irrationality, fanciful construction, distortion, and lack of understanding and had to be eliminated from or suppressed in social science research.

Postmodernists have climbed all over what they have called modern social sciences, or the social sciences of modernity, deprecating their methods and ridiculing their so-called objectivity. They have also done the same to the physical sciences and have removed value from both the physical and social sciences, saying they could offer no more truth than art or even religion—although not as sanguine with respect to the latter. But postmodernists have not perceived the racist foundationalist inclusion in or the latter's functioning in Western social science and much of its physical science.

They have also not seen the racist foundationalist intrusion in their analysis of texts. And it takes several forms. Eliminating the author completely is one of these manifestations. Another is putting the emphasis on text itself, because the latter does not necessarily focus on people, any more than many social science writings do. There is a lot of peopleless political science, sociology, psychology, and economics writing. A third manifestation of racism is the idea of audience. This is really not about people, but about structure or structural feature, textual feature, or even theory or ideology. Social science theorists, and there are still a number around, frequently refer to the theoretical problem of structure and agency. They refer to how some social scientists speak of structures as if people or humanity does not exist; this creates difficulties in trying to explain social action and social change. Many literary critics see no difficulty in explaining literary works from a textural or structural—or peopleless—point of view. They do not see how racism is a part of this approach or how unjust it is. Why should the author's voice not have representation? After all, he or she wrote the text and had things in mind when writing it and said things they wanted other people to hear and to think about. Why does this not have value? No literary critic can make a case that a text wrote itself, any more than an art critic can say, without seeming to be off the wall, that a painting painted itself. That sounds clearly and patently absurd. But text self-generation does not sound this way to many literary critics.[63] Authors of fiction or poets have been known to say that critics, as well as readers, have not understood what they have written. And deceased writers might well be astonished as to how reviewers at later times in history have reviewed their writings or poetry. This is a way of saying that there have always been authors, critics, and a reading public, and all three of these elements have (agreed as well as) differed with each other about what had been written. But there had been no interest in the past to eliminate the author. Indeed, white men were mainly the authors and therefore had no interest in eliminating themselves. And is it simply a coincidence that talk of eliminating authors in what is called postmodernity occurs at the point where white women and people of color are becoming in numerous ways authors and are projecting new and different voices? Would removing or suppressing the author beneath text or textuality silence or suppress the new voice or voices, or keep them obscured or at the margin? Would this keep the white male voice centered, in particular the voice of the white male literary critic, who is still the dominant literary critic in Western civilization?

And then there is the talk about the fictive self and the fictive person. This is where the subject of language and its role in discourse really gets an airing and a shower of accolades. It is also where language shows its relationship to the racist foundationalism of Western culture and how racism works through language. Of course, during the time of alleged modernity racism inundated English and other Western languages. And that would include maleist, sexist, and anti-Jewish racist foundationalist inundations of language, thus making language too a part of Western racist foundationalism.

Today racism has to be expressed more subtly, and the fictive self or the fictive person provides that opportunity. To talk of human beings in fictive terms, as if they were fictions and not realities, is already talk against their humanity and, indeed, a denigration and rejection of their humanity. The fictive argument is that language determines self or the person, that both are only abstractions, creations of language, with no actual embodiment. As John Murphy writes, "The self, stated simply, is not a thing but something that a person manufactures. . . . In line with the postmodern view of language, persons define or speak themselves into existence. This process, of course, is never-ending, for language cannot be exhausted. Because the self resides within language, a search for a so-called real self would be interminable."[64] Postmodernists argue that nothing exists outside language; that language determines what is understood to be reality. It constitutes representations of reality, meaning that there is no reality outside of linguistic description. For people who are supposed to be against absolutism, transcendence, and foundationalism, postmodernists have converted language into just those things. Postmodernists who employ irony as a literary device, or radical action, or as a discursive form of social theory believe that language offers certitude. As Charles Lemert has written, "Irony when applied to theory is, therefore, more than a literary tactic; it is a peculiar position in relation to reality. It holds that nothing is certain save language, yet the language is a safe and reasonable certitude. And, because of the certitude of language, one can, in language, make general statements about the order of things real."[65] For postmodern thinkers to think of certitude or even to have such a word in their vocabulary is a gross contradiction. This is a modernist word, denoting foundation or foundationalism.

But Black intellectuals and other Black people, if they were thinking critically or looking at this theory of language, that language is certain and that nothing exists outside language, would have great trouble accepting this kind of talk. Throughout their history in America, Blacks have seen themselves to be precisely outside the racist language that has depicted them, that has projected representations about them, that has proclaimed what their reality is. Du Bois said Blacks had developed a "double-consciousness," implying that it had enabled them to devise language that gave them a sense of self or who they were that enabled them to counter the racist self that Whites sought to impose on them. This indicated to Blacks that their sense of self, or their self was real and that the White racist "self" was not; it was fictional. Here we have Blacks, to set the record straight, going back to the seventeenth century, dealing with fictive and real selves, without employing this kind of terminology. It was also in the seventeenth century that they started to face the problem of Whites trying to make representations real that were not real or which did not correspond to or depict reality. These are matters that postmodernist thinkers are focusing on, but without seeing the strong racist predicate for this kind of thinking and interest.

This also means that the use of language to create fictions about people, fictive selves or fictive persons (other than in fiction writing), or to distort or misrepresent reality, or where alleged appearance or observed appearance is taken for the real, is not something that originated with postmodern thinkers and did not originate in postmodernity. These matters go back to, to use the word, modernity, and back at the beginning of modernity when it was launched in high gear in the seventeenth century. One can be even more accurate than this. These kinds of interests predated European modernity by millennia, as they have been the preoccupation of women all that time— all the fictions and misrepresentations that men have imposed upon them. White women in Europe were preoccupied with these fictions and misrepresentations at the launching of European modernity, which were carried into this new situation. Black people as well as Indians got caught up in the fictions and misrepresentations that Whites/Europeans created and imposed on both by racist beliefs and racist depictions of them.

Postmodern thinkers have no conception of the longevity of some of the matters that grip their interest. And still less do they see how they are carrying on with traditional, that is modernist modes of thought. They do not perceive these things, because they do not deal with racism, with racism's connection with modernity, or with the racist foundationalist connection with so-called postmodernity. The abstract and/or esoteric discussions of language cover up the racist foundationalism or the racist intrusions in the writings and discussions. When it is said, for instance, that the self is not real, the racist preoccupation with eliminating or suppressing humanity is part of that thinking and discussion, even if it is not discerned by those doing it. The self goes beyond language, because the self becomes real when it is internalized and regarded as being real to the individual who internalizes it and regards it as his or her own, as being who he or she is. Sambo and Coon were fictive selves that white racists created for black people and then sought to impose on them and to get Blacks to internalize as their real self-images and their real selves. Had Blacks internalized those images and selves, they would have thought themselves to be those realities and would have thought, felt, and acted on the basis of them. Indeed, what is missing from the postmodern discussion about self is the affective psychological qualities that are involved in any understanding or sense of self, such as imagination, attitudes, feelings, and emotions. A sense of self and an identity are not all intellectual. And they go beyond language. Such would not be seen by someone who makes a comment like the following: the self cannot be completed: "such closure would automatically violate the criterion of authenticity. As a result, one must constantly create and re-create an identity based upon one's ongoing experience in the world."[66] Nor would this matter be seen by Jacques Lacan,

Michel Foucault, Roland Barthes, or Gabriel Marcel, who all believe that language is something that is always changing, that the self can never be fully known. Something does to have to be fully known to be known, or fully understood to be understood. And it is simply poor psychology not to be able to see that when a self is internalized and taken to be reality by the person who has done so, this is not a construction or a reality that is going to change very quickly. When someone says that he or she is a white supremacist, this is a sense of self and an identity that are not going to change very quickly and may never change throughout the life of the person, no matter what anyone says or does to challenge or to condemn such a person's sense of being a white supremacist. Identities get rooted in psychological affectations. But even more than that, they also get rooted in the nervous system, proven by the fact that challenges to them can cause nervous-system reactions. One of the weaknesses of Marxist thinking about ideology is that Marxists did not see (with few exceptions, and the exceptions were usually not Marxists, but individuals who had some Marxist orientation, such as T. W. Adorno and his associates, who produced *The Authoritarian Personality*),[67] the psychological effects of believing in things in an ideological manner; psychological effects that get structured or "packed" into the mind, the personality, and the nervous system. When Black people took on a sense of black self or Black self or a black identity or Black identity between the 1960s and 1980s, they were not just engaged in intellectual activity or simply using language. They went beyond both things, although including both things, to turn a linguistic construction or a social construction into a reality—their reality, to which language could always draw attention. A self accepted is, at that moment, constituted, solidified, and autonomous. But this does not mean that the self, the sense of self, or an identity cannot change. Language, experiences, thought, and social pressures can bring about changes. But human beings do not change quickly from the understanding of and the feelings they have for themselves. Did not Sigmund Freud teach us this simple, basic fact?

What we have with so many postmodern thinkers is that they are making a fetish of language. It took a long time for language to become an object of study in the Western world; it mainly did so in this century. Many postmodern thinkers have taken up this study, but they are using language, not just studying it, and they are using it as a tool or weapon to attack what they call modernity and to promote and protect postmodernity. It is also being used, at bottom, to protect, and to keep trying to promote white male power and the hegemony of the White Male Voice in Western culture. When one is told that the self is fictive or fiction, this is an effort to keep people from trying to devise a self—mainly a self different from what is already in the culture, which invisibilizes them, suppresses them, excludes them, and even confuses them. Feminist Jane Flax has not been fooled by the postmodern use of language and the postmodern talk about the fictive or fiction self. She has understood how the maleist/sexist part of the racist foundationalism of Western culture has intruded in the use of language and in postmodern discussions of self:

> Postmodernists intend to persuade us that we should be suspicious of any notion of self or subjectivity. Any such notion may be bound up with and support dangerous and oppressive "humanist" myths. However, I am deeply suspicious of the motives of those who would counsel such a position at the same time as women have just begun to remember their selves and to claim an agenic subjectivity available always before only to a few privileged white men.[68]

Henry Louis Gates, Jr., has also reacted to the postmodern racist use of language, and its strong, but hidden (but not to initiates) intrusion in postmodern discussions of self and subjectivity, specifically to keep traditionally suppressed and ostracized people from developing these things:

> The classic critique of our attempts to reconstitute our own subjectivity, as women, as blacks, etc., is that of Jacques Derrida: "This is the risk. The effect of Law is to build a structure of the subject, and as soon as you say, 'well, the woman is a subject and this subject deserves equal rights,' and so on—then you are caught in the logic of phallocentrism and you have rebuilt the empire of law." To expressions such as this, made by a critic whose stands on sexism and racism have been exemplary, we must respond that the Western male subject has long been constituted historically for himself and in himself. And, while we readily

accept, acknowledge, and partake of the critique of *this* subject as transcendent, to deny us the process of exploring and reclaiming our subjectivity before we critique it is the critical version of the grandfather clause, the double privileging of categories that happen to be *preconstituted.*[69]

White male postmodern thinkers (and others as well, but not to the same degree) have not only made a fetish of language, they have been and continue to be engaged in the *languagezation* (foundationalism) of postmodernity and Western civilization. Somehow, by language alone, they are going to create something grand for assimilation and emulation, and that is going to be grand for Western civilization and the world. There are postmodernists, especially those with a Marxist orientation—to some degree—who talk about how present-day capitalism *commodifies* people and Western culture and social life. I am always annoyed by this kind of talk when it comes from postmodern thinkers who accept their own commodification, which leads to the large sale of their books, high-priced public speeches, research grants, or other kinds of remunerated public appearances. Late capitalism, as it is described, is so good to such people (and notice the phase *late capitalism*. Is late capitalism more modern than modern capitalism, which supposedly existed during modernity? And what comes after late capitalism? Will it be more modern than late capitalism?).

Many postmodern thinkers complain about commodification and even counsel counteraction or rebellion against it. But so many of these people are also caught up in their fetish: languagezation that has to be countered. Languagezation will not resolve the present crisis of Western civilization or the present crisis of white male intellectuals and white people. Nor will it bring Western civilization from its present depths of intellectual inadequacy and moral and spiritual debasement into some kind of rejuvenated and reoriented entity that will enable it to act with stature, wisdom, and humaneness on the domestic and world scenes. The postmodernists have not even realized that so much of what they think is new in the way of thought and interest, and which constitutes postmodernity, has already been dealt with by others during what they called modernity. And Black people in America are some of the people who have dealt with these things. Many postmodernists laud deconstruction, but Black people have been employers of the deconstructive method since the seventeenth century, from the first moment they heard that white people and America stood for freedom. Over their history, they have deconstructed documents, writings, phrases, words, images, and symbols. In the 1960s, Jacques Derrida employed the deconstruction method and popularized it, with it virtually being assumed that he invented deconstruction. He used it to attack the language of Western metaphysical philosophy and foundationalism and also as a method to analyze literary and other written texts. He was accused by modernists and postmodernists for not using his method to analyze the political life of Western society and to use it to help spawn revolt. Derrida felt he had contributed to the possibility of revolt by using his deconstruction method to expose the pervasiveness of hierarchy in Western thought and his own denigration of it. There have been Blacks since the seventeenth century who have attacked hierarchy in American history and social life, namely, White over Black hierarchy. They have seen that hierarchy embedded in the Declaration of Independence, the Constitution, the theory of representative government, of local government, the concepts of the "rule of law" and "state's rights," and in White usage of liberal democratic ideas and ideals. All of these numerous deconstructions have been related to Black protest and struggle in America and even related to the efforts to find allies among Whites in America, and thus to effect cooperation with Whites to try to end or mitigate oppression or to make progress.[70] But Blacks have engaged in deconstruction in a more comprehensive manner. Since the late seventeenth and the first half of the eighteenth centuries, when Black slavery was firmly planted in the British colonies in North America, many Blacks have learned to wear "masks"; that is, demeanors that mask real thoughts, feelings, and motivations. These masks were veils or shields behind which Blacks deconstructed white people: their facial expressions, the looks in their eyes, the changes in their complexion, their moods, the tones in their voices, their laughter, their bodily moves, the placement of their hands or their hand gestures. This kind of deconstruction could be related literally to life and death, which was true for Black slaves, but which was even more true for Blacks, nonslave or slave, in the late nineteenth and early twentieth centuries, when Blacks were put under the Race Etiquette System, a social code by which Blacks, at all times, had to show extreme deference to Whites, with the simplest infraction possibly ending in death. Thus, what is to be said about Blacks and their use of the deconstruction method in America is that they used it in a general way to *deconstruct life*, not just narrowly thought or written texts.

There is one other thing to say about the way Blacks have employed deconstruction in their history in America. They have used it to expose the White over Black hierarchical relationship. But in struggling against this hierarchical reality, Blacks have not done what Derrida advocated: that oppressed or suppressed people should "invert the hierarchy." It was his view that an oppressed or subordinated element had to turn the tables on those who dominated them and establish a new hierarchical relationship and social reality in which they would be the dominant element. This was necessary political resistance and political action. But this was all language and description and their substitution for historical and political reality. Inverting hierarchy does not lead to the end of hierarchy or "authentic/inauthentic" reality. It simply sets up a new hierarchical situation and a new authentic/inauthentic reality, or, more accurately, a "more-than/less-than" reality. What hierarchical inversion invariably leads to is the new dominant element seeking cultural (i.e., moral or legal) legitimacy and institutional solidification to make the new hierarchical situation permanent or to give it a long life. History is replete with these kinds of examples, with the communist and other dictatorial regimes in this century providing numerous examples.

Blacks, of course, as a small minority compared to the white population in America, were never in a position to engage in hierarchical inversion. Therefore, this was never an ideal or value of theirs (although there were doubtlessly Blacks who visualized this situation over the centuries). Deconstructing the white over black hierarchy led Blacks, along with other encouragements, such as their diunital method of cognition, to move to a different posture, or a different intellectual, perceptual, or moral premise. This was a conscious and unconscious act of resistance that enabled Blacks to have the ability to devise their own realities, to look at a reality or realities differently from others—indeed, and as a special capability, to look at the same reality that Whites looked at, but to see it differently. Whites meant certain things by the words *Negro, Colored,* or *black.* Blacks knew what they meant, but they also had their own perceptions and understandings of these names and realities, which were contrary to the perceptions and understandings of Whites. This was not just linguistic, but also intellectual, psychological, moral, and political resistance on the part of Blacks. This kind of behavior was initiated by Black slaves, who were constantly deconstructing slavery and white people on slave plantations and slave farms. White slave masters, for instance, used to try to convince slaves that taking things was stealing and was immoral. Slaves had a different way of looking at their stealing, namely, as justified behavior, given the great theft against them; as an act of personal and moral integrity; and even as an act of resistance against their servile condition. White masters endeavored to use Christian teachings to make Black slaves humble, obedient, and amenable to slavery. Black slaves used the same teachings to cloak and make use of their African religious heritages; as a means to attain an independent sense of value and worth, or human dignity; and as motivations for resistance to slavery, not a resistance that could lead to the overturning of the system, but to mitigating its oppressiveness. Today we have white scholars and Black scholars with different perceptions and understandings of ancient Egypt. Africancentricity and the Africancentric Perspective and Blackcentrism and the Blackcentric Perspective represent independent and different intellectual, perceptual, moral, and motivational postures or premises from which to view the realities of black Africa or the realities of Black people in America and the impact of both on various peoples and contexts. It indeed goes without saying that deconstruction as a methodology, especially as a general methodology that deconstructs life, the way Blacks have historically used that methodology, is augmented in its capacity and capabilities when it can be used from an independent intellectual, perceptual, moral, and motivational base. It also has to be said, to keep the record straight, that Blacks are not the only people ever to use deconstruction as a generalized critical method. Deconstruction is a method that is millennia old, including its generalized use. This is the method of subordinate or oppressed people, which makes it millennia old. This means that it was probably first used by women, even as a generalized methodology. It probably also was women who first used masks for self and group protection, as veils or shields behind which they could deconstruct men and their behavior. This would also make mask wearing millennia old, not something first devised by Blacks in America.

A number of Black intellectuals are lodged fully in the postmodern fold. As a rule, they are not there in the same way that white men and women are. They are, however, in the fold and take their cues—many of their intellectual or aesthetic cues—from postmodernity. In some ways, this has strengthened Black intellectual and aesthetic ef-

forts but, by and large, postmodernity assaults the Black mind and
Black psychology and Black cultural and social life. It is also an assault, especially when not approached or utilized cautiously and critically, to the independent source of Black intellectual capability and
activity. Specifically, the postmodern assault against the things just
mentioned occurs when Black intellectuals and other Blacks use
White cognitive systems to analyze themselves or their efforts, or
Black culture, or Black life or use these cognitive systems to utilize
and deliver postmodern assistance. Black Cognition, like the Blackcentric Perspective and Blackcentrism (and sometimes in interaction
with the Africancentric Perspective and Africancentrism), is the key
to analyzing Black history, culture, and social life, and contributions
to the same. They are also the key elements needed to construct a
Black Aesthetic, which will be discussed in the next chapter.

5.

Developing a Black Aesthetic

The crisis of Western civilization, as I talked about it in the last chapter, presents an opportunity for Black intellectuals. This is also a crisis of American civilization and in the same way. Black intellectuals emerged in America as a counter to white intellectuals and racism and slavery, but they also emerged endeavoring to ally with white intellectuals to end racism and slavery. A question is how will Black intellectuals relate to white intellectuals today, especially since they do not see white intellectuals as the voice they once were in America and even perceive them to be crippled in their ability to be a voice that can significantly help America. White postmodernists in America are showing themselves to be cut adrift with their thinking and ideas, a situation that is true of white postmodern thinkers in general in the Western world. But all over the Western world white male postmodernist thinkers are trying to hold onto the dominant intellectual position of the White Male Voice even though it has not the credence, respect, or moral stature it once had, thus deepening the crisis of white intellectuals and the American manifestation of the general Western crisis.

Let me provide a clear example. In 1968 the president of the Organization of American Historians, C. Vann Woodward, made an address in which he criticized some Black historians for arguing that white historians could not write Black history in a fair manner and should not attempt to write it. Woodward made the point, which was true, that most Black history was written by white historians. But there had been a lot of criticism of this White writing, much of which dripped of racism. Woodward acknowledged this criticism, expressing the hope that in the future white historians would keep racism out of their scholarship. He even had an expectation, because he felt that with more professional Black historians on the scene, White historians would be more cautious and circumspect. But what Woodward was really concerned about was that Black historians might be more critical of American history than white historians were. But he masked this concern by cautioning white liberal historians, the presumed allies of Black historians, not to take this approach to writing American history, feeling that they might do so out of guilt and not out of an interest to provide a deeper and more accurate reading of American history. "Equally misguided are impulses of self-flagellation and guilt that encourages the deprecation of all things European or white in our civilization and turn its history into a chorus of *mea culpas*."[1] That same year, 1968, Arthur Schlesinger, Jr., admonished the newer and younger Black historians to observe the canon of historical writing.[2] To many Black historians, these remonstrations were an outrage, which some historians expressed at the meeting of the Organization of American Historians. White historians were hardly in any position to talk about observing the canon of historical research and writing, given how so many of them, motivated by racism, had violated the canon or had shoved it aside. Black historian Sterling Stuckey expressed the sense of outrage that many Black historians had felt being scolded or "schooled" by white historians. He said white historians "have not been above lecturing blacks on how they should perceive and record their experiences. . . . Of all the people to deliver sermons to blacks, they would be among those least likely to receive a respectful hearing."[3] In his last published work, Nathan Huggins criticized white historians for still refusing to assess the impact of Black slavery and Black oppression on white people and American history. This was a reference to the silence that white historians continued to keep on these subjects: "Like the framers of the Constitution, they have treated racial slavery and oppression as curious abnormalities—aberrations—historical accidents to be corrected in the progressive upward reach of the nation's destiny."[4] But Huggins's remarks could also be directed toward Black historians who have not taken up these subjects either and who, therefore, have been helping white historians maintain the silence, which is a silence for Black people, white people, and other Americans.

Black historians have yet to write on *American* history as white historians do. They have continued to let white historians do this, as if it were their right only—even though many white historians write on Black history. This is a default of scholarship (but also of Black Politics). It specifically hurts the efforts of Black intellectuals to be a critical voice in America, a critical Black Voice, and especially to have something to say to the country that other intellectuals have not said or said well enough. The crisis of Western civilization that refracts through America requires that Black intellectuals have this capability, or there will be a continuation of white intellectuals having the floor but not saying much that will help redirect American history and American life. I personally believe that an intellectually, culturally, and morally retooled America is the key to pulling the Western civilization out of its destructive crisis.

Postmodern thought is reflective of that crisis. Not only in terms of the racism that affects the thought, the drift of that thought that seems to want and value only endless dissemination and signification, and the refusal to seek consensus or universality that alone can bind people together for common thought and common action—and for a common morality—but because many, if not most postmodern intellectuals do not seem to be too interested in being very critical of Western civilization, or American civilization for that matter. This cannot be done when it is believed that appearance and reality are the same, and the result is like saying that there is no reality and reinforcing that by the argument that there is nothing outside language. Jean Baudrillard has argued, as Nevelle Wakefield has written, "the futility of all criticism."[5] Assessing postmodern thinking, Sven Birkerts has written, "Postmodernism is, in this sense, the very apotheosis of aestheticism. Enjoy the play of surface, never mind the depths. There *are* no depths. Notions of profundity, cravings for connection and significance, must be jettisoned."[6] Some postmodernists claim there is no way to know reality, or what is, except through representation. Angela Carter writes, "We may see, hear, feel, smell, and touch it, but do we *know* it in the sense that we give meaning to it?"[7] Or, as Lisa Tickner has written, the real is "*enabled to mean* through systems of signs organized into discourses on the world."[8]

Let's start at the top in considering this list of postmodern postures. It is strange, indeed, for an intellectual like Baudrillard to resign himself to the position that it is futile to be critical, believing that it is no longer possible to be so. Clearly this kind of attitude will not help to get the Western civilization out of its deep-seated crisis. And equally clearly, intellectuals not interested in critical thinking or probing widely and deeply into reality have nothing to offer Western civilization in its time of great need. And it is a false notion that the only way to know reality is through signs or representations. Carter and Tickner both make this error, a common one, which occurred during so-called modernity as well. The error during modernity and postmodernity grew out of misunderstanding words and dichotomizing cognitive activity. Neither Carter nor Tickner made a distinction between knowing something and understanding something, knowing reality and understanding reality. It is possible for someone to be aware of something, but not really understand what he or she is aware of, or why. Knowing something, or reality, can be done by the senses alone. Think of yourself standing in the path of a speeding car. If that car runs into you, you will know reality by the senses, at least by seeing, hearing, and touching. If you win the lottery for two million dollars, you will know reality by the senses and perhaps even by some other bodily actions, such as by fainting, temporarily not being able to talk, or even by hyperventilating. Do any of these bodily actions constitute meaning or stand for signification? They do, but they indicate the signification and meaning of knowing, but not understanding.

Understanding takes knowing, because it involves at least a sense or two, and even more numerous kinds of bodily reactions. But understanding takes more than the senses, or bodily actions, because it is a more complicated activity that also involves ideas, information, or analytical activities. The problem here, at the *deep* level, is the White/Western cognitive practice of assaulting and slicing up reality, and putting reality "in its place," they way that white people have put Black people and other people in their place. Historically, and for many centuries, Whites/Europeans have separated—actually—divorced thought from social reality or social life, thought from the body, or thought from the senses—as reflected in phrases such as mind *or* body, thought *or* senses, or the body *or* soul. All four White cognitive systems have participated in this dichotomizing activity, to the point where the body and senses have been ruled out or seriously restricted in the activities of learning, acquiring information, evaluating information, or knowing or understanding reality or truth. As said earlier, cognitive psychologists dichotomize the intellectual and affective qualities of cognition and then rule out the psychological or affective qualities—in keeping with traditional White/Western cognition.

In the past, during so-called modernity, the racist argument was that people who stressed affective traits, focused on or indulged the body, or put an emphasis on feeling, were considered to be naturally inferior people, primitive people, or uncivilized people. This was what white racists said of black people in America, and black people elsewhere, but also of Indians in America, or yellow and brown people in Asia. The White cognitive practice of dichotomizing the mind and body, or the mind and the senses, or the body and soul, got anchored in the White racist foundationalism of Western history and civilization, to the point where White became synonymous with mind and soul, and black people, in particular, but also other people of color became synonymous with the body and senses. When Whites get into discussions about representations and reality, about knowing and understanding reality, or about signification, it is hard if not impossible for them to keep White racist foundationalism out of their discussions. This has been true during alleged modernity and also now during postmodernity. Intellectually avoiding the senses is psychologically avoiding black or other people of color. Thus, white intellectuals and other white people are shoved up hard against the idea that only through the mind or intellect is reality to be perceived, analyzed, or understood (language, description). And this remains an inadequate way to relate to reality, in terms of apprehending, participating, evaluating, or understanding reality or what is real. This was the inadequacy of modernist critical activity, as it is the inadequacy of postmodernist critical activity. In regard to the former, the inadequacy helped to plunge the Western civilization into its present crisis. In regard to the latter, the inadequacy assures that Western civilization will be short of the intellectual help it needs to try to emerge from its crisis.

All of this puts Black intellectuals in a propitious position with respect to the American manifestation of the Western civilization crisis, providing them an opportunity to make an intellectual contribution that might aid America in climbing out of its morass. Black intellectuals are from a people who have always understood the body and the senses and who have used and enjoyed both extensively. Jon Spencer has talked about the rhythm of black people, from Africa to what I call the Western African Extensia, and how this rhythm, which has a clear affinity with the body and senses, affects or informs the aesthetic cultural activities of black people and even their thought. In *Nobody Knows My Name*, published in 1961, James Baldwin made an oblique reference to his first novel, *Go Tell It on the Mountain*, which he finished writing in Switzerland. He said he had to draw on his two records of Bessie Smith there, which he played over and over, to finish it: "It was Bessie Smith, through her tone and her cadence, who helped me dig back to the way I myself must have spoken,"[9] so that he could produce authentic Black speech in his novel. A year later, in a recorded interview with Studs Terkel, Baldwin developed his point a little further, saying that he corrected and wrote dialogue on the basis of what he heard Bessie Smith sing, and the way J. P. Johnson played.[10] In his comments, specifically referring to the "cadence" of Bessie's Smith's lyrics, Baldwin was indicating that there was a certain rhythm in Black speech. And, obliquely, he referred to the rhythm in J. P. Johnson's musical accompaniment. So, it was expressions of Black rhythm, in speech and in music, that helped Baldwin to finish his first novel, that helped the intellectual, emotional, and artistic efforts of his first writing. But Baldwin's writings, essays and novels, are generally characterized by the two expressions of Black rhythm mentioned, even his novels *Giovanni's Room* and *Another Country*, where these expressions have not always been seen.

Jon Spencer is right to point to a general rhythm of black people from Africa to the Western African Extensia. He sees it more as a cultural, rather than a racial thing, and this makes one wonder why he insists that black people should stress their racial identity. Spencer is critical of those Black and white postmodernists who want to debunk race. There are a number of reasons that they do so. They confuse race with racism, which is the most common reason, and it is common among Black and white postmodernists who seek to debunk race. There are Black postmodernists who reject what they regard as a racial essentialism, but which more often than not is confused with racist essentialism, which not only deprecates Black humanity, but is rigorously deterministic, a bother to Black postmodern thinkers, as it is to white ones. There are Black postmodernists who have simply, intellectually, and at least to some extent, mentally, or psychologically, thrown off their racial identity and think of themselves only as individuals; and it would seem colorless individuals at that, something that raises a doubt or two about someone having thrown off race mentally or psychologically. Then there is the linguistic rejection of race, when it is argued that race is not real, but only a "social construction." Black historian Barbara Fields has rejected race on this basis.[11] Henry Louis Gates, Jr., has also rejected race on this linguistic ground and has attributed many human atrocities to the linguistic fabrication. He asserted, appealing to Black intellectuals, but to any in the postmodern fold: "our task is to utilize language more precisely, to rid ourselves of the dangers of careless usages of problematic terms which are drawn upon to limit and predetermine the lives and choices of human beings who are not 'white.' "[12] One understands the responses of Fields and Gates and others who react like them. *Race* is a word that has been abused, and people have suffered from it, particularly black people and other people of color. But this abuse could have come even if someone had defined the word *race* precisely. The abuse does not come from a word; it comes from those who want to or who do commit abuse. People can distort or misrepresent any word—*tall, short, fat, disabled, Christian, democrat,* or *intelligence*—so that they can rationalize being abusive or repressive toward people. The fault is not with the word, fundamentally, but with the people who use the word or words. It shows again the idea presented in the last chapter, that there is always something beyond language.

But on the other hand, it is illogical to be against race on the basis of the understanding that race is "socially constructed." Human beings socially construct everything. That is, they use language to describe, to identify, to characterize, to classify, and to authorize and legitimize. This is simply what human beings do, and precisely because they are human and precisely because human beings use language to devise thoughts and descriptions and to guide their social behavior. Something that is called a tree exists independently of that name. And the same goes for rock, brook, mountain, sky, and star. Each could have been called something else. But the naming of these things, or providing descriptions of them did not bring any of them into existence. They existed before the names and descriptions were applied; this is the way of many aspects of reality. This would include race, meaning a biological reality, which existed with its characteristics long before a name and description were applied to it. White men invested race with more than biological attributes, because they wanted to abuse a race or races of people. So they socially constructed race in a way to distort it, to misrepresented it, to give it characteristics and meanings it did not have—that the biological reality itself could never have given it. In short, white men devised racist fantasies or even elaborate racist doctrines to describe race, which eructed race and produced "race"; it became something that did not exist, except as an abstract, fanciful, and mystical construction. To reject race is to play into the hands of racism, not to move away from racism or to push it out of history. Rejecting race helps to leave racism in history and doing its destructive things. Rejecting race is to focus on race. The focus is not on racism, and racism is not being rejected. In his book *Race Matters*[13] Cornel West focused overwhelmingly on the subject of race, and the victimization of race, which also included his discussion of the inadequate, confused, and self-serving thinking about race done by its victims, which is typical subject fare of writings on race. West's book was not entitled *Racism Matters*. Then we would have had a different discussion, a discussion about white people, and white people as racists, and what racism has done to white people, and what white people have done to American history, culture, and social life practicing racism. Another way of looking at this is that we would have had a discussion of racist essentialism. Whenever there is talk about racist essentialism or racial essentialism by Black or white intellectuals, whether they are, in each case, postmodern intellectuals or not, the talk is always about black or Black people; and how black or Black people are subscribing to racist essentialist depictions, or how such people are alluding to certain racial or biological traits that have special qualities; not defined (usually) as superior or inferior, but as special or distinctive, that refers to difference. But the white race and white people do not come in for this kind of discussion. But in the past, white people themselves used to engage in discussions of racist or racial essentialism with respect to themselves rather frequently. These were the years, indeed, centuries, in America and Europe, when white people were publicly and blatantly racist and talked about the essential characteristics or traits of white people or the white race. Since this was mainly done in a racist manner, the discussion was mainly about racist essentialism. Today, white people in America and Europe are not so publicly blatant in their racism, so racial and racist essentialism are not publicly broadcast anymore, except by very extremist elements, who want to keep the whole thing— the history of blatant White racism and racist essentialism—going. But white racists in America and Europe are now more subtle in their racism, and they more subtly promote racial, and especially racist essentialism with respect to themselves.

But where are the Black and white intellectuals to help us understand these things? There are many in both camps, especially when they think of themselves as postmodern thinkers, who want to get rid of race. What they do is to continue to make race problematic, when race is not problematic. Racism is problematic. And if there is no focus on this reality and the kind of problems it creates, because of the kind of mephitic reality it is, then racism is abetted. It is aided in continuing its history and life. Inadequate focus allows racists and racism to draw on race as a shield to hide behind to keep perpetuating themselves.

And in this sense, black intellectuals in America or black intellectuals elsewhere are complicitous in the ongoingness of White-perpetrated racism (actually racisms). Black or black intellectuals really do not deal with racism. They deal with the consequences of racism, the victimizing consequences of it, and the people who have been obviously and grossly victimized, particularly economically and socially. This means that Black and black intellectuals are engaged in inadequate analyses and discussions. They are joining with postmodern thinkers who do not wish to be very critical thinkers. They will use souped-up phrases like *critical theory, critical analysis,* or *critical exegesis,* or even rather abstract language; but they are not very critical, and their discussions of race and racism and other things show it. But in the case of Black intellectuals in America, this kind of inadequate discussion of race and racism did not occur with the advent of so-called postmodernity. This kind of discussion has been going on for centuries. In a way, it could not have been otherwise, because white people made race so overwhelming in the life of Black people. This forced Black intellectuals and other Black people to focus on race. But the centuries of forcing Blacks to deal with race led them, and even Black intellectuals, to exaggerate how large a role race, biological characteristics, played in their lives. They were led to exaggerate the role that their race played in their oppression, to the point that they overwhelmingly believed that they were oppressed (enslaved, denied human dignity, rights, opportunities, and justice) because of their race. This put the responsibility for their oppression on their biology, on themselves, and took responsibility away from the Whites who did the oppressing, who vilified their biology. Whites perceived themselves as being guiltless, innocent, and nonresponsible and had a number of Black people, including some Black intellectuals feeding those delusions, by such people thinking, and even sometimes arguing, that Black people were responsible for their own blighted situation in America; usually put in terms of their not doing enough for themselves, not working hard enough, not having the right values or the right attitudes, or not taking advantage of opportunities when they presented themselves. There are so-called Black conservatives who talk like that right now, ignoring how Whites have never wanted most Blacks to make it in America, and all the things they have done and continue to do to make sure it does not happen. They have also failed to recognize or acknowledge how numerous Blacks (and not just themselves) have made it in America, that is, have attained the level of education, wealth, cultural sophistication, or linguistic or social competence attained by Whites, despite the horrendous obstacles put in their pathway; or because of them.

And the over-focus on race had Black intellectuals and other Black people thinking that their race, their biology, was the source of their thought, or their cultural traits or construction, or their destiny in history. Du Bois was one of the Black intellectuals who believed in the racial theory of history, as have many Black intellectuals in this century, even if the conceptualization was not there or not clear. Many Black intellectuals have and still believe in racial essentialism, and this is, as it was in the past, the basis for a racial conception of history. But in fairness to such individuals would not the White domination of America, the White domination of the planet, and the struggle of black people, red people, yellow people, and brown people against these forms of domination lead to and validate a racial theory of history?

But what Black intellectuals—to focus on them—could not always help in the past, they have to be able to get past today. While it may not have been possible to understand race or racism fully in the past, or the interaction between the two, and the way these forces impacted America and the life of Black, white, and other people of the country—these are things that Black intellectual have to understand critically and fully now. There is no way that Black intellectuals are going to become a major critical voice in America or become an intellectual force to help America pass to the other side of its civilizational crisis and be a voice to help contribute to Western civilization's passage through its crisis if they are still fleeing from, stumbling over, poorly analyzing, or inadequately thinking through very basic matters. Race, racism, and ethnicity are basic matters that have historically impacted Black people and continue to do so. Black intellectuals have to offer Black people a full understanding of these matters, as realities, and as impactful elements. These will be the same understandings passed onto Whites and other Americans.

I have tried to point out the difference between race and racism in this essay. I have also said something about ethnicity and will be saying more. I said earlier on that a race was comprised of ethnic groups. Therefore, race and ethnicity were different realities, but they were related to each other. They were different realities, but not necessarily antagonistic toward each other. I had also previously said that Black people in America should view themselves as having a racial and an ethnic identity, indicated by spelling one identity *black* and the other *Black*. Karla Holloway sees this interactive double identity, interacting on the basis of diunital logic, but prefers to think of Blacks as African-Americans: "The presence and practice of the African American community that practices this cultural work in the United States forces a convergence of memory and history, practice and progress that is both racial and ethnic."[14]

I reject Holloway's description of Blacks as African-Americans. I have been critical of this identity for Black people in America on a number of occasions in this book and have shown how Black people themselves overwhelmingly reject it. The insistence on the African-American or the Afro-American, to say nothing about an African identity for Black people, creates and maintains divisions among Blacks. The insistence on these identities by numerous Black intellectuals also goes smack to the question of whether Black intellectuals can be a strong, critical public voice in America, identified as the critical Black Voice, or as a voice to help America end an intellectual, social, moral, and spiritual crisis. But the matter is more purulent than this. Because those Black intellectuals who regard themselves and other Blacks as having some version of an African identity also talk of Black people as being black, Black, blacks, or Blacks. I referred earlier to James Baldwin's book *Nobody Knows My Name*. He was referring largely to the way that White racism had made it incredibly difficult for Black people to establish an identity and to define themselves. Black people have had a number of names in America: slave, Negro, Colored, people of color, black, Black, or nigger, and among some Black middle class people, and black intellectuals, such names as African, Africos, Afro-Americans, Aframericans, Afri-Americans, or Afriamericans, or Afrikan-Americans. No people who have that many names can know or understand who they are!

But in reality, historically, only five of the above names have had any impact on, and meaning for, the mass of Blacks in America: *slave, Negro, Colored, black*, and *nigger. Slave* is gone, so are *Negro* and *Colored. Nigger* is dying, but it has yet fully to decease. But in the 1960s and 1970s the mass of Black people, including the majority of Black middle-class people, concluded that they were black people, meaning mainly racially black. Few Blacks, then or now, see themselves as being Black, that is, as ethnically Black. In the 1960s and 1970s, Black people overwhelmingly believed, and still believe, as they have never been educated differently, that their culture was racially determined. That is, most Blacks in the 1960s and 1970s, and to this day, believe in racial essentialism—without conceptualization, of course. It means that the mass of Black people have to learn that they constitute an ethnic group and have an ethnic identity—as well as a racial identity. This is where Black intellectuals come in to help, but they have not done so, because so many of them still play around with, or are confused about, their identity and the identity of Black people. In *The Fire Next Time*, Baldwin said that people in America were very confused and were controlled by that confusion. As he remarked, "We are controlled here by our confusion, far more than we know."[15] Racism lies at the heart of it, because it has confused Blacks and Whites about themselves, about their relationship to each other, and about each's relationship to America.

Clearly Black intellectuals have to end their confusion, and certainly about basic matters that pertain to their identity and the identity of Black people, if they are to be the kind of intellectuals that it seems to me that American history and civilization and which Western history and civilization as well are calling upon, in desperation, for them to be. But the history of Black people and Black culture are sending up desperation signals as well. The future of Black culture is at stake in America. If race ceases to be a major public matter in America, owing to a better understanding of it, which will point to its lesser importance, then this will raise questions about the source, as well as the continuation of Black culture, if race is the source.[16] This will raise questions for Black literati and other Black aesthetic cultural intellectuals about positioning to do Black aesthetic culture. If Black culture is regarded as an African culture and is developed as if it were, this would suppress Black culture, as it will suppress Black ethnicity. There are Black historians who are raising a threat to this reality by interpreting Black history as African history, and Black culture as African culture. There are Black literary and other Black aesthetic intellectuals who are joining with them. This leads them to think of Black aesthetic culture as African aesthetic culture. This, of course, affects the positioning of these intellectuals to do Black aesthetic culture. Then there is a question of Black ethnicity, as a reality, and as the source of Black social and aesthetic culture, and, thus, the matter of positioning from this reality. But this latter matter, the question of a Black ethnic identity and its portent for social and aesthetic culture, is more complicated.

The reason why this is so is because *there is more than one black ethnic group in America!* This is not a reality that Black intellectuals seem to have perceived, because one sees no discussion of it in writings by Black intellectuals, or in words and understandings by other Blacks. There are black people from Africa, from South America, and the West Indies (and a small number from Central America) in the United States. None of these black people mentioned belong to the Black ethnic group. As said earlier in this essay, the Black ethnic group is composed of the direct descendants of Africans, and their descendants, Black slaves. Other black people in this country are from elsewhere, from different geographical locations, different land masses, different histories, different cultures, and also different identities. There are presently in America Nigerians, Liberians, and South Africans. There are Jamaicans, Haitians, Barbadoans, and other black people from the West Indies in the United States. And then there are black people in the country who do not form a separate ethnic group, but who are part of ethnic groups that include white people, red people, and brown people (and mixtures), such as Puerto Ricans, Cubans, or Panamanians. The history and practice of White racism in America has been to lump all black people in America together, those who are ancestral and indigenous and those who are not, and to regard them all as being of the black race—to give them all an indistinguishable racial identity and to ignore the historical, cultural, and also national sources of their identities before coming to America. But this slurring over the identities of black people in America is also done by Black intellectuals when they call all black people in the Western African Extensia, including Black people in the United States, Africans, African-Americans, or Afro-Americans.

There were black African intellectuals who, at one time, were en-
amored of the concept of *négritude*, because of the unity of
consciousness it produced, the rehabilitation it carried out on an in-
jured blackness (racial reality) and on the psychological injury from
racist, as well as colonial and imperialistic oppression, and the way it
enabled black African intellectuals to talk positively about blackness.
It aided black African aesthetic cultural development. But at a Pan-
African cultural festival in the early 1970s, in Africa, African aesthetic
intellectuals denounced négritude, as Henri Lopes did, which had a
general endorsement: "The worst danger about 'negritude' is that it
constitutes an inhibiting force for negro writers, so far as creative
activity is concerned. If it does not actually incite folklore in literature
. . . it does lead to conformity of style and content, as prejudicial to
cultural vitality as all other constraints, moral or other."[17]

The danger to Black aesthetic cultural thinking, and cultural activities, is Africancentricity, which makes no distinction between the various black people of the Western African Extensia, that recognizes no
national identities among them, or the conversion of these national
identities into ethnic identities when such people come to America
to live. The Blackcentric Perspective and Blackcentrism distinguish
Black people from other black people in America, and the Black ethnic group from other black ethnic groups in the country, which exist,
even if they are much smaller in size than the Black ethnic group,
which numbers in the tens (at least two) of millions in America. Black
literati and other Black aesthetic intellectuals have to decide which
black ethnic group they belong to and from which they will position
themselves in America. These are matters to which present Black intellectuals in America do not remotely relate. This is not a matter that
is as urgent to deal with as the question of whether positioning will
be done on the basis of race or ethnicity, or both, and in what ways.
But the question of black ethnic groups and black ethnicities will have
to be considered at some point. The different black ethnic realities in
America raise questions about the critical Black Voice in America.
There has to be certainty about that on the part of Black intellectuals
who, along with Black leaders, will mainly constitute the Black Public
Voice in America. How will other black voices relate to it? Or to
America?

The Black Public Voice will be a political and social voice, as it has
been since its inauguration in the first half of the nineteenth century.
But at its inaugural, it was not ethnically culturally directed. Northern

Black middle-class people and the Black intellectuals among them inaugurated the critical Black Public Voice in America, which emerged to attack slavery, racism, and efforts to colonize or deport non-slave Blacks from the country or efforts on the part of Blacks to promote emigration by Blacks or black people, that is, the black West Indians in the United States such as newspaper editor John Russwurm. Black ethnicity existed mainly with Black slaves who did not have, and who could not have projected, a critical Black Public Voice. Booker T. Washington combined Black culture with modernization thought and the modernization he led millions of Blacks in between the 1880s and his death in 1915. Years before the latter happened, a group of Black intellectuals, as seen earlier, had founded the American Negro Academy. The latter was racially rather than ethnically driven, with a strong belief in racial essentialism and a racial theory of history. The Harlem Renaissance did not ethnically direct the Black Public Voice. This was a period when Black literati and other Black aesthetic intellectuals extensively developed Black aesthetic culture. But these intellectuals could not or, at least, did not, develop a Black Aesthetic that would have helped other Black intellectuals and Black leaders to devise a Black Public Voice that would have had deep roots in Black ethnicity and Black culture. But the conscious rooting of such a voice would have been in race at this time anyway, not in ethnicity. While Marcus Garvey and his movement helped to stimulate and augment the Harlem Renaissance, they did not aid in the construction of a general Aesthetic for that aesthetic cultural outpouring. Garvey, like most other Black and black people in the United States—the large number of West Indians, like Garvey— thought in terms of race; of racial essentialism and a racial theory of history. It was not until the 1960s, with the advent of Black Power, that a possibility was opened up for the first time in Black history, for a Black Public Voice to be rooted strongly in Black ethnicity and to be strongly influenced by it. But Black Power scared many white people and the major Black leaders, who both attacked it publicly. The attack occurred admidst the efforts on the part of some Black intellectuals to devise a general Black Aesthetic that offered a promise of fully identifying, accepting, and publicly disclosing the reality of Black ethnicity in America and drawing strongly on the latter to devise a general Black Aesthetic. But with white racists and frightened and confused Black leaders collaborating, the Black Power Movement and the Black Politics that it proffered were suppressed. This prevented any effort—any serious effort, anyway—to establish a union between Black aesthetic intellectuals and Black political thinkers and Black political leaders, that would have made it possible to bring a general Black Aesthetic and Black Politics into a relationship that would have enabled those Politics to be nourished and given some of its direction by the Black Aesthetic, Black ethnicity, and Black aesthetic culture.

The promise of the collaboration of the 1960s and 1970s did not reach fruition. A Black Aesthetic was devised, but it was never fully developed, and it passed away as Black Power thrusts and sentiments passed away. But those who devised the Black Aesthetic, such as Amiri Baraka, Addison Gayle, Jr., Ed Bullins, Hoyt Fuller, Sarah Fabio, Larry Neal, Ron Karenga, Darwin Turner, and Carolyn Gerald, understood, fully, that a Black Aesthetic had to grow out of Black history, culture, and social life, and had to be related to Black political behavior, and that Black aesthetic intellectual and aesthetic performers, such as musicians, singers, or actors, needed a strong Black community from which to function and from which to draw support. Indeed, it has to be said that if Black intellectuals generally are to become the powerful critical voice in America that America and Western civilization presently need, there is going to have to be a strong Black ethnic community behind them, because there is going to be opposition to their playing an intellectual leadership role in America, especially one where they will also be seeking to influence and lead white people in their thinking and social behavior. In short, Black intellectuals are going to need the support of Black Power, and the latter is a product of, and also constitutes, a strong Black community. Thus, there is a need to return to Black Power theorizing, and Black Power leadership and organizing and developing activities, especially financial and economic development activities. Both Black intellectuals and the Black ethnic community in America need financial and economic strength and rootedness. Black people spend, as recently estimated, $400 billion dollars annually in the United States.[18] Black intellectuals could work with Black political, religious, and other leaders to devise a way, or ways, that Blacks could convert billions of that annual spending into annual financial and economic help for the Black community, Black intellectuals, and for Black aesthetic culture. The latter is a motor power of Black life and also a source of direction and emotional satisfaction for all Black people, not just for Black intellectuals or Black leaders. The aesthetic culture of Black people in

America is what fundamentally distinguishes them from other people in this country, other ethnic groups, and that includes distinguishing them, although not as strongly as in the case of white people or white ethnic groups from the various black ethnic groups in the country. Thus, any general Black Aesthetic has to be of a special quality, which includes being capable of change and continuous development.

The Black Aesthetic, developed initially in the late 1960s and the early 1970s, and which was part of what was called the Black Arts Movement, was an advance for Black intellectuals in America, going beyond anything that Black intellectuals had ever done before, and it was an individual and collective effort. In the 1920s and 1930s Black literati and other aesthetic elements acted individually, but also collectively, to produce the Harlem Renaissance. Black literary, art, and music critics emerged to evaluate and to guide the aesthetic cultural outpouring. Black and white contemporaries, and Black and white historians, have generally described the Harlem Renaissance as being less than a spectacular success. Cornel West just recently dismissed the Harlem Renaissance with a wave of the hand and with considerable disdain:

> Black literary artists and critics have proclaimed a Harlem Renaissance that never took place, novelistic breakthroughs that amounted to poignant yet narrow mediums of social protest (for example, *Native Son*) and literary movements that consist of talented though disparate women writers with little more than their gender and color in common. Such defensive posturing overlooks and downplays the grand contributions of the major twentieth century African American literary artists—Jean Toomer, Ralph Ellison, James Baldwin (more his essays than his fiction), Toni Morrison and Ishmael Reed.[19]

The Harlem Renaissance was the production of a people just up from slavery (with millions still slaves) who had to produce their art in an extreme racist context that disjointed and deprecated their effort. With these severe impediments, the achievements of the Harlem Renaissance are not to be sneered at and do not have to be viewed as a distraction from later Black artistic achievements. After all, later achievements were significantly aided by the earlier ones. The Harlem Renaissance is best seen as a building time (even experimental time) for Black aesthetic elements and for Black aesthetic culture. And what should specifically be seen are the kind of successes that were attained as building blocks. Alain Locke, a contemporary literary and art critic, felt that some of the Black writers and artists had developed technical competence in writing the novel and in sculpting and painting.[20] And, indeed, it was Houston Baker, Jr.'s, view that some Black writers had "mastered the form" of literary genre.[21] There were Black literary and other Black aesthetic critics who "mastered the form" of their aesthetic areas. The Black literati and other aesthetic creators learned how to incorporate Black folk material into their literary and artistic efforts. There were aesthetic questions raised in the 1920s and 1930s, questions about the role of art not only in Black life, but in relationship to the Black struggle in America. These were all questions that related to a Black Aesthetic, but the literati and other aesthetic figures did not provide full answers to these questions. Nor did they construct a general Black Aesthetic philosophy or theory.

In a volume published in 1971 entitled *The Black Aesthetic*[22] and edited by Addison Gayle, Jr., a group of Black aesthetic intellectuals collaborated on the construction of a general Black Aesthetic, not systematically, but on the basis of individual contributions. The volume had a historical dimension, as it included some writings and aesthetic views by some aesthetic intellectuals of the Harlem Renaissance. There was some overlapping and contradiction in the voices, but they, collectively, presented a Black Aesthetic, with some tenets that still have value, and that, in my view, should have a presence in any effort to continue on with Black aesthetic philosophizing or theorizing.

One of the salient and enduring features of the Black Aesthetic constructed during the Black Arts Movement, and which was also presented in the Gayle volume, was that such an aesthetic related to politics as a matter of necessity. This meant, as another salient point, also presented in the Gayle book, that a Black Aesthetic did not, and should not, have its origins in aesthetic philosophy or aesthetic theory, but in Black history, Black culture, and Black social life. This would oblige Black aesthetic creators always to look upon art or aesthetic culture as being inseparable from other parts of Black life. This projected the view that art and aesthetic culture were part of a whole and had their meaning, not only in their intrinsicness, but within the reality of the whole. These viewpoints constituted a rejection of the notion that art existed "for art's sake," that aesthetic culture existed for its own sake. Postmodernists would call these latter kinds of thoughts modernist thoughts about art or aesthetic culture, meaning, without saying it, being silent about it, White/Western thoughts about art and aesthetic culture, which flowed not only from thought, but from cognition—vertical cognition when art and aesthetic culture were separated from the rest of life or domination-subordination cognition when they were to dominate life. Max Weber had a vertical cognitive view of art, while T. W. Adorno, the critical theorist, had a domination-subordination cognitive view of art. Postmodern thought hedges about art. Postmodernists seek to debunk or subvert what they call modern art, to point out the political implications of art, and how powers that be during modernity used art for political purposes without explicitly saying so[23] (or even at times knowing that they were doing so). Postmodernists shy away from seeing art explicitly and directly as a political tool, still clinging to the modernist assumption, however obscured, that "art exists for art's sake." But in regard to the postmodern deconstruction of art, I want to refer to some comments that Du Bois made in the 1920s, during the Harlem Renaissance and as one trying to guide its development. Du Bois made his remarks in a writing that Gayle did not include in the volume of 1971. Du Bois had said that "all art is propaganda and ever must be, despite the wailing of the purists." The purists would be those who believed that art existed for art's sake, which included some Black and black intellectuals in the 1920s. Claude McKay was one of these black intellectuals. Du Bois was criticized as being a conservative in regard to the Harlem Renaissance, because he had some critical views about how black and Black literati and other black and Black aesthetic contributors were doing their work. These critics were contemporary but were also of a later period. Neither contemporary nor later critics ever made any effort to understand what Du Bois meant by his provocative statement. But his own remarks that appeared in that article, and which always seem to be overlooked, and that explained what he meant and how he deconstructed the modernist view of art were the following: "Suppose the only Negro who survived some centuries hence was the Negro painted by white Americans in the novels and essays they have written. What would people in a hundred years say of black Americans?"[24] This portrait of Black Americans might be done with the greatest skill by a novelist or essayist. But for Du Bois, it would not be, as it was not for him, simply a matter of art, or form, but also a question of content. The content

had political significance which chants about the purity of art or comments about how writers had a right to present their stories as they
wished could not obscure. Langston Hughes had argued for this kind
of writer's freedom in "The Negro and the Racial Mountain," which
was included in Gayle's volume. Du Bois favored the freedom of
artists. He praised Jean Toomer's *Cane*, and also some of the writing
of Julia Peterkin, a white writer who he felt had treated Black lower-
class people with artistic ability and honesty. What Du Bois primarily
objected to was the over-focus, and especially the over-focus on Black
lower-class life by Black writers and other aesthetic creators as if that
were all there was to Black life in America or the only kind of life to
be found among Blacks in urban areas. Du Bois saw this portraiture
of black people as having political significance, that is, feeding white
racist stereotypes, which Whites were using to suppress, exclude, and
to deny Blacks in America. This meant that Du Bois was criticizing
Black novelists and other Black contemporary aesthetic figures for
helping to abet Black oppression.

   This kind of question still has relevance for the broad range of
Black aesthetic contributors and Black aesthetic culture. The Gayle
volume of the early 1970s was without Du Bois's comments, but it
showed an interest in some of his concerns. As in the case of Du Bois,
there was a rejection of art for art's sake and a belief like his, but much
stronger, that art (as well as aesthetic culture, generally) had political
significance. The stronger Black Aesthetic view was that art and Black
aesthetic culture had to be direct means to help Blacks in their liberation struggle in America. Ron Karenga subscribed to this view, and
spelled out three ways that he understood it and wished to advocate
it, which would have found support among most of the contributors
to the philosophical and theoretical volume. Karenga argued that
Black art, broadly conceived, had to have three indispensable criteria.
It had to be functional, collective, and committed. To be functional
meant that it had to be useful to the people out of whom it came, or
who inspired it, and to whom it was logically and of necessity addressed. It had to be collective because it had to come from the people and had to return to them "in a form more beautiful and colorful
than it was in real life."[25] Black art, generally, had to be committed,
meaning that it had to be fully committed to Black liberation from racism and oppression in America and the Black attainment of full freedom in the country. Neither Karenga nor other collaborators of the

Gayle volume saw any necessary antagonism between art and political and social objectives, or between the form of art and the content of art, which were salient and in my view enduring aspects of their Black Aesthetic.[26] The contributors to the Black Aesthetic also argued that Black art, or Black aesthetic culture in general, had to show an affinity to beauty and also had to be capable of soothing the psychology or senses of Black people. Another salient point, which remains salient and durable in my view, is that Black art, or Black aesthetic culture, was that which was done by Black people. This was an effort to establish the *authenticity* of Black aesthetic cultural creators, and the black *authority* for Black aesthetic culture. In a recent book, *Liberating Voices: Oral Tradition in African American Literature*,[27] Gayl Jones stressed the view that Black writers in this century did not understand and establish their true literary identity until they threw off Euro-American modes of literary expression or turned to and utilized the oral and musical traditions of Black people—that is to say, folk cultural traditions among Black people. Sven Birkerts, in reviewing Jones's book, criticized her for not seeing how some Euro-American forms of literary expression were critical of other forms and represented alternatives or options to do literary work. Another germane criticism was that Jones did not perceive the *real* reason for the Black turn from Euro-American forms (although that was never complete, as she indicated), to the Black folk-cultural sources, which was because Black literati were making claims on those sources and were establishing their authority over them.[28] The Black folklore traditions belonged to Black people, and it was Black people, including Black aesthetic creators, who had authority over them and who had the right to determine whether they were being rendered authentically in modes of aesthetic cultural expression by Black or outside aesthetic elements. This discussion leads to the final salient and durable Black Aesthetic feature projected in the Gayle volume and which will be discussed here, that there have to be Black critics for Black aesthetic elements and Black aesthetic culture. The assumption being made here is that Black critics can evaluate Black aesthetic elements and their creations and Black aesthetic culture as well as anyone, and better than most who try, who seek to do it from a distance from, or disdainful of, the creators, the creations, and the culture. All of this meant also as well that Black critics could authoritatively establish the criteria for evaluating different kinds of Black aesthetic cultural expressions, whether they were literature, art, music, dance, or theater.

There were some aspects of the Black Aesthetic of Gayle's volume that I found as flaws of the construction, areas that I felt had to be improved upon or deleted. I regard it as necessary to reject the African-American or Afro-American identities for Black people that were projected in a number of the articles of the collection. Black people are black people, Black people, and Black Americans. Gayle entitled his book *The Black Aesthetic*. Why not *The African-American Aesthetic* or *The Afro-American Aesthetic*? The subtitle of Sterling Stuckey's book *Slave Culture*, which had much popularity among Black historians and other Black intellectuals, was *Nationalist Theory and the Foundations of Black America*. Why did Stuckey's subtitle not read "of African America? or "of Afro-America"? Stuckey insisted in his book that Black people in America were Africans. Then why the discrepancy and even contradiction with the title? And why did he call Black people in his book *black* and *blacks* and still less, why did he frequently call them *Negro* and *Negroes*?

A curious thing that has to be noted is that Black intellectuals who insist on referring to Black people as Africans, Afro-Americans, or African Americans in their writings just about as frequently refer to them as black, blacks, Black or Blacks in the very same writings. Why is this? It suggests, deep down, that these Black intellectuals know that Black people in America are black, Black, and Blacks, as well as Black Americans but just cannot, for psychological reasons, it would seem, mainly, bring themselves to do so and to chuck the various African identities.

But a Black Aesthetic in America has to chuck those identities. They are fictions or fictive persons, and they show where Black intellectuals show victimization by racism. White racists imposed fictional identities on Black people and sought to get them to internalize them. Black intellectuals and other Black people from the Black middle class, as the main elements to do this, responded, with many in both groups still responding to this racist imposition, with fantasies of their own, for themselves—fictive selves or fictive persons for themselves. The racist selves were not real, and the various African selves are not real. They should be jettisoned, as most Black people have done. Those who want to use Black aesthetic culture to aid Blacks in their quest for full freedom or to repair the racist damage done to the Black psyche or to repair damage done to the Black community or to augment that community are undermining these efforts by having names that the mass of Black people do not identify with or by giving them symbols with names and meaning that they do not regard as their own and which they reject.

A Black Aesthetic has to mean a *Black* Aesthetic. And those who construct it have to clearly project this reality and understanding. Some Black literati and other Black intellectuals have tried to emphasize the Blackness of a Black Aesthetic by Black Nationalist rhetoric. This was done in several essays in *The Black Aesthetic*. But even when Black Nationalist rhetoric did not explicitly appear in essays, it was clear that many of them were written strongly from that orientation. Recently Madhu Dubey showed her affinity with Black Nationalism in her book *Black Women Novelists and the Nationalist Aesthetic*, which also demonstrated her affinity to a Black Aesthetic and its continued construction in America. But Dubey had a criticism of the Black Aesthetic constructed in the late 1960s and 1970s:

> While initiating a radical redefinition of literary "blackness," Black Aesthetic discourse, consolidated around the sign of race, discouraged any literary exploration of gender and other differences that might complicate a unitary conception of the black experience. Black feminist literary criticism, which emerged in the wake of the Black Aesthetic movement, seeks precisely to comprehend the "creative function of difference" in black women's literature, and to render this literature readable in ways that both restructure and supplement the ideological program of black cultural nationalism.[29]

The Black Aesthetic was mainly constructed by Black men between the late 1960s and the 1970s, but they cannot be the only ones to do this constructing, and the continuous development of this philosophical or theoretical framework is going to have to involve Black women as well, as a practical and moral necessity. But this, in my view, has to be done by jettisoning the concepts, or ideologies, of Black Nationalism, Black Cultural Nationalism, or just Cultural Nationalism. Only one of these concepts or ideologies has ever had any life in Black history and Black social life. This was Black Nationalism. This was always thought and political activity of a small number of Black people in America. It involved two realities: the notion of Black people emigrating from America and going to some different or distant land to build a black country or Black people seeking to build a

Black country within the confines of geographical America. An all-Black state in America, or all-Black states are not expressions of Black Nationalism. On the one hand, they would just be an expression of Black separatism, under which Blacks sought no, or very little, contact with white people. But they could also just be acts of separation, which did not preclude Blacks' interacting with Whites and other states or with the larger America; that is to say, integrating, participating with Whites in American culture, social institutions, and social life. What is usually regarded as Black Nationalism has nothing to do with the two manifestations mentioned. And this is also true of Cultural Nationalism. The way in which both of these concepts are used by Black intellectuals, and especially since the years of Marcus Garvey, is to use them interchangeably with the concept and reality of ethnicity, or the reality of the Black ethnic community, which does not seek to leave America and go anywhere, which does not seek to separate itself from Whites or others in America or from America itself, but which is a separate community in America that also seeks fully to integrate into American history, culture, and social life. This is Black Cognition at work, and it has been pushing Black history and Black life in America on these horizontally interacting tracks of separation and integration for centuries. Richard Wright's essay "Introduction: Blueprint for Negro Writing" was included in *The Black Aesthetic*, and he argued that Black writing was motivated and informed by Black Nationalism. But Wright's discussion of Black Nationalism showed how it was not that at all, but Black ethnicity, and how Black intellectuals of his time (with many Black intellectuals today continuing the practice), misapplied Black Nationalism or Cultural Nationalism and seemed not to understand ethnicity itself: "The nationalist aspects of Negro life are as sharply manifest in the social institutions of Negro people as in folklore. There is a Negro church, a Negro press, a Negro social world, a Negro sporting world, a Negro business world, a Negro school system, Negro professions; in short, a Negro way of life in America."[30]

A Black Aesthetic cannot be related to or supportive of Black Nationalist objectives, as it has never been. But it gets put in this trajectory, when not just Black Nationalist ideology affects it, but when Africancentric thinking affects the philosophizing or theorizing. The Blackcentric Perspective and Blackcentrism center in Black ethnicity and the Black ethnic community, and reject Black Nationalism or Black Cultural Nationalism as fictive or fictional matters (when not relating to a nation-state, or nation-state construction, which are the legitimate references of nationalism, but which, and particularly properly understood, would be completely unrealistic and illegitimate for Blacks in America today). The Blackcentric Perspective and Blackcentrism have to play large roles in constructing a Black Aesthetic (and the Africancentric Perspective and Africancentrism where appropriate).

Another weakness in the fashioning of the Black Aesthetic by the Gayle collectivity and which was a weakness in terms of inadequacy and somewhat obliquely alluded to was the matter of positioning to do Black aesthetic culture. Race and ethnicity were reflected in the essays of the collection, and not just race as Madhu Dubey had said, although the concept of ethnicity was missing. Larry Neal proclaimed the legitimacy of a "Third World" positioning for Black aesthetic intellectuals and creators. There is validity in this assertion as long as it is not viewed in an either-or manner, which unfortunately is how Neal viewed it. This was not only Black Nationalism, but Africancentricity working on Neal's thinking, indicating his belief that Blacks in America had only one ancestral parent: an African parent. Blacks are also of the "First World" and because of that also have two other ancestral parents. This is a diunital matter, and a Black Aesthetic must function from that cognitive system, or it will be devised as if it were a White Aesthetic with a Black face. (This question of Black Cognition and the Black Aesthetic will be discussed more fully in the concluding chapter.)

The major weakness of *The Black Aesthetic* on positioning was that it did not explicitly develop the legitimacy and necessity of ethnic positioning. If Black people are an ethnic group in America, as I believe they are, then this represents the wholeness of a people. This wholeness would also be reflected in the concept of a Black ethnic community, which is interchangeable with Black ethnicity. Within Black ethnicity or the Black ethnic community, one finds all the things that Richard Wright talked about and even things he did not mention, such as ethnicity but also gender and social class. Thus, Black aesthetic intellectuals and creators have a number of positions from which to do aesthetic activity. None of these positions is necessarily contradictory; they do not have to be made so. But where there is conflict, it can and should be recognized and explained. Black men and Black women have had similar experiences in America, but they have also had different experiences. The differences have been suppressed by Black male aesthetic intellectuals and creators. Black women aesthetic intellectuals and creators are changing this situation. Many have been influenced by feminist or postmodern thought, which has inspired them to deconstruct Black male aesthetic work to show its suppressive activities, its limited perspectives, and its limited descriptions and discussions of Black people and Black life in America in order to open up space for the Black Female Voice in Black aesthetic culture and in the construction of a Black Aesthetic, under which the Black Female Voice will speak on the basis of equality with the Black Male Voice in both categories. There are some Black female aesthetic intellectuals who have taken on White feminist thought, White literary criticism, or White postmodern thought in a very strong manner, and without the traditional safeguard in the history of Black thought of borrowing from Whites and reinterpreting or using what was borrowed in a special manner, that enhanced understanding of Black realities and did not detract from them. In the fiction of a number of Black women novelists, the Black male or many of the Black men portrayed are portrayed essentially devoid of humanity, as the grossest type of low-life people. Such images as coward, shiftless, wastrel, drunkard, thief, rapist, drughead, and other such images can be found, for instance, in Alice Walker's *The Color Purple*, Toni Morrison's *Beloved* and Gloria Naylor's *The Women of Brewster Place*. This is racist essentialism being exhibited in these works, recognized or not.

To be certain, *The Black Aesthetic* and Black Aesthetic thinking beyond that book, which was done mainly by Black men, wanted, and unrealistically, only *positive* images projected of Black men, and generally Black people when not specifying Black gender in Black aesthetic culture. This was where Black male/Black aesthetic thinking slipped into White Cognition and when it went against wholeness, the nature of Black ethnicity, and what Black Cognition always strove for. But there are now Black female aesthetic intellectuals who have also forgotten wholeness in their effort to reconstruct the image of Black women in Black aesthetic culture, and because they have slipped into using White cognition themselves. Usage of the latter, feminist thought, and postmodern thought have even led some Black female literary critics to take the Blackness out of Black life, as they analyze it, or to analyze it.[31] Michael Awkward recently cautioned against this kind of behavior, predicating his caution on his criticism of Deborah McDowell's "de-Blacking" of Toni Morrison's *Sula*:

I believe that the Afro-American critic ought to be committed to exploring the blackness of black texts; at the very least s/he should be able, even during the process of the most energetically poststructuralist rhetorical flight, to acknowledge that there is black expressive cultural precedence for technical experimentation such as Morrison's. I do not believe that critical theory is inherently resistant to such insights, but it needs to be "reinterpreted," appropriated, blackened or *denigrated*, if you will, for use in the analysis of the blackness of Afro-American texts by critics more interested than McDowell is in "Boundaries" in such exploration.

Without such appropriation or *denigration*, the Afro-American "poststructuralist" will find him/herself almost by necessity virtually erasing the blackness out of Afro-American authorial utterance.[32]

I believe Michael Awkward to be correct in his comments. But it also seems to me that he and other black literary critics, like Deborah McDowell and others, are begging the question. Why are Black literary critics dependent upon White literary critical theories in the first place to analyze Black literary works? These theories do not just come with ideas or even methods of analysis; they also come with White cognitive systems, which guarantee their assault against a *Black* text, or the cultural (Black ethnic) reality of that text. White literary theories have to be used with great care by Black literary critics and Black writers. Henry Louis Gates, Jr., has called for a Black vernacular as a basis for constructing a Black literary criticism. But this approach, while inventive, has limitations, because all Black people do not speak in the vernacular, or at least not consistently, such as educated Blacks or other Black middle-class people. Gates's vernacularism has its roots in Black folklore traditions. That is a primary source material for constructing theories of Black literary criticism, or to do Black aesthetic culture, rural Black folk culture, or urban Black folk culture. These are other contexts within Black ethnicity for positioning to do aesthetic work.

But the folklore positioning is also hurtful to the reality and interests of the Black middle class within Black ethnicity. There still seems to be no great interest on the part of Black aesthetic intellectuals or creators to position themselves on the Black middle class to do aesthetic work. Such people and other kinds of Black intellectuals still deprecate the Black middle class. Historically, Black middle-class people have rejected and castigated white racists for viewing them through their perceptions of Black lower-class people. Some of these elements have also shown a disdain for Black folk culture. E. Franklin Frazier criticized *all* Black middle-class people for this disdain in his book *Black Bourgeoisie*.[33] Black middle-class people are no longer criticized, as in the past, for disdaining black folk culture. The primary criticisms of this class are that too many members of it are too bourgeois, too isolated, too distant, or think they are, or are trying to be white. They have abandoned or lost their roots, or they are ashamed of their roots, other things that have been said about the Black middle class.

But have Black middle-class people abandoned or lost their roots? No, on two counts. If those roots are to be defined as the Black folk culture, which was produced originally by Black slaves and carried on and developed originally by Black slaves and carried on and developed after that initial creation (which took centuries) by Black lower-class people, then a number of Black middle-class people did not abandon or lose their roots. They never had significant folk cultural roots. But many, if not most Black middle-class people still function out of the folk cultural roots; this is reflected in their diunital cognition, the Black churches they attend, the various kinds of Black music they listen to, the kind of dancing they still do, the kind of humor they engage in, the kind of body language they exhibit, and the kind of emotions they display—all activities that are linked to the folk cultural traditions, which have not remained stagnant or unchanging, as witness the realities of an old rural and a new urban folk culture. Not even Black middle-class intellectuals have really understood the Black middle class very well, as the kinds of comments they always seem to make about it show. Such people have not understood how that class has importantly mastered the lifestyle. Houston Baker, Jr., as said earlier, indicated how some black literati during the Harlem Renaissance "mastered the form"—actually forms—of literary expression and how this was an important achievement. The Black middle-class, a class that was not supposed to be in America, not only emerged and developed, but it mastered the American middle-class way of life, which was and remains an achievement. It is as hard a strike against White racism as Blacks have ever made in America. And the continuous growth of this class in the country is a continuous strike against

White racism. And that continuous growth continually carries Black folk culture along with it. The Black rhythm is found among many Black middle-class people, as found among Black lower-class people. In his book *The Rhythms of Black Folk* Jon Spencer praised R. Nathaniel Dett and Dorothy Maynor for their musical achievements, namely, their mastery of European musical forms. But Spencer said their mastery involved more than that: "In this regard, Dett's and Maynor's sophisticated renditions of the spirituals were an instance of what Houston Baker, in his book *Modernism and the Harlem Renaissance* . . . terms the 'mastery of form.' " In my own interpretation of Baker, the "mastery of form" occurs in one instance when an inner Africanism is masked behind an outer Europeanism. Musically speaking, Dett and Maynor mastered the form in such a way that the inner religious and rhythmic substance of the spirituals was maintained but encased within European musical forms."[34] Black middle-class people have not masked the Blackness of their middle-class existence in America. It may not be as thorough or as thick as that of the Black lower class, but it is still there and recognizably so.

What all this means is that Black aesthetic intellectuals cannot continue to ignore the Black middle class, because it is part of Black ethnicity and the Black ethnic community. Those intellectuals, and this is virtually all of them who say that a Black Aesthetic and Black aesthetic culture must serve Black people, cannot logically, legitimately, or morally exclude the Black middle class. And this is contradictory anyway, because the people doing the excluding are Black middle-class people themselves. Just as Black female aesthetic intellectuals are seeking to reconstruct the image of Black women in Black aesthetic culture, there has to be a reconstruction of the image of the Black middle class in that culture. It is contradictory to say the least to have Black aesthetic culture undermine the Black middle class, as resourceful, resilient, and as heroic as it has often been in America and when it is the leadership class of Black people. Is this confusion on the part of Black intellectuals? I think it is, and I think it is about time for Black intellectuals to end their confusion. And one of the things that I think will aid in achieving this objective is for Black intellectuals of all kinds, and especially aesthetic intellectuals, to turn to the full complexity of the Black historical foundation and Black identity in America. That foundation and that identity both have three sources: an African heritage, a slave experience and heritage, and a Euro-American heritage. There are Black intellectuals who like only to turn back to the African and slave heritage to do their work; this is true of many Black poets, fiction writers, playwrights, artists, and musicians who draw heavily on the folk culture heritage that comes from that combined source. But very few Black intellectuals turn to the Euro-American heritage—intellectual, cultural, and social—that has also shaped Black history and a Black identity and still less to the full tripartite historical and cultural heritage. Most Black intellectuals have yet to realize that the Eurocentric, or the broader Euro-Americancentric orientations or perspectives, are theirs as much as they are the orientations and perspectives of white people. Or, and this is true, too: they refuse to accept these orientations and perspectives as their own. But Black people are people of the Western World, citizens of America, have assimilated American culture, and have contributed greatly to it and also to Western culture. Western Europeans also exploited Black people over the centuries as slaves and nonslaves. Much of the wealth that was produced by Blacks in America, and black people elsewhere in the Western hemisphere, and especially as slaves, was transferred to Western Europe, where it was used to help finance the construction and operation of Western European governments, to help augment the financial, industrial, and commercial capacities of Western European countries, to augment the wealth and power of the upper and middle classes in Western Europe, and to help finance the art, science, and technology of the area. White Western scholars like to ignore or play down these contributions, which they invariably do when they write their accounts of matters from their Eurocentric or Euro-Americancentric perspectives. But Black intellectuals in America and most black intellectuals elsewhere in the Western hemisphere let them get away with this, because they do not seek to make use of these two Perspectives and invest them with their knowledge and angle of vision, which would give a different, broader, and more realistic view of how America and Western Europe evolved, developed, and grew to great power, great prosperity, and ascendancy in the world.

The Black middle class in America is, in a very strong manner, an outgrowth of the Eurocentric and Euro-Americancentric orientations and practices in America. But many Black middle-class people deny this heritage, minimize it, or run away from it. Most Black intellectuals have done the same, and they have been the worst offenders of all, because it has always been their task since their emergence in America, in the late eighteenth century, to help Black people know who they were in America, in the fullest sense possible, and to give them the fullest kind of intellectual guidance. But Black intellectuals, and especially Black aesthetic intellectuals usually only want to go two-thirds of the way on this matter: to provide an understanding of the African and slave heritages, but not the Euro-Americancentric one. But in order to understand the full history and identity of the Black middle class in America, it is necessary to focus on the triple heritage of Black people, in their individual and interactive forms. Being Black middle class has not meant, for the most part, Black middle-class people ignoring or abandoning their slave and African heritages. The class itself, generally, shows its affinity to all three forms of heritage. It is time that Black intellectuals caught up with it, as it is time for them to catch up to the mass of Black people who think of themselves as Black people and Black Americans.

To say it again, and emphatically, a Black Aesthetic has to make room for a Black middle-class perception of Black historical, cultural, and social reality. It also has to accept Black middle-class cultural and social existence as part of Black cultural and social existence in America, that is, as part of Black ethnicity and a Black ethnic identity. It further has to be an Aesthetic that accepts and sanctions artistic (broadly conceived) efforts to depict Black middle-class cultural and social existence by Black artists as legitimate *Black* artistic efforts and which also accepts and sanctions these creative depictions as reflections of Black aesthetic culture, and as part of the diversified, but also unified, Black aesthetic culture in America.

6.

The Black Cognition Imperative

In the end, the success in constructing a general Black Aesthetic will depend upon the use of Black Cognition. The creative effort requires dealing with great complexity. It takes a cognitive method that can deal with such complexity. Blacks have that cognitive method, including Black intellectuals, and it becomes a question of how diligently they use it. In the 1960s, it might be recalled that Jean-Paul Sartre was in search of a method to try to analyze Western history and social life, which he felt Marxism was not able to do alone. He turned to Existentialism and synthesized the two to construct a broader analytical approach. But Sartre's idea of method was largely ideas, or theories from two sets of ideas used in interaction. The interaction was done on the basis of dialectical cognition, Sartre's preferred methodology. Other intellectuals in the 1960s employed the dialectic and other forms of White cognition and attempted to synthesize thought, such as the ideas of Friedrich Nietzsche, Martin Heidegger, and Sigmund Freud to try to deal intellectually with their times. The times were the French manifestation of the Western crisis, and the intellectual effort resulted in the postmodern critique where all forms of absolutist or foundational thought, including Marxism and existentialism, were critiqued and condemned. But neither Sartre nor French postmodern thinkers, nor postmodern thinkers generally in the Western world, have realized that the search for a critical intellectual method is the search for a cognitive method that has great critical capacity. The dialectic and other White cognitive methods do not individually or collectively add up to this critical cognitive capability and to the critical cognitive capability needed by Western civilization. Western civilization had run out of useful cognitive methods.

But not totally. There was the Black Cognitive method of Western civilization. It had been forged, nourished, and developed in great complexity, and over a period of centuries. It lay at the center of Black ethnicity and Black intellectual and analytical activity. This was cognition that reached for wholeness, which accepted and related to realities that were similar or oppositional, which were different but not necessarily antagonistic, which insisted that aspects of reality interact with each other whether they were similar to each other, in opposition to each other, or different from each other but not oppositional, on a horizontal basis, so that they could interact individually and equally to each other. This was a cognitive system that was open to the wideness and variety of reality and which was patient enough to let reality reveal itself instead of abruptly eructing it, separating it, suppressing it, or trying to overcome it, with all the implications of dominating, controlling, and suppressing reality that this registered.

Black people have not had a history in America of dominating or controlling people. That was reserved for white men in particular and white people in general—and they were invested by American culture and social life with the cognitive systems to dominate and control. Black men, throughout their history in America, and on a continuous basis, had the props of domination kept away from them: requisite political power, economic power, education, even the power over their own families who, throughout most of Black history in America, were owned and/or controlled mainly by white men. Black women have always exercised power in Black families, and do so today, when there are many Black families without fathers. The general point is that Blacks did not make history in America and evolve socially, asking themselves continuously, as Whites did: whom are we going to dominate, whom are we going to exclude, whom are we going to deny, whom are we going to marginalize or lock out, or whom are we going to punish? Whom are we going to punish for being different? This was an entirely different way of looking at reality. Blacks, of necessity, had to look at reality differently from Whites, and they had to develop the cognitive means to do so, which would enable them to look at reality with an openness, with notions of accepting things, and including things, and also trying to promote harmony and unity between things. They developed diunital cognition to help them pursue and to attain these objectives.

This is not to say that this kind of cognitive success was always achieved, but it was achieved enough for Blacks to strongly develop diunital cognition and to use it as their main method of cognition. Their inability always to use it, or always to use it consistently, was owing to actual life experiences but also to the White cognitive methods that they had to learn and use to some extent. Black intellectuals and Black middle-class people mainly did this. Just as these elements among Blacks learned to speak English, but still maintained an ability to speak in the Black English dialect when the situation called for it, that is when in a Black context, they also held fast to diunital cognition while they employed forms of White cognition, usually when interacting with white people.

But it was not always done when interacting with white people. Black intellectuals, Black leaders, and other Black middle-class people used White cognitive systems to relate to Blacks, to Black social life, the Black struggle, and also to Black aesthetic culture. None of these utilizations, not even over centuries, have destroyed the Blackness of Black life, but over the centuries, they have threatened it, undermined it, and in ways diminished it. For instance, when Black intellectuals and other Black people, in a vertical cognitive fashion, said to Blacks that they should reject materialistic values and accept only spiritual values, they undermined and diminished Black life. When such people said that the truth more than power would help Blacks achieve rights, opportunities, and freedom in America, they were undermining and diminishing Black existence. And White cognitive systems threaten and undermine, as well as diminish, the efforts to construct a general Black Aesthetic.

Now this construction is in the hands of Black intellectuals, aesthetic kinds, but others as well. It is when White cognitive systems are intruded in this process that Black intellectuals have difficulty constructing and relating to the forces outside themselves and Black life who want to participate themselves or want to obstruct or diminish efforts.

Take the question, a basic one to constructing a Black Aesthetic of art and politics, or aesthetic culture and politics. The four systems of White Cognition make these two sets of realities binary and oppositional. And the consequence is, one of the paired realities in each set must be eliminated, dominated, overcome, or completely separated from the other. The postmodern effort to show how politics are reflected in art that supports them still presents these matters in a dualistic manner, as they see this reality as virtually an ironic situation, which brings it back to a binary situation. Postmodern thinkers, as they emphatically assert, are against hierarchy and binarianism. But they have no cognitive systems that can take them beyond the wish. Blacks do. In diunital cognition hierarchy is completely eliminated, as is binariansim. The latter is not just the matter of opposites, it is a matter of opposites in opposition, and this as a matter of necessity. There are no binaries in Black Cognition that are there of necessity. Aspects of reality may be oppositional, but that has to be revealed. And even when realities are in opposition, they interact with one another on a horizontal and not on a hierarchical basis, so that there is full exposure of reality. This full exposure helps to define each reality, and it is on the basis of the full exposure of reality, in diunital cognition, that not only interaction takes place, but changes in realities take place.

Clearly, in Black Cognition, art and politics, or aesthetic culture and politics, are not necessarily binary or oppositional. They are, as they exist, each in its integrity, simply different. But these differences are not incompatible. Indeed, they represent, as Black Cognition would have it, to provide more terminology, *logical differences.* These are differences that fit together in a logical manner because they are, or can be perceived to be, compatible with each other, such as men and women, husbands and wives, politics and economics, or theory and practice. Logical differences reflect, in Black Cognition, being open to realities, and to the potentials of realities, for compatible interaction, and for mutual use.

This is how Black aesthetic culture and Black Politics are to be perceived, and as they are or can be perceived with Black Cognition, as logically different or, another way of describing this situation, as *logical opposites* (not necessarily antagonistically opposite). And what has been said of Black aesthetic culture and Black Politics, and how they are perceived by Black Cognition could also be said about other kinds of realities that are all related to constructing a general Black Aesthetic, such as art form and art content, critic and artist, critic and art, artist and text, or the particular and universal. Any of these paired differences of logical opposites could be or could become antagonistic, but that would have to be revealed through diunital, horizontal interaction. The thrust of Black Cognition is to tie things together, to seek harmony, unity, and wholeness. Logical opposites or logical differences in Black Cognition reflect harmony, unity, and wholeness. While not reflecting harmony, antagonistic opposites or antagonistic differences reflect unity and wholeness or can move reality in those directions. Black Cognition endeavors to delineate reality, but also to clarify how it fits; how individual aspects of reality fit into the whole, or how they fit in relationship to another reality or realities, which establishes harmony or unity or both with fitted or related realities, which both reflects and drives towards wholeness (even the wholeness of a negative situation).

White postmodern thinkers show great hostility toward the harmony, unity, or wholeness of reality. This is not just on the basis of ideas or conceptualizations but also on the basis of the functioning of cognitive systems, which is the primary reason for this, but which is less discernible to them. But in any case, when white postmodern thinkers endeavor to analyze aspects of Black aesthetic culture with their cognitive systems and with hostility toward harmony, unity, and wholeness, they come to the task, from a Blackcentric Perspective, ill prepared to carry it out. But, on the other hand, Black aesthetic and other Black intellectuals are in error with the argument that white aesthetic intellectuals, literary and other white aesthetic critics, for instance, should not be able to analyze aspects of Black aesthetic culture. On the one hand, this is just a wasted argument, because there is no way to stop such white critics from doing the evaluating. On the other hand, they have a legitimate right to evaluate Black aesthetic culture. While Black aesthetic culture is *Black* aesthetic culture, and aesthetic culture of Black people, it is also a manifestation of American culture. Diunital cognition makes that clear, and a violation of that cognition, that is, utilizing either-or cognition, obscures that clarity. As Americans, white literary and other white aesthetic critics have a right to evaluate Black aesthetic culture, which is also a right that Black aesthetic intellectuals in the same categories have with respect to the aesthetic culture of any ethnic group in the country. And then there is the fact that when people outside one's ethnic group borrow from or extensively utilize aspects of that group's aesthetic culture, they are going to insist on being able to evaluate that culture or the selected attributes, and this would be a very natural thing to do. After all, cultural borrowing is selective, and this requires critical evaluation.

What it seems to me that Black intellectual elements have to do, and the thing that would be quite legitimate for them to do, and which the Blackcentric Perspective, Blackcentrism, and a Black Aesthetic would legitimize and insist on, is that they declare their right to evaluate those who evaluate Black aesthetic culture, in terms of their capability to do so and how well they have done so. Blacks are the *authority* with respect to their own aesthetic culture, and they have every right to exercise that authority within, vis-à-vis Black aesthetic figures, and without, vis-à-vis others.

And this brings us to a very important matter, and which is a matter of Black Cognition, as well as an important consideration for a general Black Aesthetic, and that is the question and reality of *Black Authenticity*. I have been talking about that, and it is natural for Black aesthetic and other Black intellectuals to have this assumption and understanding when talking about Black aesthetic culture. But this is an assumption and understanding that cannot automatically be held, as long as Black people in the view or in the writings of Black aesthetic and other Black intellectuals have so many different names. Simply and directly asked: is there an African aesthetic culture and African Authenticity in America, as some Black intellectuals say, or is there a Black aesthetic culture and a Black Authenticity here? Because Black intellectuals have divided on this, they have created an either-or situation in Black aesthetic culture, meaning they have brought either-or cognition into the situation that goes against Black Cognition, and which challenges it and also poses a threat to the Black aesthetic culture in America as well as to Black ethnicity generally. Black Cognition endeavors to recognize individual aspects of reality, and in their fullness, or intrinsicness. That Cognition is presented with a difficulty, when the ideas that guide its functioning are not clear and are even contradictory. Black and African are differences, not necessarily antagonistic realities. But there are Black intellectuals who make them antagonistic when they try to establish an African identity for Black people, eliminate the Black identity, or try to impose an African identity over a Black identity—or when they claim that Black aesthetic culture in America is African aesthetic culture. Either-or thinking or more-than thinking is White thinking and not Black thinking, and Blacks have to use Black thinking when constructing a Black Aesthetic. And that thinking has to eliminate fictitious names and identities of Black people for the integrity and security of their ethnicity, ethnic identity, and their ethnic aesthetic culture.

That means necessary and proper eliminations when attempting to form literary canons. And that would definitely mean eliminating fictive names and identities when attempting to form Black canons. In 1987, scholars of Black literature met in a conference to present views and to work out some of the difficulties in establishing Black literary canons. As the two editors of the volume *Afro-American Literary Study in the 1990s*, a conference collection, Houston Baker, Jr., and Patricia Redmond wrote, "The conference in April 1987 was historic: never before had leading Afro-American critics formally convened to set an agenda for the field."[1] The meeting was historic, and it would have also been historic had the scholars gathered discussed and eliminated the fictive names and identities of the Black canons. But this matter never even came up.

What was brought up, but what was not resolved, was what constituted a *Black* canon. Henry Louis Gates, Jr., who apparently presented the first paper at the conference which, along with others, was published in the anthology, said that Black canon formation had begun in the 1840s, and with what he called a dilemma that had plagued the canon ever since: "Here, then, we see the two poles of black canon-formation, established firmly by 1849: is 'black' poetry racial in theme, or is black poetry any sort of poetry written by black people? This quandary has been at play in the tradition ever since."[2] This quandary was presented in the first paper of the conference of literary critics, but the dilemma was not dealt with. Of course, the matter went beyond just Black poetry and to the matter of Black literary canons, generally. The conferees essentially let the matter pass, apparently thinking or assuming that everyone knew what was meant by a Black canon and thus not requiring significant discussion. But when it is considered that at the conference, Black literary canons had several names—African-American, Afro-American, and black (and maybe even Black, too, but editing would have eliminated that if the preponderant usage was *black* in the papers, to achieve symmetry). But a question could be asked, and could have been asked and answered at the conference: was a Black canon racial, ethnic, or both, or did it rest on other positions as well? The conferees let an important moment pass.

But it seems clear to me, as it did to the Addison Gayle, Jr., Black Aesthetic group, that a Black Aesthetic requires that Black literature, Black poetry, Black music, Black drama, and so on be done by Black people, that they be totally or mainly about Black people (as sometimes it takes white people or other people to tell a Black story). It seems to me that a Black Aesthetic can now reject the overriding racial themes and racial positions and can now insist that Black literary canons, and all forms of Black aesthetic culture, position on the broad basis of ethnicity, which takes in race but also other aspects of Black ethnicity such as gender, social class, and community. Black aesthetic intellectuals can position on any of the aspects of Black ethnicity, which will expand and enrich Black aesthetic culture, and Black ethnicity.

As to the matter of white people doing Black aesthetic culture, or Black aesthetic figures doing nonBlack aesthetic culture, there is no way to stop Whites from writing about Black people, or playing Black music, or painting Black people or Black life. But it will be *white people doing Black aesthetic culture*, and that is the category to which these efforts should belong. Black people are Americans, and they can write on any people or subject of American life and can do other people's aesthetic culture. Whites in America, from numerous ethnic groups, have done Black aesthetic culture. So Whites have no leg to stand on to complain about Blacks when the latter, thinking of themselves as Blacks and Americans, that is, thinking diunitally, insist that they have the legitimate and moral right to think of America's aesthetic cultures being open to them to do aesthetic work.

This raises another matter for creators of a Black Aesthetic. They also have to construct a *Black American Aesthetic*. This would resolve many of the difficulties they have trying to devise a Black Aesthetic and relating to Black aesthetic elements who write, paint, or who perform outside Black ethnicity and the Black aesthetic culture. Many Black literati have trouble with James Baldwin, and precisely because they don't think he was always Black enough in his writings. Baldwin, thinking diunitally, wrote as a Black writer and as a Black American writer, with the latter entitling him to write outside Black ethnicity, and on other subjects, on other people, and on the broad canvass of American life. Richard Wright was chastised by Black critics for *The Outsider* and *Savage Holiday*. And Ralph Ellison came in for criticism, too, even for *Invisible Man*, which has been criticized for its integration theme (which is one theme of the novel). Frank Yerby has long since been banished by Black literati. But a Black American Aesthetic would make it possible to claim Black aesthetic figures who do not write or perform out of Black ethnicity. But they are Black, and it may be that they want to be included in the fold, but a place must be made for them or for those Black literati or other Black aesthetic creators who do Black aesthetic culture, but who also go outside it to do their aesthetic work or who mix aesthetic cultures. There can be literary canons as well as other aesthetic cultural genres within the framework of a Black American Aesthetic.

Creating a general aesthetic theory or philosophy (and there can be more than one general theory or philosophy with the presumption that another or other general Black Aesthetics would be positioned on Black ethnicity and its multiple interactive parts) will show the capabilities of Black intellectuals to play a critical historical role in Western intellectual life and Western history and civilization. The American and broader Western crises are calling them to come forward. It is up to Black intellectuals to hear the call and to prepare themselves to answer it. The preparation involves immersing themselves widely and deeply in the knowledge of Black history, culture, and social life, and what Black intellectuals and other Blacks have said about these things. Robert Franklin has shown that Black intellectuals, in discussing Black social life also have spoken at the same time, on universal human and social themes: "These men [Booker T. Washington, W.E.B. Du Bois, Martin Luther King, Jr., and Malcolm X] spoke and wrote a considerable amount about individual life-plans, community development, social justice, and the important relationships among the three. In his own way, each of these monumental public moralists analyzed the interdependence of the self and society and worked toward optimal and humane relations between them."[3] Franklin was saying what other Black intellectuals have said over the years, that the universality of human experience can be located in an analysis of Black history and in artistic portrayal of Black life. Thus, Black thought extends to Black American thought. And Black intellectuals have to dig widely and deeply into both forms of thought, something that should be done on a diunital interaction basis, with the two forms of thought informing, augmenting, and clarifying the other. The Black historical and social experience in America is the basis for constructing various kinds of social theories with universal implications and applications. This is simply something for Black intellectuals to realize and to set their sights on doing. Indeed, this is something that they have to do if they are to provide a critical voice in America that can relate directionally to the American and Western crises. Black intellectuals cannot play this kind of critical intellectual role by simply focusing their attention and writing on the Black historical, cultural, and social experiences in America. Nor can they do this simply by providing a marvelous aesthetic culture that serves them and America. Black intellectuals have to use all of these means to excavate knowledge, truths, and understandings about human beings, human behavior, and human aspiration that will serve as messages to America and Western civilization that will invest both with thought, energy, and motivation to help them climb from their present crises. Du Bois once said that Blacks would one day give America and the world a "Message." Was this prediction or prophecy? It is up to Black intellectuals to provide us with an answer—to provide America and Western civilization with an answer.

Notes

PREFACE

1. E. Franklin Frazier, "Failure of the Negro Intellectual," in *E. Franklin Frazier on Race Relations, Selected Writings,* edited and with an Introduction by G. Franklin Edwards (Chicago: University of Chicago Press, 1968), pp. 267–279.

2. Harold Cruse, *The Crisis of the Negro Intellectual* (New York: William Morrow, 1967).

CHAPTER 1: THE REALITY OF BLACK INTELLECTUALS

1. Reginal Horsman, *Race and Manifest Destiny: The Origins of American Racial Anglo-Saxonism* (Cambridge, MA: Harvard University Press, 1981), pp. 56–57.

2. W. E. B. Du Bois, *The Autobiography of W. E. B. Du Bois: A Soliloquy on Viewing My Life From the Last Decade of Its First Century,* edited by Herbert Aptheker (New York: International Publishers, 1960), p. 143.

3. Quoted in Joel Williamson, *The Crucible of Race: Black-White Relations in the American South Since Emancipation* (New York: Oxford University Press, 1984), p. 120.

4. Du Bois, *The Souls of Black Folk* (Millwood, NY: Kraus-Thomson Organization Limited, 1973), p. 184.

5. Du Bois, "The Training of Negroes for Social Power," in *W. E. B.*

Du Bois Speaks: Speeches and Addresses, 1890–1919, edited by Dr. Philip S. Foner (New York: Pathfinder Press, 1970), p. 131.

6. W. D. Wright, "The Faces of Racism," *Western Journal of Black Studies* 11, no. 4 (1987), pp. 168–176.

7. Quoted in John Hope Franklin, *Racial Equality in America* (Chicago: University of Chicago Press, 1976), p. 50.

8. Quoted in Jan Nederveen Pieterse, *White on Black: Images of Africa and Blacks in Western Popular Culture* (New Haven, CT: Yale University Press, 1992), p. 34.

9. Quoted in Martin Bernal, *Black Athena: The Afroasiatic Roots of Classical Civilization, Volume I: The Fabrication of Ancient Greece 1785–1985* (New Brunswick, NJ: Rutgers University Press, 1987), p. 241.

10. Alfred A. Moss, Jr., *The American Negro Academy: Voice of the Talented Tenth* (Baton Rouge, LA: Louisiana State University Press, 1981).

11. Quoted in Gregory U. Rigsby, *Alexander Crummell: Pioneer in Nineteenth-Century Pan-African Thought* (Westport, CT: Greenwood Press, 1987), p. 168.

12. Ibid., p. 1

13. W. E. B. Du Bois, "The Conservation of the Races," in *W. E. B. DuBois Speaks . . . 1890–1919*, pp. 73–85.

14. Allison Davis, "Our Negro Intellectuals," *The Crisis* 35, no. 8 (August 1928), p. 286.

15. Jon Michael Spencer, *The Rhythms of Black Folk: Race, Religion, and Pan-Africanism* (Trenton, NJ: Africa World Press, 1995), p. 1.

16. George M. Frederickson, *The Black Image in the White Mind: The Debate on Afro-American Character and Destiny, 1817–1914* (New York: Harper & Row, Publishers, 1971), pp. 105–109.

17. Davis, "Our Negro Intellectuals," p. 285.

18. Molefi Kete Asante, *Malcolm X as Cultural Hero and Other Afrocentric Essays* (Trenton, NJ: Africa World Press, 1993).

19. Clarence E. Walker, *Deromanticizing Black History: Critical Essays and Reappraisals* (Knoxville: University of Tennessee Press, 1991).

20. Vernon J. Dixon and Badi G. Foster (eds.), *Beyond Black or White: An Alternative America* (Boston: Little, Brown, and Company, 1971).

CHAPTER 2: FROM AN AFRICAN TO A BLACK IDENTITY

1. Eric J. Sundquist, *To Wake the Nations: Race in the Making of American Literature* (Cambridge, MA: Harvard University Press, 1993), p. 567.

2. Ibid.

3. Cf. J. A. Rogers, *Sex and Race*, 3 vols. (St. Petersburg: Helga M. Rogers, 1942, 1967).

4. St. Clair Drake, *Black Folk Here and There, Volumes I–II* (Los Angeles: CASS Publications, 1987, 1990).

5. George G. M. James, *Stolen Legacy* (San Francisco: Reprinted by Julian Richards Associates, Publishers, 1985).

6. Chancellor Williams, *The Destruction of Black Civilization: Great Issues of a Race from 4500 B.C. to 2000 A.D.* (Chicago: Third World Press, 1987).

7. Frank M. Snowden, Jr., *Blacks in Antiquity: Ethiopians in the Greco-Roman Experience* (Cambridge, MA: Harvard University Press, 1970); Snowden, *Before Color Prejudice: The Ancient View of Blacks* (Cambridge, MA: Harvard University Press, 1983).

8. Cheikh Anta Diop, *The African Origins of Civilization: Myth or Reality* (Westport, CT: Lawrence Hill & Company, 1974); Diop, *Civilization or Barbarism: An Authentic Anthropology* (Brooklyn, NY: Lawrence Hill Books, 1991).

9. John G. Jackson, *Introduction to African Civilizations* (Secaucus, NJ: Citadel Press, 1970).

10. Yosef ben-Jochannan, *African Origins of the Major "Western Religions"* (Baltimore, MD: Black Classic Press, 1991); ben-Jochannan, *Africa: Mother of Western Civilization* (Baltimore, MD: Black Classic Press, 1988).

11. Ivan Van Sertima, *They Came Before Columbus* (New York: Random House, Inc., 1976).

12. Quoted in Clinton M. Jean, *Behind the Eurocentric Veils: The Search for African Realities* (Amherst: University of Massachusetts Press, 1991), p. 74.

13. Donald Johnson and Maitland A. Edey, *Lucy: The Beginnings of Humankind* (New York: Simon and Schuster, 1981).

14. John Noble Wilford, "Skull in Ethiopia Linked to Earliest Man," *New York Times*, March 8, 1994, pp. A1, A8.

15. "Anthropologists Conclude Africans Were First to Make Tools About 90,000 Years Ago," *Jet*, 88, no. 1 (May 15, 1995), p. 5.

16. John Tierney, Lynda Wright, and Karen Springen, "The Search for Adam and Eve," *Newsweek*, January 11, 1988, p. 51.

17. Luigi Luca Cavalli-Sforza and Francesco Cavalli-Sforza, *The Great Human Diasporas: The History of Diversity and Evolution* (Reading, MA: Addison-Wesley Publishing Company, 1995).

18. "Did Flies Drive Man from Paradise?" *New Haven Register*, March 1, 1992, p. B8.

19. Quoted in "Does Academic Correctness Repress Separatist or Afrocentrist Scholarship?" *Journal of Blacks in Higher Education*, no. 2 (Winter 1993/1994), p. 42.

20. Quoted in "Does Academic Correctness Repress," p. 45.

21. Cornel West, *Prophetic Fragments* (Grand Rapids, MI: William B. Eerdmans Publishing Company, 1988), p. 48.

22. West, "The Dilemma of the Black Intellectual," *Journal of Blacks in Higher Education*, no. 2 (Winter 1993/1994), p. 62.

23. Asante, *Malcolm X as Cultural Hero*, p. 39.

24. West, "Dilemma of the Black Intellectual," p. 66.

25. Steven Best and Douglas Kellner, *Postmodern Theory: Critical Interrogations* (New York: Guilford Press, 1991).

26. But a racist truth regime in America was and is a falsehood regime. This is a term that Blacks would have no difficulty accepting. It is a critical concept, portending critical analysis. Foucault's truth regime does not have these attributes, although it might appear so. Analyzing what is perpetrated as truth, without analyzing the premises of the projections, is more or less to sanction or to approve the projections, even to provide them with intellectual (and, perhaps, even) moral legitimacy. The purported critical or radical analysis would not be so critical or radical.

27. West, "Dilemma of the Black Intellectual," p. 67.

28. Paul Gilroy, *The Black Atlantic: Modernity and Double Consciousness* (Cambridge, MA: Harvard University Press, 1993), p. 190.

29. Snowden, *Blacks in Antiquity*, p. 7.

30. Quoted in Frederick Newsome, "Black Contributions to the Early History of Western Medicine," in *Blacks in Science Ancient and Modern*, edited by Ivan Van Sertima, New Brunswick, NJ: Transaction Books, 1984), p. 137.

31. Denesh D'souza, *The End of Racism: Principles for a Multiracial Society* (New York: Free Press, 1995), p. 367.

32. Richard Osborne, "The History and Nature of Race Classification," in *The Biological and Social Meaning of Race Edited by Richard Osborne* (San Francisco: W. H. Freeman, 1971), p. 165.

33. Molefi K. Asante, *Afrocentricity: The Theory of Social Change* (Buffalo, NY: Amulefi, 1980); Asante, *The Afrocentric Idea* (Philadelphia: Temple University Press, 1987).

34. Asante, "Racism, Consciousness, and Afrocentricity," in *Lure and Loathing: Essays on Race, Identity and the Ambivalence of Assimilation,* edited and with an Introduction by Gerald Early (New York: The Penguin Press, 1993), p. 139.

35. Asante, *Malcolm X as Cultural Hero*, p. 41.

36. Kwame Anthony Appiah, *In My Father's House: Africa in the Philosophy of Culture* (New York: Oxford University Press, 1993), p. 139.

37. Ali Mazrui, "On the Concept of 'We Are All Africans,' " *American Political Science Review* 58, no. 1 (March 1963), p. 90.

38. M. Itua, "Africans Do Not Want to Be Africans," in *The Black Think Tank*, edited by Naiwu Osahon (Lagos: International Coordinating Committee of the 7th Pan African Congress, 1992), p. 4.

39. Appiah, *In My Father's House*, p. 177.

40. Henrico Stephano, *Thesaurus Graecae Linguae, Vols. 1–2* (Paris Excudent Ambrosius Firmin Didot 1831–1856), p. 2703.

41. Robert E. Hood, *Begrimed and Black: Christian Traditions of Blacks and Blackness* (Minneapolis, MN: Fortress Press, 1994), p. 25.

42. Charles T. Lewis and Charles Short (eds.), *A Latin Dictionary* (Oxford: Clarendon Press, 1966), p. 69.

43. Joseph E. Holloway (ed.), *Africanisms in American Culture* (Bloomington: Indiana University Press, 1990), p. xx.

44. Sterling Stuckey, *Slave Culture: Nationalist Theory and the Foundations of Black America* (New York: Oxford University Press, 1987), p. 43.

45. Lee Sigelman and Susan Welch, *Black Americans' Views of Racial Inequality: The Dream Deferred* (New York: Cambridge University Press, 1991), p. xi.

46. "Poll Says Blacks Prefer to Be Called Black," *Jet* 79, no. 17 (February 11, 1991), p. 8.

47. *Jet*, 86, no. 17 (August 1994), p. 46.

48. *Jet* 85, no. 4 (May 30, 1994), p. 37.

49. Nikki Giovanni, "Black Is the Noun," in *Lure and Loathing*, edited by Gerald Early, p. 122.

50. John Henrik Clarke, *Christopher Columbus & the Afrikan Holocaust: Slavery and the Rise of European Capitalism* (Brooklyn, NY: A&B Books Publishers, 1992).

51. There were Africans who contributed to the African Holocaust, as well as to the African-Black Holocaust, by capturing Africans, or selling them into slavery.

CHAPTER 3: BLACK COGNITION

1. Gunnar Myrdal, *An American Dilemma: The Negro Problem and Modern Democracy* (New York: Harper & Row, Publishers, 1994).

2. Sidney W. Mintz and Richard Price, *The Birth of African-American Culture: An Anthropological Perspective* (Boston: Beacon Press, 1992), p. 10.

3. Michael Awkward, *Negotiating Difference: Race, Gender, and the Politics of Positionality* (Chicago: University of Chicago Press, 1995), p. 35.

4. Quoted in Awkward, *Negotiating Difference*, p. 37.

5. Clifford Geertz, *The Interpretation of Cultures* (New York: Basic Books, 1973), p. 14.

6. Houston A. Baker, Jr., *The Journey Back: Issues in Black Literature and Criticism* (Chicago: University of Chicago Press, 1980), p. xvi.

7. Ibid.

8. Anthony J. Sanford, *Cognition and Cognitive Psychology* (New York: Basic Books, 1985), p. 1.

9. Joel Kovel, *White Racism: A Psychohistory* (New York: Columbia University Press, 1984).

10. Ivan Van Sertima, "Race and Origins of the Egyptians," in *Egypt Revisited*, edited by Ivan Van Sertima (New Brunswick, NJ: Transaction Publishers, 1989), p. 4.

11. Chukwunyere Kamalu, *Foundations of African Thought: A Worldview Grounded in the African Heritage of Religion and Philosophy, Science and Art* (London: Karnak House, 1990), p. 6.

12. Janheinz Jahn, *Muntu: An Outline of the New African Culture* (New York: Grove Press, 1961), p. 97.

13. Jacques Maquet, *Africanity: The Cultural Unity of Black Africa* (New York: Oxford University Press, 1972).

14. V. Y. Mudimbe, *The Invention of Africa: Gnosis, Philosophy, and the Order of Knowledge* (Bloomington: Indiana University Press, 1988), pp. 30–31.

15. Tejumola Olaniyan, *Scars of Conquest/Masks of Resistance: The Invention of Cultural Identities in African, African-American, and Caribbean Drama* (New York: Oxford University Press, 1995), p. 46.

16. Du Bois, *The Souls of Black Folk*, p. 3.

17. Du Bois, "The Souls of White Folk," in *W. E. B. Du Bois: A Reader*, edited and with an introduction by Meyer Weinberg (New York: Harper and Row, Publishers, 1970), p. 304.

18. Du Bois, *Black Reconstruction in America: An Essay Toward a History of the Part Which Black Folk Played in the Attempt to Reconstruct Democracy in America, 1860–1880* (New York: Atheneum, 1970), p. 727.

19. Albert Murray, *The Omni-Americans: Some Alternatives to the Folklore of White Supremacy* (New York: Random House, 1970), p. 79.

20. Mary White Ovington, *Half a Man: The Status of the Negro in New York* (New York: Hill and Wang, 1969), p. 100.

21. Lerone Bennett, Jr., *The Negro Mood* (Chicago: Johnson Publishing Company, 1964), p. 51.

22. Joseph White, Jr., "Guidelines for Black Psychologists," *Black Scholar* 1, no. 5 (March 1970), p. 57.

23. Quoted in *Black Women Writers at Work*, edited by Claudia Tate (Harpenden, Herts, England: Oldcastle Books, 1983), p. 122.

24. Du Bois, *The Souls of Black Folk*, p. 4.

25. Quoted in W. D. Wright, "The Cultural Thought and Leadership of Alain Locke," *Freedomways* 14, no. 1 (First Quarter 1974), pp. 43–44.

CHAPTER 4: THE MODERNITY AND
POSTMODERNITY DECEPTIONS

1. Quoted in Gianni Vattimo, *The End of Modernity: Nihilism and Hermeneutics in Postmodern Culture* (Baltimore, MD: Johns Hopkins University Press, 1988), p. vi.

2. Best and Kellner, *Postmodern Theory*, p. ix.

3. Anthony Giddens, *The Consequences of Modernity* (Stanford, CA: Stanford University Press, 1990), p. 3.

4. Ibid., p. 45.

5. Agnes Heller, *Can Modernity Survive?* (Berkeley and Los Angeles: University of California Press, 1990), p. 170.

6. Ibid., p. 169.

7. Stanley Rosen, *The Ancients and the Moderns: Rethinking Modernity* (New Haven, CT: Yale University Press, 1989).

8. Ross Poole, *Morality and Modernity* (New York: Routledge, 1991), p. ix.

9. Cornel West, *Prophetic Thought in Postmodern Times* (Monroe, ME: Common Courage Press, 1993).

10. Best and Kellner, *Postmodern Theory*, p. 1.

11. Hans Sluga, *Heidegger's Crisis: Philosophy and Politics in Nazi Germany* (Cambridge, MA: Harvard University Press, 1993), pp. 70–74.

12. Quoted in Neville Wakefield, *Postmodernism: The Twilight of the Real* (London: Pluto Press, 1990), p. 48.

13. Quoted in Philip S. Foner (ed.), *The Life and Writings of Frederick Douglass, Volume III: The Civil War Era, 1861–1865* (New York: International Publishers Co., 1952), p. 126.

14. W. E. Burghardt Du Bois, *The Suppression of the African Slave Trade to the United States of America, 1638–1870* (Baton Rouge: Louisiana State University Press, 1969), p. 199.

15. James P. Comer, *Beyond Black and White* (New York: Quadrangle/ New York Times Book Company, 1972), p. 118.

16. I may not always use terms such as *alleged, supposed,* or *so-called* when discussing modernity and postmodernity, but I want it fully understood that I do not regard either of them as having ever existed. What exists presently is contemporary Western thought that has been given a decorative, but false name that has in turn resulted in a decorative and false name being given to a past time in Western history.

17. Postmodern intellectuals criticize the hierarchical pretenses of Western culture, even calling the pretenses expressions of racism, but at the same time, uphold the hierarchical pretenses of Western modernity, which they do by asserting its existence and critiquing it, which they have yet to see as racist intellectual activity.

18. W. E. Burghardt Du Bois, *The Negro* (New York: Oxford University Press, 1970), p. 90.

19. Max Weber, *The Protestant Ethic and the Spirit of Capitalism* (London: Allen & Unwin, 1948).

20. Zygmunt Bauman, *Modernity and the Holocaust* (Ithaca, New York: Cornell University Press, 1989).

21. Actually the Slavic Holocaust which Hitler expanded in the 1940s, was initiated in the 1930s by Stalin.

22. Bertrand Russell, *A History of Western Philosophy* (New York: Simon & Schuster, 1972), p. 3.

23. George Sarton, *Ancient Science through the Golden Age of Greece* (New York: Dover Publications, 1980), p. 116.

24. Joan M. Erikson, *Legacies Prometheus Orpheus Socrates* (New York: W. W. Norton & Company, 1993), p. 78.

25. Ivan Van Sertima, "The Moor in Africa and Europe," in *Golden Age of the Moor*, edited by Ivan Van Sertima (New Brunswick, NJ: Transaction Publishers, 1992), p. 16.

26. Mary Lefkowitz, *Not Out of Africa: How Afrocentrism Became an Excuse to Teach Myth as History* (New York: Basic Books, 1996), p. 85.

27. Joseph Kaster, ed., quoted from the Heliopolitan theology in *The Wisdom of Ancient Egypt: Writings from the Time of the Pharaohs*, translated by Joseph Kaster (New York: Barnes & Noble Books, 1968), p. 49.

28. Lefkowitz, *Not Out of Africa*, p. 77.

29. Ibid., p. 78.

30. Classicist Mary Lefkowitz seemed not to know what Cicero said about the Egyptians and astrology: "The Egyptians are the authors of many inventions, such as that which determines according to the day on which a man is born, and what his character and spirit will be." Quoted in Jacques Champollion, *The World of the Egyptians* (Geneva, Switzerland: Minerva, 1971), p. 58. Cicero did not use the word *astrology*, but it is clear that this was what he was talking about.

31. Charles S. Finch, "The Kamitic Genesis of Christianity," in *Nile Valley Civilizations*, edited by Ivan Van Sertima (Journal of African Civilizations, Ltd., 1985), p. 186.

32. Wayne Chandler, "Of Gods and Men: Egypt's Old Kingdom," in *Egypt Revisted*, edited by Van Sertima, p. 148.

33. Gay Robins, "Mathematics, Astronomy, and Calendars in Pharaonic Egypt," in *Civilizations of the Ancient Near East, Volume I*, edited by Jack M. Sasson, John Baines, Gary Beckman, and Karen S. Robinson (New York: Charles Scribners's Sons, 1995), pp. 1812–1813.

34. Ibid., p. 1812.

35. Beatrice Lumpkin, "Mathematics and Engineering in the Nile Val-

ley," in *Egypt Child of Africa*, edited by Ivan Van Sertima (New Brunswick, NJ: Transaction Publishers, 1995), p. 331.

36. Robert Palter, "Black Athena, Afrocentrism, and the History of Science," in *Black Athena Revisited*, edited by Mary R. Lefkowitz and Guy Maclean Rogers (Chapel Hill: University of North Carolina Press, 1996), p. 228.

37. George Feuerstein, Subhash Kak, and David Frawley, *In Search of the Cradle of Civilization* (Wheaton, IL: Theological Publishing House, 1995), p. 10.

38. Palter, "Black Athena, Afrocentrism, and the History of Science," p. 238.

39. Ibid.

40. Ibid., p. 242

41. Robins, "Mathematics, Astronomy, and Calenders in Pharaonic Egypt," p. 1809.

42. W. G. Hardy, *Origins and Ordeals of the Western World: Lessons from Our Heritage in History* (Cambridge, MA: Schenkman Publishing Company, 1968), p. 73.

43. Quoted in Kaster, ed., *The Wisdom of Ancient Egypt*, p. 12.

44. Palter, "Black Athena, Afrocentrism, and the History of Science," p. 254.

45. P. Ghalioungui, *The House of Life: Magic and Medical Science in Ancient Egypt* (Amsterdam: B. M. Israel, 1973).

46. Charles S. Finch III, M.D., "Science and Symbol in Egyptian Medicine: Commentaries on the Edwin Smith Papyrus," in Van Sertima, ed., *Egypt Revisited*, p. 326.

47. H. W. F. Saggs, *Civilization Before Greece and Rome* (New Haven. CT: Yale University Press, 1989), pp. 254–255.

48. Kent R. Weeks, "Medicine, Surgery, and Public Health in Ancient Egypt," in Sasson et al., eds., *Civilizations of the Ancient Near East, Volume I*, p. 1797.

49. Ibid.

50. D'souza, *The End of Racism*, pp. 367–368.

51. Fred Gladstone Bratton, *A History of Egyptian Archeology* (New York: Thomas Y. Crowell Company, 1968), p. 25.

52. Ibid., p. 22.

53. Kaster, *The Wisdom of Ancient Egypt*, p. 12.

54. Quoted in Kamalu, *Foundations of African Thought*, p. 4.

55. Hans Goedicke, *The Report About the Dispute of a Man with His Ba* (Baltimore, MD: Johns Hopkins University Press, 1970), p. 3.

56. John W. Murphy, *Postmodern Social Analysis and Criticism* (Westport, CT: Greenwood Press, 1989), pp. 4–6.

57. Pauline Marie Rosenau, *Post-Modernism and the Social Sciences: Insights, Inroads, and Intrusions* (Princeton, NJ: Princeton University Press, 1992), p. 7.

58. Quoted in Vattimo, *The End of Modernity*, p. xxi.

59. Sven Birkerts, *American Energies: Essays on Fiction* (New York: William Morrow and Company, 1992), p. 26.

60. But another point has to be made about removing strict boundaries between subject matter or aspects of reality. This is not something that has to be done. While science and myth have things in common, they are not the same things. Men and women have things in common, but they are not the same things. Historical monographs and novels have similar features, even similar objectives, but they are still different things. It is not an advance in thought to blur reality or to diminish autonomy as so many postmodernist thinkers seem to think it is or write as if it is. To me, this is not only inadequate thinking, but it seems to reflect a lack of will, or a lack of will to thought, which is damaging in intellectuals. But there is also a deep basis for this inadequacy and confusion. Postmodern thinkers convey the view that they exalt differences. That being so, seeking to end or blur boundaries or to diminish or end autonomy is contradictory behavior. It sounds similar to alleged modernists saying that people are different and are entitled to their differences, but then such people end up being ridiculed, suppressed, segregated, or killed for being different. Postmodernists, exalting difference, and then attacking it and diminishing it, show racist foundationalism intruding in their thinking, as modernists had it intrude in theirs, even if not with the same intensity or violent expressions.

61. Charles Lemert, "General Social Theory, Irony, Postmodernism," in *Postmodernism and Social Theory*, edited by Steven Seidman and David G. Wagner (Cambridge, MA: Basil Blackwell, 1992), pp. 21–34.

62. Nathan I. Huggins, "Afro-American History: Myths, Heroes, Reality," in *Key Issues in the Afro-American Experience, Volume I, to 1877*, edited by Nathan I. Huggins, Martin Kilson, and Daniel Fox (New York: Harcourt Brace Jovanovich, 1971), p. 5.

63. Granted, a broad cultural context or textuality, for example, for writing a novel or a poem, exists prior to individual writers or poets and influences them and their work. But a writer or poet is not passive in the face of a cultural context or textuality; they give shape, color, motion, and even meaning to that context or textuality, as a means to do their literary work. Thus, a writer or poet is influenced by contextuality or textuality but also helps to define it—and invigorate it—so that it can be of help to influence literary efforts. Literary figures and contextuality or textuality are inseparable. Each has an impact on the other. This should be the context for analysis or literary evaluation.

64. Murphy, *Postmodern Social Analysis and Criticism*, p. 118.

65. Lemert, "General Social Theory, Irony, Postmodernism," p. 23.

66. Daniel Joseph Singal, "Towards a Definition of American Modernism," in *Modernist Culture in America*, edited by Daniel Joseph Singal (Belmont, CA: Wadsworth Publishing Company, 1991), p. 12.

67. T. W. Adorno, E. Frenkel-Brunswick, D. J. Levinson, and R. N. Sanford, The *Authoritarian Personality* (New York: Harper & Row, 1950).

68. Jane Flax, *Thinking Fragments: Psychoanalysis, Feminism, and Postmodernism in the Contemporary West* (Berkeley and Los Angeles: University of California Press, 1989), p. 220.

69. Henry Louis Gates, Jr., *Loose Canons: Notes on the Culture Wars* (New York: Oxford University Press, 1992), pp. 35–36.

70. Many postmodern thinkers reject the ideal of progress. Invariably, these people are white men. Given the continuing development of science, technology, social organization, communication, and delivery systems, why would people not still think in terms of historical and human progress? Could it be that the white male postmodern thinkers who reject the idea of progress are trying to discourage Blacks, white women, and other men and women from challenging white men who dominate and control resources, institutions, and delivery systems, and schedules; and who, therefore, stand in the way of their making progress? Is this not a racist, even racist reactionary posture, covered up by the "no progress" discourse itself that does not even mention race or racism?

CHAPTER 5: DEVELOPING A BLACK AESTHETIC

1. C. Vann Woodward, "Clio with Soul," *Journal of American History* 56, no. 1 (June 1969), p. 18.

2. Arthur Schlesinger, Jr., "Nationalism and History," *Journal of Negro History* 54, no. 1 (January 1969), 19–31.

3. Quoted in John Blassingame, "The Afro-Americans: From Mythology to Reality," in *The Reinterpretation of American History and Culture*, edited by William H. Cartwright and Richard L. Watson (Washington, DC: National Council for Social Studies, 1973), p. 54.

4. Nathan Irvin Huggins, *Black Odyssey: The African-American Ordeal in Slavery* (New York: Random House, 1990), p. xii.

5. Quoted in Wakefield, *Postmodernism*, p. 3.

6. Birkerts, *American Energies*, p. 28

7. Quoted in Linda Hutcheon, *The Politics of Postmodernism* (New York: Routledge, 1989), p. 33.

8. Quoted in Hutcheon, p. 33.

9. James Baldwin, *Nobody Knows My Name: More Notes of a Native Son* (New York: Dell Publishing Company, 1961), p. 18.

10. "James Baldwin: Black Man in America: An Interview with Studs Terkel" (Chicago: WFTM Radio Station, 1963).

11. Barbara J. Fields, "Ideology and Race in American History," in *Region, Race, and Reconstruction: Essays in Honor of C. Vann Woodward*, edited by J. Morgan Kousser and James McPherson (New York: Oxford University Press, 1982), pp. 143–144.

12. Henry Louis Gates, Jr. (ed.), *Black Letters in the Enlightenment: Race, Writing, and Difference* (New York: Oxford University Press, 1990), p. 5.

13. Cornel West, *Race Matters* (Boston: Beacon Press, 1993).

14. Kara F. C. Halloway, *Codes of Conduct: Race, Ethics, and the Color of Our Character* (New Brunswick, N.J.: Rutgers University Press, 1995), p. 6.

15. James Baldwin, *The Fire Next Time* (New York: The Dial Press, 1963), p. 103.

16. The problem of dealing with race is not only discursive. Race also exists as a category of American law and of court rulings. Ferreting it out of these institutional structures without damaging Blacks might prove a difficult task.

17. Henri Lopes, "Negritude: A Sober Analysis," in *New African Literature and the Arts*, edited by Joseph Okpaku (New York: The Third Press, 1973), p. 79.

18. *Jet*, 86, no. 17 (April 29, 1995), p. 22.

19. Cornel West, *Keeping Faith: Philosophy and Race in America* (New York: Routledge, 1993), p. 40.

20. Wright, "The Cultural Thought and Leadership of Alain Locke," pp. 39–40.

21. Houston A. Baker, Jr., *Modernism and the Harlem Renaissance* (Chicago: The University of Chicago Press, 1987).

22. Addison Gayle, Jr. (ed.), *The Black Aesthetic* (Garden City, N.Y.: Doubleday & Company, Inc., 1971).

23. Hutcheon, *The Politics of Postmodernism*, p. 3.

24. W. E. Burghardt DuBois, "Criteria of Negro Art," in *Writings in Periodicals Edited by W. E. B. DuBois: Selections from the Crisis Volume 2 1926–1934*, compiled and edited by Herbert Aptheker (Millwood, N.Y.: Kraus-Thomson Organization Limited, 1983), pp. 447–448.

25. Ron Karenga, "Black Cultural Nationalism," in Gayle, *The Black Aesthetic*, p. 34.

26. It has always been and remains nonsensical to speak of art for art's sake. Art has no sake. An individual has a sake. People have sakes. The word *sake* means "purpose, motive, end." An artist has a sake in producing art. People have sakes in relating to art. Anything that human beings create— art, science, technology, religion, music, knowledge, truth, buildings, machines, dams, automobiles, or whatever—does not exist in, of, or for itself.

They were created by human beings, motivated to do so, with certain purposes or ends (or goals) in mind. If any of these things created themselves, and invested themselves with purpose, motive, or end, then it could be said or argued that they existed for their own sake or sakes. The "for its own sake" argument is someone's effort to cloak dominance, hierarchy, and the exercise of great power. Postmodernists have invested language with its own sake, as they have words such as *dissemination, plurality, relativism, difference, play, poetics*, and other things in their intellectual serving. It reflects their interest, like the so-called modernists before them, in dominance, hierarchy, and the exercise of great power. Giving the objects of human creators a sake leads to their having a purpose, motive, end, and even will of their own, that could lead to the objects dominating and controlling their creators, or other people—or an entire society. Another way of looking at this is that for-its-own-sake thinking is reified thinking that results in the objects of human creation (or human appropriation), including abstract beliefs, ideas, ideals, or morality being invested with a materiality or embodiment, and even a will, motivation, and purpose of their own that could incline them to seek to dominate and control their creators or investors, as well as others, or an entire society. Postmodernists proclaim they are against reified thinking, but their body of thought indicates otherwise. And it indicates that they have not left the so-called modernist mode.

27. Gayl Jones, *Liberating Voices: Oral Tradition in African American Literature* (New York: Penguin Books, 1991).

28. Birkerts, *American Energies*, pp. 171–173.

29. Madhu Dubey, *Black Women Novelists and the Nationalist Aesthetic* (Bloomington, IA: Indiana University Press, 1994), p. 1.

30. Richard Wright, "Introduction: Blueprint for Negro Writing," in Gayle, *The Black Aesthetic*, p. 337.

31. Such usage has also led many Black women writers to portray Black women in a negative light, without seeing that they have done so. With the focus on Black men of low character and social behavior, many Black women writers have given Black women primarily only these kinds of Black men to relate to or to choose from. These writers might well have depicted the selfless, courageous, resourceful, regenerative, or heroic way these women have related to these men. But this context of writing also simultaneously deprecates Black women, as it constantly shows them relating to or choosing to be with men of shallow character and low-life dimensions. They seem incapable of making other kinds of selections or show a fear of doing so or of being with men of quality: that they can only be selfless, courageous, regenerative, resourceful, or heroiness with debased or weak Black men. This raises questions about the character and sense of self of the portrayed Black women and the authenticity or value of their personal achievements interacting with Black men.

32. "Response Michael Awkward," in *Afro-American Literary Study in the 1990s*, edited by Houston A. Baker, Jr. and Patricia Redmond (Chicago: The University of Chicago Press, 1989), p. 76.

33. E. Franklin Frazier, *Black Bourgeoisie* (Glencoe, IL: The Free Press, 1957).

34. Spencer, *The Rhythms of Black Folk*, pp. 5–6.

CHAPTER 6: THE BLACK COGNITION IMPERATIVE

1. Baker and Redman, *Afro-American Literary Study in the 1990s*, p. 1.

2. Henry Louis Gates, Jr., "Canon-Formation, Literary History, and the Afro-American Tradition: From the Seen to the Told," in *ibid.*, p. 32.

3. Robert Michael Franklin, *Liberating Visions: Human Fulfillment and Social Justice in African-American Thought* (Minneapolis, MN: Fortress Press, 1990), p. 4.

Selected Bibliography

Appiah, Kwame Anthony. *In My Father's House: Africa in the Philosophy of Culture*. New York: Oxford University Press, 1993.

Asante, Molefi K. *Afrocentricity: The Theory of Social Change*. Buffalo, NY: Amulefi, 1980.

———. *The Afrocentric Idea*. Philadelphia: Temple University Press, 1987.

———. *Malcolm X as Cultural Hero and Other Afrocentric Essays*. Trenton, NJ: Africa World Press, 1993.

———. "Racism, Consciousness, and Afrocentricity." In *Lure and Loathing: Essays on Race, Identity and the Ambivalence of Assimilation*, ed. Gerald Early. New York: Penguin Press, 1993.

Awkward, Michael. *Negotiating Difference: Race, Gender, and the Politics of Positionality*. Chicago: University of Chicago Press, 1995.

Baker, Houston, Jr. *The Journey Back: Issues in Black Literature and Criticism*. Chicago: University of Chicago Press, 1980.

———. *Modernism and the Harlem Renaissance*. Chicago: University of Chicago Press, 1987.

———, and Patricia Redman, eds. *Afro-American Literary Study in the 1990s*. Chicago: University of Chicago Press, 1989.

Baldwin, James. *Nobody Knows My Name: More Notes of a Native Son*. New York: Dell Publishing Company, 1961.

———. *The Fire Next Time*. New York: Dial Press, 1963.

Bauman, Zygmunt. *Modernity and the Holocaust*. Ithaca, NY: Cornell University Press, 1989.

ben-Jochannan, Yosef. *Africa: Mother of Western Civilization.* Baltimore, MD: Black Classics Press, 1988 (orig. 1970).

————. *The African Origins of the Major "Western Religions."* Baltimore, MD: Black Classics Press, 1991 (orig. 1971).

Bennett, Lerone, Jr., *The Negro Mood.* Chicago: Johnson Publishing Company, 1964.

Bernal, Martin. *Black Athena: The Afroasiatic Roots of Classical Civilization. Volume I: The Fabrication of Ancient Greece, 1785–1985.* New Brunswick, NJ: Rutgers University Press, 1987.

Best, Steven, and Douglas Kellner. *Postmodern Theory: Critical Interrogations.* New York: Guilford Press, 1991.

Birkerts, Sven. *American Energies: Essays on Fiction.* New York: William Morrow and Company, 1992.

Blassingame, John. "The Afro-Americans: From Mythology to Reality." In *The Reinterpretation of American History and Culture,* ed. William H. Cartwright and Richard L. Watson. Washington, DC: National Council for Social Studies, 1973.

Cavalli-Sforza, Luigi Luca, and Francesco Cavalli-Sforza. *The Great Human Diasporas: The History of Diversity and Evolution.* Reading, MA: Addison-Wesley Publishing Company, 1995.

Chandler, Wayne. "Of Gods and Men: Egypt's Old Kingdom." In *Egypt Revisted,* ed. Ivan Van Sertima. New Brunswick, NJ: Transaction Publishers, 1989.

Clarke, John Henrik. *Christopher Columbus & the Afrikan Holocaust: Slavery and the Rise of European Capitalism.* Brooklyn, NY: A&B Books Publishers, 1992.

Comer, James P., M.D. *Beyond Black and White.* New York: Quadrangle/ New York Times Book Company, 1972.

Davis, Allison. "Our Negro Intellectuals." *The Crisis* 35 (August 8, 1928): 268–269, 284–286.

Diop, Cheikh Anta. *The African Origins of Civilization: Myth or Reality.* Westport, CT: Lawrence Hill & Company, 1974.

————. *Civilization or Barbarism: An Authentic Anthropology.* Brooklyn, NY: Lawrence Hill Books, 1991.

Dixon, Vernon J., and Badi G. Foster, eds. *Beyond Black or White: An Alternative America.* Boston: Little, Brown, and Company, 1971.

Drake, St. Clair. *Black Folk Here and There. Volumes I–II.* Los Angeles: CASS Publications, 1987, 1990.

Dubey, Madhu. *Black Women Novelists and the Nationalist Aesthetic.* Bloomington: Indiana University Press, 1994.

Du Bois, W. E. Burghardt. *The Suppression of the African Slave Trade to the United States of America, 1638–1870.* Baton Rouge: Louisiana State University Press, 1969.

————. "The Conservation of the Races." In *W. E. B. Du Bois Speaks: Speeches and Addresses, 1890–1919*, ed. Dr. Philip S. Foner. New York: Pathfinder Press, 1970.

————. "The Training of Negroes for Social Power." In *W. E. B. Du Bois Speaks: Speeches and Addresses 1890–1919*, ed. Dr. Philip S. Foner. New York: Pathfinder Press, 1970.

————. "The Souls of White Folk." In W. E. B. *Du Bois: A Reader*, ed. Meyer Weinberg. New York: Harper and Row, Publishers, 1970.

————. *Black Reconstruction in America: An Essay Toward a History of the Part Which Black Folk Played in the Attempt to Reconstruct Democracy in America, 1860–1880*. New York: Atheneum, 1970.

————. *The Souls of Black Folk*. Millwood, NY: Kraus-Thomson Organization Limited, 1973.

Erikson, Joan M. *Legacies Prometheus Orpheus Socrates*. New York: W. W. Norton & Company, 1993.

Feuerstein, Georg, Subhash Kak, and David Frawley. *In Search of the Cradle of Civilization*. Wheaton, IL: Theological Publishing House, 1995.

Fields, Barbara J. "Ideology and Race in American History." In *Region, Race, and Reconstruction: Essays in Honor of C. Vann Woodward*, ed. J. Morgan Kousser and James McPherson. New York: Oxford University Press, 1982.

Finch, Charles S. III, M.D. "The Kametic Genesis of Christianity." In *Nile Valley Civilizations*, ed. Ivan Van Sertina. Journal of African Civilizations, Ltd., 1985.

————. "Science and Symbol in Egyptian Medicine: Commentaries on the Edwin Smith Papyrus." In *Egypt Revisited*, ed. Ivan Van Sertima. New Brunswick, NJ: Transaction Publishers, 1989.

Flax, Jane. *Thinking Fragments: Psychoanalysis, Feminism, and Postmodernism in the Contemporary West*. Berkeley and Los Angeles: University of California Press, 1989.

Foner, Philip S., ed. *The Life and Writings of Frederick Douglass. Volume III. The Civil War Era, 1861–1865*. New York: International Publishers Co., 1952.

Franklin, John Hope. *Racial Equality in America*. Chicago: University of Chicago Press, 1976.

Franklin, Robert Michael. *Liberating Visions: Human Fulfillment and Social Justice in African-American Thought*. Minneapolis, MN: Fortress Press, 1990.

Frazier, E. Franklin. *Black Bourgeoisie*. Glencoe, IL: Free Press, 1957.

Frederickson, George M. *The Black Image in the White Mind: The Debate on Afro-American Character and Destiny, 1817–1914*. New York: Harper & Row, Publishers, 1971.

Gates, Henry Louis, Jr. "Canon-Formation, Literary History, and the Afro-

American Tradition: From the Seen to the Told." In *Afro-American Literary Study in the 1990s*, ed. Houston A. Baker Jr. and Patricia Redman. Chicago: University of Chicago Press, 1989.

————, ed. *Black Letters in the Enlightenment: Race, Writing, and Difference*. New York: Oxford University Press, 1990.

————. *Loose Canons: Notes on the Culture Wars*. New York: Oxford University Press, 1992.

Gayle, Addison, Jr., ed. *The Black Aesthetic*. Garden City, NY: Doubleday & Company, 1971.

Geertz, Clifford. *The Interpretation of Cultures*. New York: Basic Books, 1973.

Ghalioungui, P. *The House of Life: Magic and Medical Science in Ancient Egypt*. Amsterdam: B. M. Israel, 1973.

Giddens, Anthony. *The Consequences of Modernity*. Stanford, CA: Stanford University Press, 1990.

Gilroy, Paul. *The Black Atlantic: Modernity and Double Consciousness*. Cambridge, MA: Harvard University Press, 1993.

Giovanni, Nikki. "Black Is the Noun." In *Lure and Loathing: Essays on Race, Identity and the Ambivalence of Assimilation*, ed. Gerald Early. New York: Penguin Press, 1993.

Goedicke, Hans. *The Report About the Dispute of a Man with His Ba*. Baltimore, MD: Johns Hopkins Press, 1970.

Halloway, Kara F. C. *Codes of Conduct: Race, Ethics, and the Color of Our Character*. New Brunswick, NJ: Rutgers University Press, 1995.

Hardy, W. G. *Origins and Ordeals of the Western World: Lessons from Our Heritage in History*. Cambridge, MA: Schenkman Publishing Company, 1968.

Heller, Agnes. *Can Modernity Survive?* Berkeley and Los Angeles: University of California Press, 1990.

Holloway, Joseph, ed. *Africanisms in American Culture*. Bloomington: Indiana University Press, 1990.

Hood, Robert E. *Begrimed and Black: Christian Traditions of Blacks and Blackness*. Minneapolis, MN: Fortress Press, 1994.

Horsman, Reginal. *Race and Manifest Destiny: The Origins of American Racial Anglo-Saxonism*. Cambridge, MA: Harvard University Press, 1981.

Huggins, Nathan I. "Afro-American History: Myths, Heroes, Reality." In *Key Issues in the Afro-American Experience. Volume I. To 1877*, ed. Nathan I. Huggins, Martin Kilson, and Daniel Fox. New York: Harcourt Brace Jovanovich, 1971.

————. *Black Odyssey: The African-American Ordeal in Slavery*. New York: Random House, 1990.

Hutcheon, Linda. *The Politics of Postmodernism.* New York: Routledge, 1989.

Itua, M. "Africans Do Not Want to Be Africans." In *The Black Think Tank,* ed. Naiwu Osahon. Lagos, Nigeria: International Coordinating Committee of the 7th Pan African Congress, 1992.

Jackson, John G. *Introduction to African Civilizations.* Secaucus, NJ: Citadel Press, 1970.

Jahn, Janheinz. *Muntu: An Outline of the New African Culture.* New York: Grove Press, 1961.

Jean, Clinton M. *Behind the Eurocentric Veils: The Search for African Realities.* Amherst, MA: University of Massachusetts Press, 1991.

Johnson, Donald, and Maitland A. Edey. *Lucy: The Beginnings of Humankind.* New York: Simon and Schuster, 1981.

Jones, Gayl. *Liberating Voices: Oral Tradition in African American Literature.* New York: Penguin Books, 1991.

Kamalu, Chukwunyere. *Foundations of African Thought: A Worldview Grounded in the African Heritage of Religion and Philosophy, Science and Art.* London: Karnak House, 1990.

Karanga, Ron. "Black Cultural Nationalism." In *The Black Aesthetic,* ed. Addison Gayle, Jr. Garden City, NY: Doubleday & Company, 1971.

Kaster, Joseph, ed. *The Wisdom of Ancient Egypt: Writings from the Time of the Pharaohs.* New York: Barnes & Noble Books, 1968.

Kovel, Joel. *White Racism: A Psychohistory.* New York: Columbia University Press, 1984.

Lefkowitz, Mary. *Not Out of Africa: How Africanism Became an Excuse to Teach Myth as History.* New York: Basic Books, 1996.

Lemert, Charles. "General Social Theory, Irony, Postmodernism." In *Postmodernism and Social Theory,* ed. Steven Seidman and David G. Wagner. Cambridge, MA: Basil Blackwell, 1992.

Lewis, Charles T., and Charles Short, ed. *A Latin Dictionary.* Oxford: Clarendon Press, 1966.

Lumpkin, Beatrice. "Mathematics and Engineering in the Nile Valley." In *Egypt Child of Africa,* ed. Ivan Van Sertima. New Brunswick, NJ: Transaction Publishers, 1995.

Lopes, Henri. "Negritude: A Sober Analysis." In *New African Literature and the Arts,* ed. Joseph Okpaku. New York: Third Press, 1973.

Maquet, Jacques. *Africanity: The Cultural Unity of Black Africa.* New York: Oxford University Press, 1972.

Mazrui, Ali. "On the Concept of 'We are All Africans.' " *American Political Science Review* 58, no.1 (March 1963): 88–97.

Mintz, Sidney, and Richard Price. *The Birth of African-American Culture: An Anthropological Perspective.* Boston: Beacon Press, 1992.

Moss, Alfred A., Jr. *The American Negro Academy: Voice of the Talented Tenth*. Baton Rouge: Louisiana State University Press, 1981.

Mudimbe, V. Y. *The Invention of Africa: Gnosis, Philosophy, and the Order of Knowledge*. Bloomington: Indiana University Press, 1988.

Murphy, John W. *Postmodern Social Analysis and Criticism*. Westport, CT: Greenwood Press, 1989.

Murray, Albert. *The Omni-Americans: Some Alternatives to the Folklore of White Supremacy*. New York: Random House, 1970.

Myrdal, Gunnar. *An American Dilemma: The Negro Problem and Modern Democracy*. New York: Harper & Row, Publishers, 1994.

Newsome, Frederick. "Black Contributions to the Early History of Western Medicine." In *Blacks in Science Ancient and Modern*, ed. Ivan Van Sertima. New Brunswick, NJ: Transaction Books, 1984.

Olaniyan, Tejumola. *Scars of Conquests/Masks of Resistance: The Invention of Cultural Identities in African, African-American, and Caribbean Drama*. New York: Oxford University Press, 1995.

Osborne, Richard. "The History and Nature of Race Classification." In *The Biological and Social Meaning of Race*, ed. Richard Osborne. San Francisco: W. H. Freeman, 1971.

Ovington, Mary White. *Half a Man: The Status of the Negro in New York*. New York: Hill and Wang, 1969 (orig. 1911).

Palter, Robert. "Black Athena, Afrocentrism, and the History of Science." In *Black Athena Revisited*, ed. Mary R. Lefkowitz and Guy Maclean Rogers. Chapel Hill: University of North Carolina Press, 1996.

Pieterse, Jan Nederveen. *White on Black: Images of Africa and Blacks in Western Popular Culture*. New Haven, CT: Yale University Press, 1992.

Poole, Ross. *Morality and Modernity*. New York: Routledge, 1991.

Rigsby, Gregory U. *Alexander Crummell: Pioneer in Nineteenth-Century Pan-African Thought*. Westport, CT: Greenwood Press, 1987.

Robins, Gay. "Mathematics, Astronomy, and Calendars in Pharaonic Egypt." In *Civilizations of the Ancient Near East. Volume I*, ed. Jack M. Sasson, John Baines, Gary Beckman, and Karen S. Rubinson. New York: Charles Scribner's Sons, 1995.

Rogers, J. A. *Sex and Race*. 3 vols. St. Petersburg: Helga M. Rogers, 1942, 1967.

Rosen, Stanley. *The Ancients and the Moderns: Rethinking Modernity*. New Haven, CT: Yale University Press, 1989.

Rosenau, Pauline Marie. *Post-Modernism and the Social Sciences: Insights, Inroads, and Intrusions*. Princeton, NJ: Princeton University Press, 1992.

Russell, Bertrand. *A History of Western Philosophy*. New York: Simon & Schuster, 1972.

Saggs, H. W. F. *Civilization Before Greece and Rome*. New Haven, CT: Yale University Press, 1989.

Sanford, Anthony J. *Cognition and Cognitive Psychology*. New York: Basic Books, 1985.

Sarton, George. *Ancient Science through the Golden Age of Greece*. New York: Dover Publications, 1980.

Schlesinger, Arthur, Jr. "Nationalism and History." *Journal of Negro History* 54 (January 1969): 19–31.

Sertima, Ivan Van. *They Came Before Columbus*. New York: Random House, 1976.

———. "Race and Origins of the Egyptians." In *Egypt Revisited*, ed. Ivan Van Sertima. New Brunswick, NJ: Transaction Publishers, 1989.

———. "The Moor in Africa and Europe." In *Golden Age of the Moor*, ed. Ivan Van Sertima. New Brunswick, NJ: Transaction Publishers, 1992.

Sigelman, Lee, and Susan Welch. *Black Americans' Views of Racial Inequality: The Dream Deferred*. New York: Cambridge University Press, 1991.

Singal, Daniel Joseph. "Towards a Definition of American Modernism." In *Modernist Culture in America*, ed. Daniel Joseph Singal. Belmont, CA: Wadsworth Publishing Company, 1991.

Sluga, Hans. *Heidegger's Crisis: Philosophy and Politics in Nazi Germany*. Cambridge, MA: Harvard University Press, 1993.

Snowden, Frank, Jr. *Blacks in Antiquity: Ethiopians in the Greco-Roman Experience*. Cambridge, MA: Harvard University Press, 1970.

———. *Before Color Prejudice: The Ancient View of Blacks*. Cambridge, MA: Harvard University Press, 1983.

Spencer, Jon Michael. *The Rhythms of Black Folk: Race, Religion, and Pan-Africanism*. Trenton, NJ: Africa World Press, 1995.

Stephano, Henrico. *Thesaurus Graecae Linguae. Volumes 1–2*. Paris: Excudent Ambrosius Firmin Didot, 1831–1856.

Stuckey, Sterling. *Slave Culture: Nationalist Theory and the Foundations of Black America*. New York: Oxford University Press, 1987.

Sundquist, Eric J. *To Wake the Nations: Race in the Making of American Literature*. Cambridge, MA: Harvard University Press, 1993.

Tate, Claudia, ed. *Black Women Writers at Work*. Harpenden, Herts, England: Oldcastle Books, 1983.

Tierney, John, Lynda Wright, and Karen Springen. "The Search for Adam and Eve." *Newsweek*, January 11, 1988: 46–52.

Vattimo, Gianni. *The End of Modernity: Nihilism and Hereneutics in Postmodern Culture*. Baltimore, MD: Johns Hopkins University Press, 1988.

Wakefield, Neville. *Postmodernism: The Twilight of the Real*. London: Pluto Press, 1990.

Walker, Clarence E. *Deromanticizing Black History: Critical Essays and Re-appraisals.* Knoxville: University of Tennessee Press, 1991.

Weeks, Kent R. "Medicine, Surgery, and Public Health in Ancient Egypt." In *Civilizations of the Ancient Near East. Volume I*, ed. Jack M. Sasson, et al. New York: Charles Scribner's Sons, 1995.

West, Cornel. *Prophetic Fragments.* Grand Rapids, MI: William B. Eerdmans Publishing Company, 1988.

———. *Prophetic Thought in Postmodern Times.* Monroe, ME: Common Courage Press, 1993.

———. *Race Matters.* Boston: Beacon Press, 1993.

———. "The Dilemma of the Black Intellectual." *Journal of Blacks in Higher Education* 2 (Winter 1993/1994): 59–67.

White, Joseph, Jr. "Guidelines for Black Psychologists." In *Black Scholar* 5 (March 1970): 52–57.

Wilford, John Noble. "Skull in Ethiopia Linked to Earliest Man." *New York Times*, March 8, 1994: A1, A8.

Williams, Chancellor. *The Destruction of Black Civilization: Great Issues of a Race from 4500 B.C. to 2000 A.D.* Chicago: Third World Press, 1987.

Williamson, Joel. *The Crucible of Race: Black-White Relations in the American South Since Emancipation.* New York: Oxford University Press, 1984.

Woodward, C. Vann. "Clio with Soul." *Journal of American History* 56 (June 1969): 5–20.

Wright, Richard. "Introduction: Blueprint for Negro Writing." In *The Black Aesthetic*, ed. Addison Gayle, Jr. Garden City, NY: Doubleday & Company, 1971.

Wright, W. D. "The Faces of Racism." *Western Journal of Black Studies* 11, no.4 (1987): 168–176.

———. "The Cultural Thought and Leadership of Alain Locke." *Freedom-ways* 14, no.1 (First Quarter 1974): 35–50.

Index

Adorno, Theodor W., 122, 147
Afer, 43
Africa: African essentialism, 19; African identity accepted in retrospect, 45; *basic rhythm* of, 19, 157; black African intellectuals' rejection of *négritude*, 142; Black loss of African culture 44–48; Blacks returning to Africa, 5–6; Egypt removed from Africa, 27, 30, 36; European denigration of black African thinking, 66–68; European disparagement of, 35; impact on Greek and Roman civilizations, 25–26; origins of human beings and human culture, 28, 29; parentage of Black people, 34, 46; problems with African identity, 41–45
Africa for Africans, 42
African-American. *See* Black people
African-Black Holocaust, 50
Africancentric knowledge, 40, 46, 51
Africancentric Perspective: and the African-Black Holocaust, 50; indicates cultural links between ancient Egypt and West African cultures, 64; initi-

ated by Black intellectuals in America, 28; limited means to analyze Black American slavery, 48; limited means to analyze Black history, culture, and social life, 128; limited means to help construct a Black Aesthetic, 153; longevity of, 26, 30; not same as Afrocentric Perspective or Afrocentricity, 19; related to Africancentricity and Africancentrism, 19, 30–31, 35; related to Blackcentric Perspective and Blackcentrism, 46
Africancentrism: aids understanding Black history and life, 35; analytical limitations, 38–39; main focus is on black Africa, 78; not secessionist in higher education, 30–31; relates to Africancentric Perspective and Africancentrism, 30–31, 35; reveals general blackness of ancient Egypt, 90; white intellectuals helped to construct, 3
African consciousness, 43
African descent, 39
African Diaspora, 39
African Episcopal Church, 15

About the Author

W. D. WRIGHT is Professor of History at Southern Connecticut State University.

ISBN 0-275-95542-7

90000>

EAN

9 780275 955427

HARDCOVER BAR CODE